Praise for *Letter to a Young*

"[Suzanne Koven's] wisdom as a doct⟨...⟩ ⟨...⟩er, and a woman finding her way in the world shin⟨...⟩ ⟨...⟩n."

—Colleen M. Farrell, MD, *Rumpus*

"An excellent memoir about growing up and growing in confidence as an adult woman, and about coping with changing relationships with parents as they age."

—Jim Higgins, *Milwaukee Journal Sentinel*

"[Readers who have trained in medicine] may also find themselves uncomfortably familiar with the routine denigration of foreign-born physicians, or the overtly classist preference for 'prestige' residencies. . . . Refusing to cast herself in a heroic, prescient, or moral role, Koven's faithful depiction of her acceptance of such practices allows us to consider our own blind spots, which is in effect what enables ongoing institutional cowardice and injustice to become more viscerally visible."

—Rana Awdish, *Los Angeles Review of Books*

"Funny, touching, and self-deprecating. . . . [A] thought-provoking and inspiring memoir."   —*Booklist*

"[I] was immediately engrossed. . . . [A] wise, must-read memoir. . . . [S]o many of us tend to see doctors as gods, yet [Suzanne Koven] show[s] the tender parts—the insecurities, the fears, especially as women."

—Caroline Leavitt, *New York Times* best-selling author of *Pictures of You,* via *CarolineLeavittville*

"Monumental . . . a disarmingly honest account of what it has been like, over the course of four decades, to be a woman in the medical profession." —Dale DeBakcsy, *Women You Should Know*

"A fine graduation present for a newly minted female M.D."
—*Kirkus Reviews*

"Suzanne Koven has written a remarkable memoir about her life as a doctor that is at once heartwarming, poignant, and breathtaking in its precision; this is a book about the essence of medicine, and will be invaluable to any doctor. But in its compassionate reflections on caring for the human body, it is also a book about life, and what makes a good one. I couldn't stop reading."
—Meghan O'Rourke, author of *The Invisible Kingdom*

"A how-to on becoming a doctor from the inside out. Addressed to women; good for all. Koven is wise, funny, and crazy honest. Essential reading for anyone who wants to be a doctor, or even see a doctor."
—Lisa Sanders, MD, *New York Times* "Diagnosis" columnist

"In *Letter to a Young Female Physician*, Suzanne Koven charts both the real and the spurious demands that the medical system makes on those who become doctors and care for us all. Her memoir is by turns reassuring and disturbing, comical and tragic, hopeful and dire. Medicine has advanced, but the particular difficulties facing young physicians have grown no less steep, and the impediments women continue to face even as they take a majority place in medical schools are considerable. Koven writes with style and wit and grace—but, more significantly, with insight and compassion."

—Andrew Solomon, author of *Far From the Tree*

"I devoured Dr. Suzanne Koven's memoir, *Letter to a Young Female Physician*, in a matter of days. . . . I imagine that this is a book I could return to at many points in my career, and it would reveal to me different truths. I am reminded of the power of narrative, which is like a buoy in the ocean of medical training, bringing me up to see the horizon."　　—Vidya Viswanathan, MD, *Doctors Who Create*

"Writing with honesty, warmth, and humility, internist Koven covers a lot of medical territory in illuminating the life of a female physician. . . . She must balance multiple roles as wife, mother, daughter of aging and sick parents, teacher, and doctor. Yet she finds comfort in listening, strength in stories."

—Tony Miksanek, MD, NYU Literature Arts Medicine Database

"*Letter to a Young Female Physician* is intimate, moving, piercing, and funny. In its pages, Dr. Suzanne Koven illuminates what it's like to be a doctor, what it's like to be a woman, and—in both roles—what it's like to be a human being, open to the pain and joys of the world."

—Lucy Kalanithi, MD, widow of Paul Kalanithi, author of
When Breath Becomes Air

LETTER

TO A

YOUNG FEMALE

PHYSICIAN

Notes from a Medical Life

❖ ❖ ❖

Suzanne Koven

W. W. NORTON & COMPANY
Independent Publishers Since 1923

The author gratefully acknowledges the publications in which several of these essays originally appeared, some in very different form: "Letter to a Young Female Physician," "Mom at Bedside, Appears Calm," "The Disease of the Little Paper," "The Doctor's New Dilemma," "Head and Shoulder," and "They Call Us and We Go" in the *New England Journal of Medicine*; "Prerequisites," originally published as "An Inherited Condition" in *Post Road*; "Admissions" and "Things Shameful to Be Spoken About" in the *Lancet*; "The Noncompliant Patient" in *Future Health Index*; "The Hateful Patient" in the *Boston Globe*; "Off the Charts" in the *American Journal of Medicine*; and "Science and Kindness," published as "Empathy, Examined" in the *Los Angeles Review of Books*.

Excerpt from "The Necessary Pleasures" from *And the Time Is: Poems, 1958–2013*, by Samuel Hazo. © 2014 by Samuel Hazo. Reprinted by permission of Syracuse University Press.

Excerpt from "The Dodo" by Leslie McGrath is reproduced with the gracious permission of the estate of Leslie McGrath.

For information about permission to reproduce selections from this book, write to Permissions, W. W. Norton & Company, Inc., 500 Fifth Avenue, New York, NY 10110

For information about special discounts for bulk purchases, please contact W. W. Norton Special Sales at specialsales@wwnorton.com or 800-233-4830

Manufacturing by LSC Communications, Harrisonburg
Book design by Ellen Cipriano
Production manager: Lauren Abbate

Library of Congress Cataloging-in-Publication Data

Names: Koven, Suzanne, author.
Title: Letter to a young female physician : notes from a medical life / Suzanne Koven.
Description: First edition. | New York, NY : W. W. Norton & Company, [2021]
Identifiers: LCCN 2021000742 | ISBN 9781324007142 (hardcover) |
ISBN 9781324007159 (epub)
Subjects: LCSH: Koven, Suzanne. | Women physicians—United States—Biography. |
Physicians—United States—Attitudes. | Medicine—Vocational guidance—United States.
| Physician and patient—United States. | Sexism in medicine—United States. | Sex discrimination in medicine—United States.
Classification: LCC R154.K65 A3 2021 | DDC 610.92 [B]—dc23
LC record available at https://lccn.loc.gov/2021000742

ISBN 978-1-324-02190-2 pbk.

W. W. Norton & Company, Inc., 500 Fifth Avenue, New York, N.Y. 10110
www.wwnorton.com

W. W. Norton & Company Ltd., 15 Carlisle Street, London W1D 3BS

1 2 3 4 5 6 7 8 9 0

For Carlo, who knew all along

Look wise, say nothing, and grunt.
Speech was given to conceal thought.

—SIR WILLIAM OSLER

Tell me everything.

—MY MOTHER

CONTENTS

AUTHOR'S NOTE

In these pages I have changed the names of my patients, colleagues, family members, and friends and altered potentially identifying details about them. I have also reconstructed scenes and dialogue and conflated certain events and people.

LETTER
TO A
YOUNG FEMALE
PHYSICIAN

INTRODUCTION

Letter to a Young Female Physician

May 18, 2017

This past June, I participated in an orientation session during which new interns were asked to write self-addressed letters expressing their hopes and anxieties. The sealed envelopes were collected and then returned six months later, when I'm sure the interns felt encouraged to see how far they'd come. This exercise, in which the intern serves as both letter writer and recipient, both novice and veteran, offers a new twist on an old tradition. In 1855, James Jackson published *Letters to a Young Physician Just Entering Upon Practice*. More recent additions to this epistolary canon include Richard Selzer's *Letters to a Young Doctor*, which appeared in 1982, and *Treatment Kind and Fair: Letters to a Young Doctor*, which Perri Klass published in 2007 on the occasion of her son's entry into medical school.

When I started my internship thirty years ago, I wasn't invited to share my hopes and anxieties in a letter—or anywhere else, for that matter. In fact, I recall no orientation at all, other than lining up to receive a stack of ill-fitting white uniforms, a tuberculin skin test, and a hasty and not particularly reassuring review of CPR. Perhaps the memory of my own abrupt initiation explains my response as I sat at the conference table watching the new interns hunched earnestly over their letters: I was filled with longing. I wanted so much to tell them, particularly the women—more than half the group, I was pleased to note—what I wished I'd known. Even more, I yearned to tell my younger self what I wished I'd known. As the interns wrote, I composed a letter of my own.

Dear Young Female Physician:

I know you are excited and also apprehensive. These feelings are not unwarranted. The hours you will work, the body of knowledge you must master, and the responsibility you will bear for people's lives and well-being are daunting. I'd be worried if you weren't at least a little worried.

As a woman, you face an additional set of challenges, but you know that already. On your urology rotation in medical school, you were informed that your presence was pointless, since, as you were told by an attending, "no self-respecting man would go to a lady urologist." There will be more sexism, some infuriating, some merely annoying. As a pregnant resident, you inquired about your hospital's maternity-leave policy for house officers and was told that it was a great idea and you should draft one. Decades into practice, when you call in a prescription, some pharmacists still ask for the name of the doctor you are calling for.

And there will be more serious and damaging discrimination as well. It pains me to tell you that, as I'm nearing the end of my career, female physicians annually earn on average $20,000 less than our male counterparts (even allowing for factors such as numbers of publications and hours worked); are less likely than men to receive academic promotions; are still underrepresented in leadership positions, even in specialties such as OB–GYN in which we are a majority; and are subjected to sexual harassment ranging from unwelcome "bro" humor in operating rooms and on hospital rounds to abuse so severe it causes some women to leave medicine altogether.

And there's another, more insidious, obstacle that you'll have to contend with—one that resides in your own head. At least, that has been the case for me. You see, I've been haunted at every step of my career by the fear that I am a fraud. This fear, sometimes called "imposter syndrome," is not unique to women. Your male colleagues also have many moments of insecurity, when they're convinced that they alone among their peers are incapable of understanding the coagulation pathway, tying the perfect surgical knot, or detecting a subtle heart murmur.

I believe that women's fear of fraudulence is similar to men's, but with an added feature: not only do we tend to perseverate over our inadequacies, we also often denigrate our strengths. While women like me—white, cisgendered, without disabilities, from privileged backgrounds—commonly experience these feelings of self-doubt, they are even more common and intense for women of color, members of the LGBTQ community, women with disabilities, and first-generation college graduates from poor and working-class families who may arrive at medical school having internalized the prejudices that have been directed at them all their lives.

A 2016 study suggested that patients of female physicians have superior outcomes. The publication of that finding prompted much speculation about why it might be so: perhaps women are more intuitive, more empathic, more attentive to detail, better listeners, or even kinder? I don't know whether any of those generalizations are true, but *my personal experience and observations make me sure of this: when women do possess these positive traits, we tend to discount their significance and may even consider them liabilities. We assume that anyone can be a good listener, be empathic—that these abilities are nothing special and are the least of what we have to offer our patients.*

I have wasted much time and energy in my career looking for reassurance that I was not a fraud and, specifically, that I had more to offer my patients than the qualities they seemed to value most.

Early on, I believed that displaying medical knowledge—the more obscure the better—would make me worthy. That belief was a useful spur to learning, but ultimately provided only superficial comfort. During my first-year clinical-skills course, an oncologist asked me to identify a rash. "Mycosis fungoides!" I blurted out, since it was one of the few rashes whose name I knew and the only one associated with cancer. My answer turned out to be correct, causing three jaws to drop at once—the oncologist's, the patient's, and my own—but the glow of validation lasted barely the rest of the day.

A little further on in training, I thought that competence meant knowing how to do things. I eagerly performed lumbar punctures and inserted central lines, and I applied for specialty training in gastroenterology—a field in which I had little interest—thinking that I could endoscope my way to self-confidence.

My first few years in practice, I was sure that being a good doctor meant curing people. I felt buoyed by every cleared chest x-ray, every normalized blood pressure. Unfortunately, the converse was also true: I took cancer recurrences personally. When the emergency room paged to alert me that one of my patients had arrived there, I assumed that some error on my part must have precipitated the crisis.

Now, late in my clinical career, I understand that I've been neither so weak nor so powerful. Sometimes even after I studied my hardest and tried my best, people got sick and died anyway. How I wish I could spare you years of self-flagellation and transport you directly to this state of humility!

I now understand that I should have spent less time worrying about being a fraud and more time appreciating about myself some of the things my patients appreciate most about me: my large inventory of jokes, my knack for knowing when to butt in and when to shut up, my hugs. Every clinician has her or his own personal armamentarium, as therapeutic as any drug.

My dear young colleague, you are not a fraud. You are a flawed and unique human being, with excellent training and an admirable sense of purpose. Your training and sense of purpose will serve you well. Your humanity will serve your patients even better.

> *Sincerely,*
>
> *Suzanne Koven, MD*
> *Harvard Medical School*
> *Massachusetts General Hospital*
> *Boston, Massachusetts*

1

Risk Factors

In elementary school my friend Lisa and I spent hours playing board games at her family's home or mine in the leafy Ditmas Park neighborhood of Brooklyn. Our favorite was Careers. Like Life, another game then popular, Careers aimed to instill in young Baby Boomers solid postwar American values. The goal was to select an occupation (doctor, lawyer, engineer, and so on) and accumulate "victory points" for fame, money, and happiness. Each player enjoyed distinct advantages—the engineer got extra points for landing on a particular square, and so forth—except the doctor. The only advantage to being the doctor was that you got to pretend you were a doctor.

I always chose to be the doctor.

It wasn't an obvious choice. My father was a doctor and so were most of the men in the couples who made up my parents' social circle. But none of the women were, except one, a psychoanalyst who practiced from her home in a wheelchair. She'd been paralyzed by spinal anesthetic while giving birth. Once, when I was about fourteen, I asked my mother whose fault it was that this woman was paralyzed. Was it the obstetrician's? The anesthesiologist's? My mother had just

entered law school after years as a housewife and volunteer active
in civic organizations, and I knew this was now the kind of thing
that interested her. During our morning commutes together to our
respective schools in her faux-wood-paneled station wagon she often
presented me with legal dilemmas. One concerned the claims of two
plaintiffs: a cattle breeder who sold a farmer a barren cow that turned
out to be with calf and thus worth much more than the farmer had
agreed to pay for it and a woman who sold a colorful stone to a jeweler for a dollar, neither of them realizing that it was a rough diamond. Should the breeder have been allowed to cancel the sale of
the cow that wasn't barren? Ought the jeweler be required to return
the woman's stone to her? I shrugged a teenage shrug. My mother
explained to me with obvious pleasure that in both cases the mistake
had been mutual. One party hadn't intentionally misled the other, so
the contract was valid. The farmer kept the cow and the jeweler the
diamond. It was all a matter of the contract. Didn't I see?

As to the psychoanalyst, my mother said she supposed if you
really thought about it, you could say her husband was to blame for
her disability, since he had impregnated her. The word "impregnated" sounded painful to me, like a punishment.

My father didn't encourage me to become a doctor, nor did he
discourage me. He never spoke of his work at home. He seemed
to have decided very early in his career to maintain a separation
between his medical and personal lives. My mother often told a
story about when my parents were newlyweds, living in Iowa City,
where my father was completing his residency in orthopedic surgery. He called one evening to tell her he'd be late for dinner
because he had to perform an emergency amputation. Assuming

that this task would dull my father's appetite, especially for meat, my mother put the leg of lamb she'd planned to serve in the icebox and, when my father returned from the hospital, presented him with a plain omelet. Why would he want *that* after a hard day's work? he asked. When my mother explained her reasoning he gently set her straight. "Amputations are my *job*," my father said.

Some afternoons I rode the city bus two and half miles from my high school in Brooklyn Heights to my father's office near the main branch of the public library and helped answer the phones, held injured limbs still, and developed x-rays until he'd finished seeing his patients and could give me a ride home. He practiced orthopedic surgery assisted by a staff of three vivid characters who played cameo roles in my childhood: a chain-smoking secretary named Bernice, who wore a nurse's uniform and starched white cap, though she was not a nurse; an x-ray technician named Sheila, who favored bright-red rouge and gargantuan false eyelashes; and a Trinidadian man named Skippy, who came by twice a week to remove plaster casts from arms and legs with a whining circular saw. I began writing in my forties, about the same age my mother was when she started law school, and in my first published essay I compared my father's orthopedic practice with mine in primary care. I recalled Bernice and Sheila and Skippy and the beribboned bottles of Chivas Regal and "World's Greatest Doctor" figurines my father received from his patients every December, and I speculated about why my patients so rarely brought me gifts.

In the years when Lisa and I played Careers, I had a watch that came with patent-leather bands in various colors that could be interchanged. In the '60s everyone was mad for color, but the only band I ever wore was the white one, which I associated with being a doctor. I glanced at it as I moved my doctor-shaped piece around the Careers board, admiring the bones in my wrist, a doctor's wrist, I thought. Even then I must have known that a doctor would never wear a white patent-leather watch band—a nurse, maybe, but not a doctor. Still, I wore the watch with the white band, chose to be the doctor in Careers, and admired my doctorly wrist.

I hated wearing dresses, and especially loathed tights. In public school girls were required to wear dresses, which meant, for most of the school year, wearing tights. I dreaded going to school because I equated school with tights. They gripped, they itched, they were not me. I sometimes stood bare- and flat-chested in front of the mirror in the bathroom I shared with my oldest brother, flexing my biceps, "making muscles." And sometimes I holed up in my parents' bathroom, carefully extracted the blade from my father's safety razor, smeared my face with Barbasol, and spent hours pursing my lips and shifting them side to side to expose my smooth cheeks, one and then the other. I cut my hair short and wore ribbed turtlenecks and straight Levi's and a newsboy cap—imitating not Twiggy, but John Lennon. I watched *Casablanca* and wanted to be Humphrey Bogart, not Ingrid Bergman. I watched *On the Waterfront* and wanted to be Marlon Brando, not Eva Marie Saint.

I didn't want to be a man, but I didn't want to be a woman, either, or what I thought a woman was. Or what my mother was, in my earliest memories of her, in the years before she went to law school, with her committees, her hats, and her boredom. It seemed so much easier to be a boy. Boys didn't wear tights. Boys didn't graduate from tights to garter belts to girdles that left red dents in their skin like the ones I saw on my mother's thighs each time she undressed. Things only got worse for girls.

One evening, when Lisa and I were playing at her house, her father entered through the front door and rushed past us. He was a doctor, too, but quick and lithe, unlike my heavy and slow-moving father. On this occasion, Lisa's father wore green scrubs and one of those surgical caps that ties neatly at the back of the head, not one of those floppy ones that resembles a shower cap. His scrubs and his shoes were spattered red. For many years I replayed this scene in my mind, the lean, handsome surgeon, so dashing in his fitted cap, covered in blood, in a hurry, his whole body radiating urgency.

Lisa was one of my best friends, but we had an uneasy relationship. Or, at least for me it was uneasy. She was petite, with golden tan skin, straight hair, light eyes, and unblemished knees. She had pristine penmanship and received 100% on every arithmetic quiz. I felt ungainly next to her: too tall, too large, my hair too curly, my knees rough and scabby, my handwriting smeary, my papers pocked with our teacher's red *x*'s. Lisa had, as far as I could tell, only one imperfection: a mole beneath her left eye that I longed to pluck off. But even that seemed perfect, since it was Lisa's. She was the first person I ever knew who seemed to have what I would later call the Answer.

On Sunday mornings I accompanied my father to the Brooklyn Jewish Hospital, where he, my mother, my brothers, and I were all born and where he performed surgery and visited his patients afterward. In the '80s, nearing bankruptcy, it merged with an Episcopal medical center and it's since been converted into an apartment complex. When I was a child "The Jewish" was a massive brick

monument to the royalty of midcentury Brooklyn: doctors like my
father and their wives. While my father checked on his patients, he
left me in one of two places: I preferred the Hospitality Shop, an
old-fashioned soda fountain located just off the lobby. I'd belly flop
and spin on the barstools, supervised by the mildly amused count-
erman. I liked it less when my father left me alone in the doctors'
lounge, where stern men in suits with celluloid collars and watch
fobs stared at me from oil portraits lining the walls, the Brooklyn
Jewish version of paintings I would later see at Johns Hopkins and
then at Harvard.

The trip to Louie's Appetizing after my father's hospital rounds
came to be linked in my child's mind with doctors, too, though
there was hardly anything medical about the wooden barrels of
pickles, sour and half-sour; the brightly lit refrigerated case of
metallic whitefish; the crank and ding of the old brass cash register;
the stacks of "shoe leather"—sheets of waxed paper coated with a
paste of ground-up dried apricots. My father always bought me my
own sheet, which I ate on the ride home, my tongue rolling over its
rough concretey surface. My father was a quiet, distant man who
often retreated, when he wasn't working, to his bed and his books.
He was nearly forty when I was born and while not inclined to rem-
inisce as my mother was, he did occasionally mention to me that
serving as a field surgeon in World War II had been the best part
of his life, that is: the best part of my father's life had ended long
before my birth. Sunday mornings at the Jewish Hospital and Louie's Appetizing were our special times together, though it's possible
that in my memory I've turned a handful of outings into a regular routine.

My mother did not work yet back then. I've read somewhere that it's a woman's job to make life less awful for everyone else. Life was not awful for us, but the point still holds. When we came home from Louie's she would run to the door and greet us, fully dressed, hair styled, smiling, animated, "peppy" as she liked to say—a quality she valued—and take the paper bag full of greasy packages and lay everything out on blue-and-white bone china, garnished with sliced lemons and capers and sprigs of parsley from her garden. This is what I understood: my father brought home the greasy brown bag and my mother turned it into something lovely. On her gravestone reads this fragment from Milton: *Beauty and grace in everything she does.*

Sometimes when I can't sleep I close my eyes and tour my childhood home. I rake my toes through the baby-blue shag carpeting I picked out for my bedroom; I see my hazy reflection in the yellow tile of the upstairs hall bathroom. I linger, especially, in the dining room. Dark-blue wallpaper flocked with black-velvet blossoms. A polished mahogany dining-room table and six matching chairs with needlepoint seat cushions. A crystal chandelier hanging from the carved ceiling. In 1949, when my parents returned from their honeymoon in Bermuda, my mother, aged twenty-one and, armed with a marriage manual that she hid in her underwear drawer, furnished her new home in her mother's ornate taste. The bay window looks out onto the backyard at the white picket fence covered with red roses. In 1970, when everything changes, my mother will rip out the fence and the roses and also the backyard lawn and install an austere slate patio bordered with compact, low-maintenance shrubs. She will apply to law school, trade the Jackie Kennedy knit suits from Loehmann's designer discounts that she wears to luncheons at the League of Women Voters for color-coordinated polyester pant-and-turtleneck sets like Diana Rigg wears in *The Avengers*. One powder-blue outfit, one mustard-yellow: clothes for women who don't have time to think about clothes. "My school uniforms," my mother will call them. She'll store away the bone china and buy dishwasher-safe plates and bowls made in Denmark, white rimmed with black.

But everything has not changed yet.

My mother, worried that my father should be properly catered to, honored, announces his arrival with a high pitched: *Your father's home!*, interrupting my television time and whatever my older brothers are doing in their rooms. My father has worked a long day and a man deserves a home-cooked meal. Standing rib roast. Liver and bacon. His face is stained with grease and his gray flannel pant legs and wingtip shoes are speckled with white casting plaster, which is also caked under his nails. My father sits at the head of the table and my oldest brother, six years older than me, at the other end. My mother sits to my father's left, and my other brother, four years older than me, sits to her left. I sit to my father's right, across from my mother. Our housekeeper, a Black woman named Essie, serves and clears, and when she is not serving or clearing she waits in the kitchen behind a swinging door. A sterling silver dinner bell meant to be used to summon Essie, a gift from my father's elegant mother, sits by my mother's place, but my mother never rings it.

◆　◆　◆

I'm not certain that the afternoons I spent at my father's medical office made us closer, especially. I am sure that watching my father practice medicine didn't give me the idea that I might one day become a doctor myself, or at least not at the time. Neither did my playing the doctor in Careers. As a child, I assumed to be a doctor you had to be a man and then in high school and college, I assumed to be a doctor you had to be good at science, both of which disqualified me. It wasn't until years later, after I graduated as an English major, that I decided to take the courses required to apply to medical school. When I told my father my plan he asked me whether it might just be easier for me to become a nurse. I raged at him—or, rather, at my mother *about* him—for being dismissive of my ambition, for his sexism. I'm still sometimes tempted by the belief that my father would have preferred that my brothers, who expressed no interest in medicine, had followed in his footsteps rather than that I did. But I knew even then that my father wasn't really a sexist. After all, he had fully supported my mother's desire to stop being a housewife and enter law school, pretty progressive for a husband fifty years ago. What hurt me about his comment was that he didn't mean it, that it was a throwaway line, intended to keep me at a distance.

Once I started medical school, I briefly harbored the fantasy that I might become an orthopedic surgeon and take over my father's practice one day, but he retired when I was barely halfway through, so that was never a possibility. Just before he ended his career, I thought I should watch him perform surgery at least once. The operation was the repair of a fractured wrist. Before sending me to the nurses' locker room to change, my father explained that he would make an incision, isolate the vital nerves and blood vessels so as not to injure them, and then stabilize the broken bone with metal plates and screws. When I joined him in the operating room the patient had already been anesthetized and his draped arm left partially exposed. A nurse positioned a bright lamp over the patient's limb and my father took up the knife.

Though I'd visited his office many times, though I'd grown up in a home where the telephone often rang late at night, a car with MD license plates sat parked in the driveway, and prescription drug samples filled the medicine cabinets, it was not until that moment that I truly understood that my father was a doctor.

Richard Selzer, one of my favorite physician-writers, recalls in his memoir, *Down from Troy*, that though his father, a general practitioner, died when "Dickie" was twelve, he felt that becoming a doctor himself drew him close to his father, even if only in memory. "It is the fellowship of those who labor in the same vineyard," Selzer writes. When I read this not long ago I had a similar thought, for the first time, about my own father: I'd graduated from medical school twenty years before he died and so, for the last two decades of his life, he was not only my father, but also my colleague.

Once, after my father died, my mother and I were talking about the Brooklyn days, when all the men were doctors, and I mentioned Lisa's father, the handsome surgeon. My mother said, "Oh, no, he wasn't a surgeon like Daddy." Only in my memory had Lisa's father been spattered with blood. "He was a medical man," my mother told me. That's what they called primary care doctors when I was a girl: medical men.

2

Prerequisites

The only thing I remember from my introductory chemistry course is that Einstein calculated Avogadro's number (6.022×10^{23}) using grains of pollen. I never understood what Avogadro's number was, but I enjoyed picturing that wild-haired genius with his loupe and tweezers painstakingly dissecting the sex organs of flowers. I struggled with the pre-med science courses I crammed in during the two years after I'd graduated from college. Science felt unnatural to me. I worked hard, earned good grades, and learned the rudiments by rote but I never became fluent in science, never dreamed in its language.

I found all the courses I took during those two years tedious except one: a virology seminar taught by a young biologist. I think his name was Kent Something, though it may be that I simply associate the name "Kent" with this man's appearance: lanky with long straight hair brushed back and cut bluntly just below his ears. Kent wore wide-wale corduroy pants, chambray shirts, and a tan. He tended to lean languidly against a desk, a lab bench, or a wall as if he couldn't bear to stand up unsupported. His posture gave me the impression that he didn't want to be where he was, and so I saw in him an ally.

The seminar required the usual midterm and final exams but, atypical for an undergraduate science class, also an essay to be presented orally. We could choose any topic as long as it related in some way to viruses. I'd just read Susan Sontag's *Illness as Metaphor*, published three years earlier, and proposed to Kent that since Sontag argues in the book that language can be misused to victimize people with cancer ("cancer victim" is one of the examples she gives) and since we'd learned about oncoviruses that cause cancer, an essay outlining Sontag's thesis would fulfill the assignment. Kent smiled broadly. I recall he had very white teeth, in an era before teeth whitening became popular.

In *Illness as Metaphor* Sontag writes disparagingly of our propensity to think of people with diseases as types. She calls out as myths the so-called tubercular personality (sad, romantic, overly passionate) and the cancer personality (emotionally repressed, asexual, and, as Sontag, a cancer patient herself, puts it unsparingly, "one of life's losers"). She quotes an Auden poem, "Miss Gee," about a spinster, "with her clothes buttoned up to her neck," who arrives at a doctor's office with a far-advanced tumor. That evening over dinner, the doctor tells his wife that " 'Cancer's a funny thing' " most likely to strike " 'childless women' " and " 'men when they retire' " " 'as if there had to be some outlet/For their foiled creative fire.' "

I didn't say this in front of the class or anywhere else, but the poem reminded me of my mother's unmarried sister, Paula, who had recently been diagnosed with leukemia and would die within a year, at fifty. Falling into the trap about which Sontag warned,

I'd wondered privately whether Paula's singleness, her childlessness had, like Miss Gee's, somehow brought on her cancer.

I don't remember much of what I said about Sontag in my presentation for Kent's virology seminar or the response of my classmates, an assortment of undergraduate pre-meds who, though they were only two or three years younger than me, seemed of a different generation. My talk was entirely pitched toward Kent, whom I wanted very much to impress. For one thing, I needed letters of recommendation for medical school and, though my workmanlike performances in the other pre-medical courses had earned me good grades, they were, I was sure, unmemorable to my instructors. More important, I wanted confirmation that I had crossed the void between what came more naturally to me and what did not; that I had, in some way, made sense of science.

My presentation was a success. I knew this because Kent, who stood leaning against a lab bench, nodded and smiled his white smile throughout. His grin broadened when I threw in a story of tenuous scientific relevance: A law school classmate and friend of my mother's who became a prominent attorney in New York had been interviewed on a local television news show and, soon afterward, she'd received a call from a geneticist at the Mayo Clinic. The geneticist explained that he was studying a rare familial syndrome that causes a dramatic white, skunklike streak in the hair of those who inherit the gene. He'd seen her on television and wanted to know if she'd consider becoming a subject in his research. My mother's friend laughed and told the geneticist that she couldn't help him. She'd dyed her hair that way. She was trying to look like Susan Sontag.

The class didn't laugh, but Kent laughed and that was all that mattered. I'd hit it out of the park. I wasn't at all surprised when, at the end of the next class, Kent asked me to stay behind for a few minutes. My heart raced and my ego dilated. He's going to ask me if he can write me a recommendation! I thought. Kent invited me to sit down while he stood and leaned. "Suzanne," he said, "I have a concern I want to share with you." This was going to be even better than I thought! I thought. He's going to *confide* in me! "My concern is this," he continued, "and it's a very serious one." He folded his arms. "I'm concerned that what you presented yesterday was not your own work." I felt something inside me collapse. Nothing hit out of the park, no recommendation; if Kent pursued this, maybe, no medical school. "But why?" I asked. "You said it was good!" "It *was* good," he said. "*Too* good."

I gathered myself and demanded nothing less than complete exoneration and an apology, which, to my surprise, Kent offered. "Yeah," he said, "I may have been reacting to the fact that your choice of topic was so unusual." A graduate student in an ill-fitting lab coat poked his head in the half-closed door just then. "President Reagan's been shot," he said. Kent turned back to me and said, "Well, I can't get too upset about *that*." His coldness repelled me. The value of his approval plummeted. The A I received in virology would be tainted in my mind, though he did write me a recommendation, which helped get me into medical school.

Just recently, I told the story of my alleged plagiarism to a friend and she observed that of course I never would have been accused of delivering "too good" a presentation if I'd been a male student. In all these years this thought had never occurred to me. I'd felt humiliated by Kent, not because I thought he was sexist, or even because he'd accused me of cheating—the charge had been halfhearted and quickly retracted—but, rather, because I felt unmasked for what I was: a mediocre science student trying to pull a fast one by talking about Susan Sontag instead of viruses.

3

Admissions

I applied to medical school because I panicked. I'd wanted, when I graduated from college, to be a journalist, specifically, George Orwell in *Homage to Catalonia* or *Down and Out in Paris and London*: to have exotic adventures, meet fascinating people, and write books that would change the world. Instead, I secured a job as the assistant to the assistant editor of a low-circulation trade magazine in an inadequately air-conditioned office in Washington, DC. I barely lasted the summer. I decided to become a physician the day my boss, a kind woman who took her role as my mentor seriously, invited me to lunch at an outdoor café near our office building in Dupont Circle. As we sweated and squinted in the blistering sun, she leaned across our wilting salads and informed me that if I continued to work very, very hard I might one day hope to have her job. Even organic chemistry and physics weren't more daunting than the prospect of spending my twenties in a cubicle, trying to attain a position as stultifying as the one I already had.

I didn't say any of this in my medical school admissions essay. What I did say was that I believed that my undergraduate study of English literature had prepared me well for a career in medicine and that I hadn't so much changed my mind about what interested me as taken the next step in a carefully laid-out plan. I must have been convincing because I received several acceptance letters. One admissions officer who interviewed me asked for permission to share my essay with his teenage daughter who loved poetry and hated science and whom he hoped might become a doctor.

I see now that what felt like a shameful truth, that I was propelled less toward medicine than away from boredom, was, like what I wrote in my application, just a story, and when I arrived at medical school, I presented my new classmates with a yet another one. I told them that my childhood dream of becoming a doctor had been thwarted by having attended an all-girls' school at which science and math were given scant attention. It had taken extra time and effort for me to overcome my substandard education. Never mind that the school, in fact, had several devoted math and science teachers and that many of my classmates went on to study these subjects in college. I repeated this tale, which cast me in a flatteringly plucky light, so often over the years that I came to believe it.

◆   ◆   ◆

Every doctor has his or her own personal origin myth, a story we tell about how and why we embarked on the profession. These myths are not unlike those humans have always crafted to explain natural phenomena and the very existence of the universe: stories that give meaning and structure to a process that can seem unsatisfyingly random. During the years I served on medical school admissions and internship-selection committees I heard many such

stories from earnest young men and women dressed in dark gabar-
dine. They often recalled a relative who was a physician or a sick
family member or an illness they'd experienced themselves. How
the doctors they'd encountered while growing up had exuded mas-
tery, wisdom, and compassion. How they wanted to be *that*.

Oddly, even though I spent hours after school tagging along
while my father practiced orthopedics, I didn't associate my desire
to visit his medical office with a desire to be a doctor. What I
wanted, I think, during those afternoons when I dipped x-rays into
vats of sharp-smelling chemicals and held down limbs as the circular saw screeched through plaster casts, was to be close to my father,
about whom I was endlessly curious. I went to his office, in part, to
discover clues as to why he had chosen a profession for which he did
not seem to have obvious enthusiasm. I also wanted, I now realize,
to witness at close range the freedom of men. My father, unlike my
mother, left the house early and didn't return home until after dark.
He wore the pants and he made the money. I wanted *that*.

Though I began my medical career with less than genuine passion, as a friend of mine once told me about her arranged marriage, in time I fell in love. What I loved at first was the drama, the
derring-do. I was thrilled when my pager went off, when I joined
the white-coated stampede racing toward a patient who had suffered
a cardiopulmonary arrest, when I came upon the obscure diagnosis,
the great save, the great case. By my final year in medical school,
though, I'd already lost my taste for these excitements. At the end of
our advanced medicine rotation we were required to deliver a grand
rounds-style presentation of a patient we'd admitted. One after
another my classmates rose to the podium to discuss aortic dis-

section, the pulmonary manifestations of rheumatoid arthritis, the cryptosporidiosis and cytomegalovirus infections to which patients with AIDS, then common and almost always fatal, are susceptible. In comparison, my own choice was, depending on your perspective, either very bold or very timid. I presented the case of a middle-aged woman who wasn't even sick, at least not physically. Her diagnosis was Briquet's syndrome which would later be called somatoform or somatization disorder and, still later renamed somatic symptom disorder. She was the daughter of a minor Hollywood star, an actress who had been a fixture of my childhood. In those days, psychiatric admissions were long and allowed for leisurely conversations during which I learned about this woman's unhappy years growing up in Tinseltown, the overweight and awkward daughter of a glamorous, if not especially talented, mother. She'd had many unnecessary surgeries and her list of allergies was so long—it included adhesive tape *and* adhesive tape remover—that she carried it around in a special notebook. Her fixation on her many symptoms and diagnoses consumed her. She couldn't hold on to a job or a relationship and appeared to be most at ease in the presence of doctors and nurses. Unlike other patients I'd met she seemed to actually enjoy being hospitalized. During the month I spent on the psychiatry unit I detected no progress in this woman's insight into the connection between her preoccupation with illness and the difficulty of her life. When the staff tried to help her make this connection, she responded that of course her life was difficult—she was sick!

In retrospect, my own self-awareness was little better. I didn't see then how the fact that I'd chosen a psychiatric patient for the final presentation in my advanced medicine rotation had any significance. I'd loved my time on psychiatry and considered becoming a psychiatrist, the specialty to which I felt most temperamentally suited—and had decided against it precisely because of that. I reasoned, unreasonably, that anything that came at all naturally to me wasn't worth doing. I may also have been influenced by a medical joke my father told me more than once as I was growing up: *The internist knows everything and does nothing; the surgeon knows nothing and does everything; the psychiatrist knows nothing and does nothing; and the pathologist knows everything and does everything a day too late.* None of this is really true, but I feared I'd be seen as the doctor who knows nothing and does nothing and so I went with my second choice: internal medicine.

In fact, internal medicine, especially primary care, isn't so different from psychiatry. Primary care doctors provide about a third of all mental healthcare in the United States, and it's estimated that 70 percent of a primary care doctor's practice involves mental health. I'd say these numbers are low. Each winter I see more patients with seasonal affective disorder than the flu, and the tissues in my exam room dry tears far more often than they muffle sneezes. And this is just fine with me. I find my patients much more interesting than their diseases.

I wonder whether, just as we take recertification exams every few years, we might be required, at intervals, to rewrite our medical school admissions essays, to articulate at each stage of our careers just what sort of doctors we aspire to be. Origin myths are meant to be retold and reinterpreted again and again.

I never asked my father why he became a doctor. When I was young, I developed my own theory. He was, after all, as much shaped by his times as my mother was. Being a doctor represented, especially for a middle-class boy who'd survived the Great Depression and World War II, the apogee of conventional masculinity. I reassessed this theory when, a few years ago, I learned of some severe financial reverses his family experienced when he was an adolescent and of which I hadn't been aware. Medicine, I assumed, must have seemed a safe harbor for him, whether he liked it or not. Then, just recently, I reconsidered this narrative too. I allowed my mind to wander back to those afternoons at his office in Brooklyn near the main branch of the public library, the grinding of the window air conditioners competing with the screech of the circular saw, my father's cigarette smoke mingling with the plaster dust. I pictured his large craggy face leaning intently toward a patient as she described her pain, and, years after my father's death, I understood something I hadn't understood before: I'd never seen him happier.

4

Clinical Skills

I knocked shyly on the open door of Albert Blake's hospital room. All I knew about him was that he was fifty-four years old and that he had leukemia. As I watched him doze for a few long seconds before knocking again more firmly, I took in his gaunt, ashen face and withered arms and observed that Mr. Blake, as we'd been taught to record in our notes, "appeared older than his stated age." He opened his eyes, smiled, and nodded toward the chair beside his bed, inviting me to sit down. Suddenly he seemed younger, healthier. I felt as if I were looking at one of those holograms where two images alternate, one shifting into the next, in Mr. Blake's case: *sick/ well, patient/person.*

I'd been assigned to interview Mr. Blake in the spring of my first year of medical school during a course called Clinical Skills. A few weeks earlier my classmates and I sat excitedly in a lecture hall and each received, courtesy of a pharmaceutical company, a starched white coat and a monogrammed black leather doctor's bag equipped with an otoscope, an ophthalmoscope, a stethoscope, and a reflex hammer. Once a week we'd put on the coats and carried the bags to the hospital to meet, in groups of four or five, an instructor who taught us how to record patients' histories and how to use our tools. We walked through the hospital corridors on the way to these sessions hoping that we wouldn't be mistaken for doctors—and also hoping that we would.

Long before deciding on a medical career, years before I wanted to be a journalist, I'd aspired to be an actor and my new costume and props made me feel as if I were onstage, a sensation reinforced by the scripts I'd newly memorized, long lists of questions we were supposed to ask our patients: Did they have headaches, double vision, ear pain, bloody noses? Had they been exposed to exotic birds or eaten unpasteurized cheese? Did they have chest pain, and did the pain occur when they took a deep breath, or when they ate or walked? So many questions, all of them as abstract to us as philosophy since we did not yet know which diseases could be transmitted by birds or cheese, or what the symptoms we elicited meant, much less how to treat them.

In the following three years, when we knew more, patients would be chosen for us to interview and examine based on whether they had interesting diseases or dramatic findings on their physical exams. We'd be sent to see the patient with sarcoidosis; listen to the chest of the woman with rhonchi, rattling breath sounds so loud even a novice couldn't miss her pneumonia; introduce ourselves to the man with Wernicke's encephalopathy, in which chronic heavy alcohol consumption obliterates short-term memory, then we'd wait five minutes, return to the room, and introduce ourselves again to the patient who would, in that short interval, have forgotten meeting us entirely.

In Clinical Skills, though, patients were selected for being . . . patient. Those who agreed to have medical students practice on them might have dozens troop by to ask the same questions again and again. *What brought you into the hospital? When did this symptom begin? Have you ever had anything like this before? What brought you into the hospital? What makes it better or worse? What brought you into the hospital?*

Mr. Blake was patient. He was also a natural raconteur who said he didn't mind passing the hours during his tedious hospitalizations by chatting with students. He'd told his story many, many times. Still, when my turn came to settle into the chair by his bed with my clipboard, Mr. Blake did not stint. What had brought him into the hospital? Well, he said, leaning back on his pillows and drawing a leisurely breath, it was like this: One afternoon about a year earlier he was coaching his ten-year-old grandson's baseball team. He'd been spending more time with the boy since his mother, Mr. Blake's daughter, had gotten involved with drugs and acquired a boyfriend who was, in Mr. Blake's opinion, a stone-cold loser. Anyway, there he was, standing behind home plate, urging one of the kids to keep his eye on the ball, when suddenly he'd felt light-headed. He held on to the chain-link fence to keep from falling and as he looked at his fingers, wrapped tightly through the metal wire, he noticed how pale they were.

And on Mr. Blake went, through the arrival of the ambulance, his grandson running in crying from left field, the first and the second and the third rounds of chemo during which his wife held everyone up as she always had, including the Blakes' daughter, who, not long after the onset of her father's illness, had ditched the drugs and the boyfriend and would be coming by to visit shortly with his favorite cookies, though he doubted he'd have enough appetite to eat them.

I transcribed all of this information and a few days later, after my instructor had approved my report, tucked it away for sentimental reasons only, thinking I'd be unlikely ever to look at it again.

Just a few months afterward, though, I dug through my desk drawers looking for my note about Mr. Blake. I was now at the end of my second year and rotating on the oncology ward, where he had again been admitted. I asked if I might be assigned to help take care of him. Mr. Blake didn't remember me, and he was sicker than when I'd last seen him, but he greeted me as he had before with a warm smile and an encouraging wave. And he again tolerated my history-taking, which remained plodding, though was somewhat more efficient now that I had a better idea of what to ask and so could spare him my slavish recitation of all the questions I'd committed to memory. I asked Mr. Blake how he was feeling, got an update on his treatment, which was not going well, and left the room to copy down his medications, allergies, test results, and other data at the nurses' station. As a new clinical student, I wasn't expected to finish my note before leaving for the day and considered myself lucky to have waiting at home a thorough account of the onset of Mr. Blake's illness that I could easily add to what I'd just recorded.

Tucked into a folder containing papers I'd written in college, I found it. My florid descriptions of Mr. Blake's pale fingers clutching the chain-link fence, his grandson's tears, the addicted daughter and her loser boyfriend made me cringe. None of that was important. All that counted now were Mr. Blake's daily fever charts and lab values, his IV fluids and urine output, his chemotherapy regimen. These were matters of life and death, unlike his story, which, however engagingly Mr. Blake had shared it with me, was irrelevant to his current medical care. I tossed my old note back in the folder with my essays on *Bleak House* and *Mrs. Dalloway*, having concluded that it was, like they were, useless. Then I wrote my new note as if I'd never met Mr. Blake before, as if I'd never heard his story.

5

Mnemonics

As a medical student I loved mnemonics, those acronyms, often as hard to remember as the facts themselves, that served as temporary containers for the information served up daily in such large portions they seemed in danger of spilling out of our brains. Bones and muscles, chemical bonds and hormones, antibodies and enzymes, symptoms and diseases could all be reduced to acronyms and, at least for a few hours before a test, mastered, even when the concepts themselves remained opaque. Most of my classmates had majored in the sciences and were, unlike me, right out of college and living in the dorm across the street from the hospital, not in apartments with spouses and wedding-present china. But even they admitted that, try as they might, it was impossible to remember everything.

At our thirtieth reunion, I confided to a classmate who had studied biochemistry as an undergraduate that I'd spent much of our first year in medical school crying in frustration in the ladies' room next to the lecture hall. She told me this could not have been true. Sipping a glass of white wine, her other hand tucked tightly across the chest of her cocktail dress as if protecting herself from the pain of an old wound even as we laughed about it, she said, "*I was always crying in that ladies' room and I never saw you there. In fact, I thought you had it all together, so much more mature than I was, so married.*"

We spent considerable time in those days comparing ourselves unfavorably to one another. We'd all been top students in our high schools and colleges, able to learn all the material in any course. Now even the most hardworking among us could barely keep up. Except that each of us felt *especially* inadequate. In the middle of the night, a week before a physiology midterm during my first year, I became extremely anxious and woke my husband. "What's wrong?" he asked. We'd met at Yale as English majors and he, like me, had completed his pre-medical requirements after college. He was now two years ahead of me in medical school and I frequently looked to him for reassurance. "Tell me," he said, wrapping his arms around me. "The pancreas!" I cried. "I don't understand the pancreas!"

I'm not sure why it didn't occur to us then that we could *all* become excellent doctors. I think it had something to do with the fact that for the first two years of medical school our entire class sat in the same lecture hall or lab all day, five days a week. My mother intuited the effect this claustrophobic arrangement had on us. Once I called home after receiving a poor grade on an anatomy test for which the class average had been high. In a rare instance when I didn't find one of her platitudes irritating, my mother told me that my classmates and I needn't compete with one another; there would be plenty of room for all of us once we left the confines of medical school. Still, I, and the woman I met at the reunion, and no doubt many others in my class, felt isolated in our misery. I now

know—and it took a very long time for me to appreciate this—
that shame incorrectly insists on its uniqueness, invariably, just as
I know that you can't sneeze with your eyes open and that with
age, everyone loses the ability to accommodate for near vision, no
exceptions, two things I learned in medical school and had no difficulty remembering.

One of the first mnemonics everyone learns is for the cranial
nerves, the tiny structures that allow us to see and smell and hear and
stick out our tongues and smile and wink and shrug our shoulders,
among other functions. There are twelve of them: Olfactory, Optic,
Oculomotor, Trochlear, Trigeminal, Abducens, Facial, Auditory,
Glossopharyngeal, Vestibulocochlear, Accessory, and Hypoglossal.
As I list them here, I rely on the nonsensical chant I learned back
then: *On Old Olympus Towering Tops A Finn And German Viewed A
Hops.* There are other versions, including: *Oh, Oh, Oh, To Touch And
Feel A Girl's Vagina, AH!* Many mnemonics are similarly bawdy, rel-
ics from the days when nearly all medical students were men. Mem-
orization of the numerous and confusing carpal bones of the wrist,
for example—Scaphoid, Lunatum, Triquetrum, Pisiforme, Trape-
zium, Trapezoid, Capitate, and Hamate—has been aided by: *Some
Lovers Try Positions That They Can't Handle*; *She Looks Too Too Pretty
To Catch Her*, and *Scabby Lucy Tried Pissing Hours after Copulating
Two Twins.* Perhaps are there new mnemonics, now that the majority of students in American medical schools are women? Scabby
Lucy's revenge.

We did have several female instructors, especially in the first
two years. One was a dermatologist who taught us the trick for
remembering the characteristics of melanoma, the most dangerous

form of skin cancer. If you see a mole you look for ABCDE: *Asymmetry, irregular Borders, more than one or uneven Color, a large Diameter, Evolving and changing.* The dermatologist was young, not much older than we were, fair and freckled with red hair, exactly the coloring that puts one at risk for melanoma. I remember wondering if this dermatologist had the disease in her family. Or whether she'd had it herself.

At the very end of the lecture, the dermatologist turned off the slide projector, stepped out in front of the podium, and asked that the auditorium lights be turned back on, signaling that what she was about to say would not be on the exam. Her whole affect changed. She relaxed the way an actor might, after a scene is shot. Though she still wore a starched white coat, she now seemed more like a friend, or an older sister. "Listen," the dermatologist said, "after seeing all these photos of skin cancer, you're going to go home and find something on your own body, and you'll be convinced you're dying. We call that 'medical student's disease.' And when this happens, I want you to call me and come right over to my office so I can reassure you."

I think some of my classmates took the dermatologist up on her offer, but not me. I didn't suffer from that medical student's disease. But I did have another affliction, an even more common one, I think: the fear that I wouldn't remember everything. That, despite all the mnemonics, all the lectures and labs and late nights, I wouldn't know enough. That I would miss something. That I would kill someone. That I would look foolish.

We Have a Body

I chose internal medicine for my first clinical rotation at the end of my second year of medical school and was sent to the old Baltimore City Hospital, which, unlike Johns Hopkins Hospital just a couple of miles away in the Black neighborhood of East Baltimore, served mostly white, working-class patients, many of them employed at the nearby Bethlehem Steel plant. My first day at City the senior resident on my team assigned me a patient named Mary who was, he informed me, a "great medical student case." By this he meant that she had, as he put it, "interesting pathophysiology." He sat me down in the charting room, grabbed a piece of progress note paper, and drew out Mary's problem. She had metastatic ovarian cancer, which had studded her internal organs and caused fluid to leak into her abdomen. Her cancer had taken away her appetite, so she was poorly nourished and thus didn't have much protein in her blood. An adult human body contains about forty liters of water distributed between the cells, the tissues, and the blood vessels to which fluid is attracted by salt and protein. If the vessels are leaky and the protein level is low, fluid wanders out of the blood vessels and into the interstitial tissues, causing the limbs and abdomen to swell. Mary, the resident said, looked like the Pillsbury Dough Boy, with so much fluid in her tissues that you could stick a finger in her belly or legs and leave a dent. This phenomenon is called "third spacing," since the excess fluid isn't in the blood vessels or the organs—the first two spaces— but in the in-between tissues, the third space.

The problem with third spacing, the resident explained, was that it put the medical team—and Mary—in an impossible posi- tion: if they gave Mary diuretics to remove the excess fluid, she would quickly become dehydrated and her blood pressure would drop dangerously low since she wouldn't have enough volume in her circulatory system. But if they gave her fluid to try to increase her circulatory volume, it would end up in the third space and increase Mary's swelling. I wanted to ask how a problem so clearly under- stood could be so difficult to solve, but I was afraid that this was a stupid question and I wanted to make a good impression.

Armed with my clipboard, to which I'd attached the resident's drawing, I entered Mary's room with some trepidation. A nurse had told me that the other reason I'd been assigned this patient, besides her interesting pathophysiology, was that the residents didn't like her. The nurse said Mary snarled at the staff, no matter how much they did for her. I now recognize that the hopelessness of Mary's condition, as codified by the Do Not Resuscitate order on her chart, was likely a large part of what made her so unpopular. Doctors don't like feeling ineffective and often unconsciously blame patients with conditions that are hard to diagnose or treat for making us feel that way. Then, though, I simply accepted that my role as a novice med- ical student—perhaps the only role I felt competent to fulfill—was to spend time at the bedside of a patient my superiors would just as soon avoid.

I stood in the doorway of her room watching Mary breathe, wondering which would reflect more poorly on me in the eyes of the resident: waking a sleeping patient or failing to examine the first patient he'd assigned to me. Mary's eyes were closed and her face was as white as the sheet tucked neatly across her chest. I'd read her chart before going to see her, and knew that Mary was sixty-two years old, that she was single and lived alone, and that before illness had forced her to retire, she'd worked as a secretary at an insurance company. Still, the swollen body lying in the bed seemed to me as ageless and genderless and anonymous as the cadaver I'd dissected in anatomy class a year earlier had seemed.

With her eyes still closed, Mary said, in a low, gravelly voice at once forceful and barely audible: "Come here." I approached slowly, stopping a few feet away from her, and announced, "I'm the medical student on the team." Her eyes still shut and her voice barely above a whisper, Mary commanded: "Come *here*." I obeyed and stood an inch from the side of her bed, waiting for my next instruction. Mary slowly withdrew her left arm from the tightly tucked sheet and said: "Sit down." I sat. Then Mary said: "Hold my hand," and I did.

Something happened next. I wasn't sure what, at first. Mary opened her mouth, and her breath came out in small bubbles, which I watched inflate and deflate, more and more slowly, until the bubbles formed and remained. I stared at the bubbles. I gripped Mary's cool, damp fingers between my own. And then I understood what had happened. Mary had died.

◆ ◆ ◆

Growing up Jewish, I'd never attended a wake with an open casket and so had never viewed a corpse. In fact, no one I knew died when I was young except for a girl in my third-grade class named Debbie Weitzman who wore plaid jumpers and formed her capital D's, when we learned cursive that year, like billowing sails, and who, mysteriously, didn't return to school after the summer when fourth grade started. Some older kids said that she'd been playing with a relative's gun and had shot herself by accident, but our teachers never mentioned Debbie's name again. Death lingered in the background of my childhood like a rumor. My father had fought in the war, as everyone's father had, and though he didn't talk about it much he made it clear that vigilance would be required if we were to avoid sharing the fate of 6 million murdered Jews. "Vigilance," for our family, consisted of not buying any products made in Germany and resolving never to set foot on German soil. My own contribution was my fantasy that an attic closet crammed with luggage and old furniture under the eaves of our Victorian home would make a perfect place to hide when the Nazis arrived in Brooklyn.

My mother's father, Samuel, for whom I was named according to the Jewish custom of giving a baby a name with the same first letter as that of a deceased relative's name, had died two years before I was born. My mother liked to recall, somewhat morbidly, I thought, that she was pregnant with me at the unveiling of his headstone a year later. She often said that the only salve for her grief after her father died was to plant flowers, to plunge her bare hands into the earth. Despite the fact that my mother frequently spoke of missing him in such a visceral way, my grandfather's corporeal absence didn't preoccupy me. Rather, as a child, I scanned the clouds to see if Grandpa Sam, dressed in the World War I doughboy's uniform he wore in the framed photograph that stood on my mother's dresser, might be smiling down on me.

Death remained vague until one winter morning when I was a senior in high school. It seems preposterous to me now, as a mother and as a doctor, that any responsible adult thought it was a good idea for our AP biology class to take a field trip to the Medical Examiner's Office of the City of New York to witness the autopsy of a nursing student from the Bronx who'd been stabbed to death the night before by her boyfriend. But the father of one of my classmates was a coroner and he had offered to host us. So, with the enthusiastic approval of our teacher, the written permission of our parents, and, presumably, the blessing of the school's administration, off we went. On the short subway ride from our small, private all-girls' high school in Brooklyn Heights to First Avenue and East Twenty-Sixth Street in Manhattan, where the Medical Examiner's Office was and still is, the coroner's daughter told us that her father had gotten up from the breakfast table that morning to answer the telephone and, sitting back down, had announced: "Well, we have a body for you girls." Perhaps this seems an indelicate thing for him to have said, especially to a teenage daughter. And yet, I like to think that the coroner's words implied respect for her toughness, and by extension, ours.

I remember that the day was cold and sunny and that the walk from the subway to the medical examiner's office was windy. In fact, I remember everything about the trip to view the autopsy except for the name of the dead woman, though I do recollect that of the handsome young man who lay on the gurney next to hers in the morgue, naked and with a single bullet hole in the center of his forehead: James Narducci. He was, I read a few days later in the *New York Times*, a pre-med at City College who had tried to intervene in the robbery of a hardware store. In addition to the details I recall, I've filled in imaginary scenes, no less vivid: the argument between the nursing student and her boyfriend; the thrust of the knife; my classmate's father returning to his breakfast from the telephone, placing his napkin back on his lap, pouring another cup of coffee.

What I remember most about the autopsy, though, is that I felt I must not flinch or look away as many of my classmates did. That to do so would be girly, and undoctorly, though I had not clearly articulated then any ambition to be a doctor. I also intuited that to flinch or look away would be to acknowledge the reality that this young woman, barely two years older than me, with long straight hair parted in the middle such as I had always wanted for myself and wearing a rust-colored suede jacket similar to one I'd seen in *Glamour* magazine and coveted, was like me and that I was like her, just a knife and a jealous boyfriend away from the autopsy table. She was, in a way, my first patient.

◆   ◆   ◆

My second body was the cadaver I dissected in my first year of medical school. During gross anatomy, or "gross" as it's sometimes called, students learn the name, structure, and location of all 206 bones in the human body as well as those of the lobes of the brain and lung, every muscle, tendon, ligament, and nerve, the abdominal and pelvic organs, the chambers and valves of the heart, and the intricate components of the eye and ear—knowledge that, besides being more or less necessary to practice medicine, depending on your specialty, admits you to that exclusive society of people who possess it. Less often mentioned but perhaps more significant, cutting up a dead person is the student's first lesson in what's been called the "hidden curriculum of medical school," an inaccurate but comforting message that asserts that doctors do not belong to quite the same species as our patients; that we are less vulnerable, more likely to wield the knife than to lie beneath it.

Anatomy left me cold. Literally. All that fall I couldn't shake a chill that I associated with the brightly fluorescent-lit lab, the gleaming steel tables on which the cadavers lay. The formaldehyde stink didn't leave my hands or hair for weeks, despite the fact that we wore rubber gloves and plastic aprons during dissection, and changed into clothes that we'd left in a locker outside the lab, in my case: an old T-shirt of my husband's bearing the logo of his high school and a pair of too-tight khaki pants from Casual Corner.

The first day of gross we were divided up alphabetically by last name and assigned four to a table. My team, another *K*, an *L* and an *M*, included two Black men, an Asian woman, and me, a misleading diversity unrepresentative of our predominantly white and male class. We called ourselves the Mod Squad but did not, as some students did, name our cadaver, a woman who, we discovered when we removed the plastic wrappings from her face late in the semester, wore in death a menacing scowl. She was large, heavy, and hard to maneuver.

What I remember most about anatomy was that it was uncomfortable, but not emotionally. I was bored and my feet hurt from hours of standing. Spatial orientation is not my strong suit and acquiring the necessary habit of thinking diagonally—the patient's right is the doctor's left as they face each other—which students first develop in anatomy class, gave me a headache. I didn't associate the bloated, smelly, log over which we labored with my own mortality or anyone else's. Nor did I deflect, consciously or unconsciously, the idea of such an association. We weren't reminded, particularly, of our cadavers' humanity. At the end of the course there was no memorial service, there were no candles, no songs, and no prayers of gratitude, as there often are in medical schools today, to honor the people our bodies had once been.

In our anatomy course there was also no harassment of women by male classmates such as had occurred in years past. Archival photographs document instances in which white male students posed their cadavers, often poor Black people, some of whose bodies had been stolen, in grotesque positions or brandished severed body parts. In addition to their inherent racism these pranks were no doubt intended, at least in part, to drive away the male students' few female classmates. Title IX, passed by Congress in 1972, outlawed gender discrimination in education resulting in the enrollment of more women in American medical schools. By the time I arrived a decade later, though still in the minority, our numbers had diluted the culture in which misogynistic practical jokes were acceptable. As it turned out, the closest I came to being harassed in anatomy was when one of my classmates, a G at a neighboring table, announced to me midsemester over an awkward coffee that though he knew I was married he wanted me to know that he "really, *really* liked" me.

In my second year of medical school we were given an assignment in our microbiology class far less dramatic than dissecting a cadaver and yet, to me, more profound. My lab partner in micro was my classmate Kevin, a pale, skinny young man with a wispy mustache who wore wire-rimmed aviators and rugby shirts. On the first day of the course, we were instructed to stick a Q-tip into our partner's nostril and then smear a Petri dish with it. Over the next week we would observe the growth of bacteria on the dish and record our observations. Kevin and I took turns donning surgical gloves and solemnly inserting a Q-tip in each other's nose in silence, without giggling or even smiling. I think we sensed that to do so would be to "break scene," to acknowledge the strangeness of the act, this proximity to another person's body, not for love or affection, but for a new kind of intimacy altogether. Perhaps I'm being oversensitive or making too much of such a small moment, but consider: if the lesson were only about nasal bacteria, wouldn't we have been asked to simply swab our own noses?

◆ ◆ ◆

The summer between my second and third years, after the rotation at City where I'd briefly met Mary, I signed up for inpatient oncology at Johns Hopkins Hospital. Rotating first on internal medicine and then next on a medical subspecialty made me feel slightly more competent than I might have felt in, say, OB-GYN. Adding to this flicker of self-confidence was something that makes me ashamed to recall: The intern on the oncology team, a year out of medical school in Mexico, was visiting from his training program at a local community hospital. By the time I arrived on the oncology ward he'd been working there for only a couple of days, not really enough time for anyone to fairly assess his competence. Nevertheless the resident, a self-possessed woman named Patricia, and the oncology fellow, a linebacker of a man named Joe who had finished his residency and was now doing subspecialty training, had already sized up José as the weak link on the team. Patricia and Joe pulled me aside the first day of my rotation to tell me that I would have to function above the level of the usual medical student to compensate for José. The implication was clear: his foreign training and low-prestige residency—and possibly his dark skin and his accent—made him less qualified. Medicine is much more diverse now—many of the residents in my hospital are not white and many are foreign-born—and saying such a thing to a medical student would be less likely today, though it certainly does still happen. But it seemed normal then, at least to me, which again, I'm ashamed to admit.

A few years ago, I visited a mentor of mine who had been a dean at Hopkins when I was a medical student. A retired pediatrician, Henry was in his eighties then. He told me a story about when he was a resident in the late 1940s, rounding with the legendary pediatric cardiologist Helen Taussig, one of very few women doctors then on the staff of Johns Hopkins Hospital. Dr. Taussig invented a novel corrective surgical procedure for infants with certain congenital heart defects. The procedure became known as the "blue baby operation" and, more formally, as the Blalock-Taussig shunt. Alfred Blalock, the surgeon who first performed the operation, took top billing. Blalock's lab technician, a Black man named Vivien Thomas, the grandson of a slave, played a key role in perfecting the procedure, a version of which is still performed today, but attempts to rename it the Blalock-Thomas-Taussig shunt haven't stuck. As Henry was rounding with Dr. Taussig they walked by the blood bank. Until the 1950s the blood bank as well as hospital wards, bathrooms, the cafeteria, and even the morgue were segregated at Hopkins. White patients were transfused with white donors' blood and Black patients with Black donors' blood. In an emergency, a Black person might receive a white person's blood, but never vice-versa. One argument against hiring female doctors in the early days of the hospital was that white women couldn't possibly be asked to provide medical care to Black men. Dr. Taussig pointed to the blood bank and stated aloud what everyone knew: that the blood of Black people and the blood of white people were stored separately there. She then asked Henry: "Doesn't this strike you as very wrong?" Henry had grown up in racially and ethnically diverse Passaic, New Jersey. His family was not unlike the many immigrant families Henry's pediatrician, William Carlos Williams, described in his writings. Henry told me he was horrified to realize that though he'd walked past the blood bank countless times and was well aware of its segregation policy, he'd never questioned it.

When Henry told me this story, not long before his death in 2010, I thought about the de facto segregation still in place at Hopkins during my residency in the 1980s. The private service, overseen by experienced physicians, admitted mostly white patients from the suburbs of Baltimore as well as those who jetted in from all over the world to receive care at one of the great academic medical centers.

By contrast, the ward service admitted mostly poor Black patients who lived in housing projects surrounding the hospital, who had no private health insurance, and whose doctors were us residents. The ward service was called Osler, in honor of Sir William Osler, the Father of Modern Medicine, who was appointed the first professor of medicine at Johns Hopkins in 1889. We residents told ourselves that we provided our Osler patients superb care, even better than the private patients received from more experienced physicians.

I don't recall ever speaking with my fellow-residents about the racism reflected in the way the hospital was organized, and, in a way, white residents had no motivation to do so. The hospital's segregation reinforced the reassuring message of the hidden curriculum, that we were fundamentally unlike our patients. We residents, mostly white, either upper middle class or on our way to that socioeconomic status, would never suffer from the diseases our Osler patients suffered from: AIDS and bacterial endocarditis from injecting drugs intravenously, amputations and blindness from poorly controlled diabetes, emphysema and asthma from smoking and air pollution. Public-health experts now recognize that poverty, not race, predisposes people to these conditions. Then we were taught to identify patients according to their color during our presentations on morning rounds—*This is a fifty-year-old Black man with diabetes*—as if Blackness alone were a risk factor for disease. The racism implicit in this assumption validated what we as white trainees told ourselves, consciously or not: that we weren't like our Osler patients, so we were safe. The private patients were more like us but, for the most part, we were too young to worry about whether the coronary disease and colon cancer that plagued them would affect us.

Of course, the experiences of the few residents of color in our program were different from mine, but I learned this only years later when I thought to ask. At my mentor Henry's memorial service I reconnected with Edward, one of the few Black students in my medical school class and also in my residency. He's now an infectious diseases specialist in Philadelphia. I told Edward that I'd been thinking about how little aware I'd been of the segregation of patients during our training, even though it had been hiding in plain sight. But it had never been hidden for Edward. He told me that he'd forged bonds with many of our Black patients on Osler that he was certain were closer than white residents had. And several of the white patients on the private service had refused to be treated by him.

Regarding José, as a second-year medical student I was just grateful to be considered more competent than *anyone*. He and I took call together that first night. Patricia would take the next night, and a resident working that month in an outpatient clinic would be pulled to cover the night after that, and so we would rotate, every third night. Joe would arrive each morning to assess our work and, with the help of an attending physician, oversee the ward during the day.

The patients on the oncology ward were very sick. Hospitalized patients were generally less ill than they are now because insurance companies today are much less likely to pay for hospitalizations than they were then—you have to be practically dying to get more than the briefest admission covered. Back then it was not unusual for someone with a mysterious fever or diarrhea or some other non-acute symptom to stay for a week or two or even three, especially on the floors for privately insured patients. These patients might be seen by every specialty consultant in the hospital and, if none of them could make a diagnosis, they'd be discharged. Especially when I was an intern and had to do all the work associated with these prolonged investigations, they seemed wasteful, indulgent of the rich and hypochondriacal. My fellow interns and I scornfully dubbed such hospital stays "dinner and Dalmane," after a sleeping pill then popular among the well-heeled.

Oncology was not dinner and Dalmane. Most of the patients, in the throes of chemotherapy, didn't eat any meals at all. They were thin and bald, lying listlessly in bed watching movies from the limited selection in the floor's VHS library or TV, which then featured few channels. Deaths were common that month. One woman, younger than me, with a platelet count so low that her blood didn't clot, hemorrhaged from a stomach ulcer, spewing red across the beige linoleum floor as we watched in horror. Even Patricia, whose calmness I admired and had decided to emulate, placed her hand over her mouth at the sight of so much blood.

When it came time for José and me to divide up the new patients coming in that first day, I was relieved when he took the two sicker-sounding ones and told me to take the one who would be more stable. José might have been aware of the low esteem in which Patricia and Joe held him, but he was, after all, a doctor, and I was only a student, with just two months of clinical experience at that.

My new patient's name was Colette. She was Black, a lifelong resident of East Baltimore, twenty-seven years old, and twenty-seven weeks pregnant. She'd been referred to oncology from the obstetrics clinic. Her pregnancy had been uneventful other than a nagging cough in her second trimester. Because of the cough, she'd been given a skin test for tuberculosis, a disease with a high incidence in her neighborhood. The test was positive. A positive skin test can indicate past exposure to TB, which may lie dormant in the lungs and elsewhere in the body for decades, or signify active infection. The first step in sorting out dormant from active TB is obtaining a chest x-ray. Though doctors are reluctant to expose pregnant women to radiation, Colette's obstetrician had rightly determined that it was important to know if she had active TB, which could affect her unborn baby if left untreated. Her protruding midsection was draped with a lead-lined cloth and a chest x-ray was done. It didn't show tuberculosis. It showed a large lung mass, which, when biopsied, proved to be adenocarcinoma, the most common type of lung cancer among nonsmokers like Colette. She was now being admitted so that our team could formulate a solution for a most challenging problem: how to kill the rapidly dividing cells of Colette's tumor without harming the rapidly dividing cells of her growing fetus.

I entered Colette's room early that evening expecting to find an emotionally devastated but physically stable young woman. I'd rehearsed how I would introduce myself to her. We were exactly the same age. I'd never been pregnant but hoped to be in the next few years. I could imagine being pregnant like Colette, but I couldn't imagine being pregnant and having lung cancer like her. I planned to tell Colette some version of what I was thinking that sounded sympathetic but not too personally revealing: that while I couldn't pretend to know exactly how she felt, I would do everything I could to help her.

I never had a chance to deliver my speech. When I walked into Colette's room, I found her sitting straight up, gripping the bedrails, sweat streaming down her face, gasping for air. I ran for her nurse. I ran for José. I ran for Patricia and Joe. Within moments, the room was full. A technician appeared with a portable machine to take a chest x-ray, this time without a lead drape since there was none readily available. I stationed myself on the right side of Colette's bed, holding her hand, feeling her pulse. Her heart rate was irregular, but in a curiously regular way. It started, and then, at even intervals, it paused. I soon realized that Colette's heartbeat stopped when she inhaled and started up again when she exhaled. I looked at the veins in Colette's neck. They bulged when she breathed in, flattened when she breathed out.

My mind detached from Colette's struggle to breathe, her wild-eyed panic, and I nearly smiled. I'd read about this. What was it called? It had a name, this thing that happens to the neck veins and the pulse when the pericardial sac surrounding the heart fills with fluid. The fluid squeezes the heart, impeding blood flow from the veins back to the heart especially during inhalation. What was it called? Kussmaul's sign! Suddenly, like pieces of a puzzle assembling themselves effortlessly and in speeded up motion, the facts of Colette's suffering became clear to me: Her lung cancer had metastasized to her pericardium, which was now full of bloody, tumorous fluid that pressed upon her heart and slowed blood flow from her veins to her heart, more so each time she inhaled. A young woman, seven months pregnant, lay before me acutely short of breath and my mind wandered from her distress as I pictured, not without pleasure, exactly what was happening at that moment in her heart and lungs.

Patricia dispatched me to the radiology department to look at Colette's x-ray, which confirmed the diagnosis. The outline of her heart appeared abnormally round, the classic "water bottle" shape of a pericardial sac full of fluid. I'd read about this too. When I ran back to the ward to report this finding, Joe, the oncology fellow, had arrived at Colette's bedside. He palpated the rock-hard, cancerous lymph nodes on either side of the young woman's neck and, as his eyes scanned down to her pregnant belly, he whispered something low but audible to everyone in the room, something that revealed emotion such as our Clinical Skills instructors, who had taught us how to use a stethoscope, percuss a liver, and comport ourselves at the bedside, had advised us never to show, something that displayed a lack of the calm imperturbability that Osler believed was the most valuable characteristic of any physician. Joe whispered: "Jesus fucking Christ."

With Colette lying awake in her hospital bed, a sterile paper drape over her chest and abdomen, a cardiologist inserted a large needle into her pericardial sac and removed several syringes full of bloody fluid. Colette sank back onto her pillows and took a deep breath. I had not yet given birth myself, but in remembering her relief the only thing I can compare it to is the moment when the baby emerges and the pain, intense and overwhelming, ends.

But as the cardiologist pointed out, the fluid would soon reaccumulate if we didn't do anything more. So, late that night, we took Colette to the operating room and a surgeon cut a small window in her pericardium and left a plastic drain in place attached to a collecting bag. Amir, a young cardiologist who, like me, observed this procedure, had been a resident a couple of years earlier and had supervised my husband when he was an intern. He was known as one of the smartest residents at our hospital in recent memory. When Colette's drain was in place, we removed our surgical masks and I introduced myself to Amir as the medical student on the case and the wife of one of his former interns. He'd already heard that a medical student had made the diagnosis of cardiac tamponade and he smiled. "So, *two* stars in your family," he said, and again, my mind strayed from Colette, lying on the table, sedated, with a fluid collection bag hanging by a slender tube from her heart, to my own swelling pride.

The next day, Colette's baby girl, Kayla, was delivered by c-section. In the 1980s the prospects for a twenty-seven-week preemie were not great, but Colette had no chance of surviving her metastatic cancer without immediate and aggressive treatment that would kill her unborn baby. Now she lay in her bed on the oncology ward with staples in her flattened midsection while little Kayla lay in the NICU connected to a ventilator. I'd been awake for more than twenty-four hours and was preparing to go home when the oncology attending arrived and asked me if Colette had seen her baby yet. I stammered something about how that didn't really seem possible under the circumstances and he said: "Make it happen."

An hour later a nurse and I wheeled Colette, with her tubes and bags, through the hospital basement and up to the NICU, where presumably she was able to touch her daughter with a gloved hand, through the incubator's porthole. "Presumably" because I have no memory of this poignant scene. I do remember calling the NICU and arranging the visit and my satisfaction in having done so, knowing that my attending would be pleased.

Finally, I went home to bed. The night seemed especially dark and the next morning unusually bright. Sunlight filled Colette's room when I arrived, as did the wails of her mother and her boyfriend who had hurled themselves across her still, silent body. Her mother screamed at me: "Get him some Tylenol! *Do* something for him!" By "him" she meant Colette's boyfriend, Kayla's father, whose grief had thrown him from the bed to the floor, where he lay sobbing.

Two years later I rotated on pediatrics. I'd saved pediatrics for my senior year because I knew I would hate it, and I did. Though I wanted to have children of my own one day, I found them tedious as patients since I couldn't really talk to them. Plus, pediatricians were so much more careful with their patients than internists were. It annoyed me to listen to long deliberations on morning rounds about whether a kid really needed a blood test. It was simpler to take care of adults, whose discomfort did not require quite so much consideration.

One day I was sitting in the doctors' charting area of the emergency room with one of the senior pediatric residents. It was a slow shift and so we got to chatting. He told me he planned to specialize in childhood leukemia and, stupidly I now realize, I asked him if that wouldn't be depressing. He answered: "Would it be less depressing if kids have leukemia and I *don't* take care of them?" Embarrassed,

I changed the subject. Had he ever heard of a baby named Kayla, a preemie who would be about two now, if she'd survived, born to a mom with lung cancer who had died the day after delivering her? "Oh sure," he said. Everyone knew *that* story. He told me that Kayla had indeed survived and was doing OK.

◆   ◆   ◆

Amir, the brilliant cardiologist, died of AIDS in 1993. As a resident he'd stuck his hand while drawing blood from a patient who'd had multiple transfusions. He had a fever and a rash briefly after that incident and then forgot about it for a couple of years until he began getting the opportunistic infections to which people with immune deficiency are susceptible. Rumors went around among the residents that Amir had acquired AIDS while visiting prostitutes or shooting drugs. The possibility that he could have gotten the fatal virus doing something that all of us did all the time was too frightening for us to contemplate. During the last years of his life Amir became an activist for improved occupational safety protections for healthcare workers. There's an old clip of him on YouTube testifying before Congress. His wife, also a physician, and a daughter who was a toddler when Amir died, survived him.

◆   ◆   ◆

Not long ago, on a visit to New York, I found myself walking along First Avenue past the Medical Examiner's Office, whose dingy white-brick facade looks quite unchanged since I was in high school. As if waking from a dream, I asked myself if it could possibly be true, that our teacher thought a trip to see an autopsy of a murdered girl barely a year or two older than my classmates and me, was appropriate—or that none of our parents had objected to the outing. I considered contacting a couple of classmates with whom I'd not spoken in decades but whose current email addresses were listed on a message I'd saved from our class secretary a few months earlier in which she'd asked for news to post in our school's alumni magazine. I didn't. I feared that I wouldn't receive an answer, or that I would receive an answer which said *No, I don't remember anything like that*, which, since I remembered the trip so vividly myself, would have given me a lonely feeling. But I realized I had another option. I recalled the name of the nursing school the dead girl had attended, and I entered it in the Google search box along with the word "murdered" and the year I took AP biology.

Elaine Moriarty.

◆　◆　◆

Patricia, the resident, is dead too. She was killed in a car accident in 1990, three months pregnant with her first child. By coincidence, Patricia's family lived in the same town in Maryland as my in-laws. Though we'd moved to Boston from Baltimore earlier that summer, we happened to be visiting them when Patricia died. I left my husband and our baby daughter at my in-laws' house and drove to the wake. I arrived feeling self-conscious, wearing the flowery sundress that was the only remotely suitable clothing I had with me. The first person I saw as I entered the funeral home was a woman who'd been a resident from Patricia's year. Her husband would die young, too, just a couple of years later, from a rare cancer. I burst into tears when I saw her and, though we barely knew each other, she took me in her arms and patted my back. "I know," she said. "I know." I wouldn't be comforted. I pulled back from her embrace and asked her, demanded of her, "But how? How? How could such a thing have happened?"

Things Shameful to Be Spoken About

I'll tell you a secret: the day I graduated from medical school was the happiest day of my life. I was happy on my wedding day, but I threw up as soon as my husband and I arrived at our hotel after the reception—something I've never confided to anyone before. I was happy, too, of course, on the days I gave birth to my children, but that happiness was alloyed with pain and fear. The day I became a doctor I experienced no pain or fear or even gastrointestinal upset—those would come just a few weeks later when I started internship—just joy. And furthermore, the joy was mine alone, me in my Boy George haircut shaved to the skull on one side, outsized disc earrings, and billowing two-piece chartreuse ensemble with enormous shoulder pads. I looked ridiculous, which I think I knew even then. I didn't care. I was a doctor. An MD. For one glorious day I didn't doubt myself. I knew exactly who I was. I had never felt and would never again feel less embarrassed.

My favorite moment of that most wonderful day was when the graduates, in black gowns adorned with three dark-green velvet stripes on each sleeve representing our new medical degrees, rose in unison to raise our right hands and take the Hippocratic Oath.

A legendary physician—I thought of him as the Great Old Doctor, or GOD—then in his seventies and known as much for his humanity as for his clinical wisdom, administered it. Everything about this scene appealed to me then and appeals to me now no less in memory. The solemnity of the ancient oath; the camaraderie of my classmates; GOD's kindly smile, his snow-white hair combed straight back from his forehead.

We recited the final lines, which, in older translations, speak ominously to the possibility that new doctors might fail to honor the oath and suffer consequences:

> Now if I carry out this oath, and break it not, may I gain for ever
> reputation among all men for my life and for my art; but if I break
> it and forswear myself, may the opposite befall me.

More recent translations are sunnier:

> If I do not violate this oath, may I enjoy life and art, respected
> while I live and remembered with affection thereafter. May I
> always act so as to preserve the finest traditions of my calling and
> may I long experience the joy of healing those who seek my help.

I don't recall which version we recited, but I remember clearly that when we finished, before he motioned for us to sit down, GOD appended a line of his own: *See in the face of every patient the face of someone you love.*

By the time my husband and I retreated to our student apartment with our families to eat the miniature quiches and tarts filled with lemon curd I'd prepared myself, trying to follow my mother's example as both an accomplished professional *and* a perfect hostess, I was still glowing from the ceremony. My glow was undiminished by my pragmatic maternal grandmother's skeptical assessment of GOD's ad lib. "But really," she said, no doubt thinking of the widows with whom she socialized ambivalently in Miami Beach, "how could you love those *kvetches*?" Granny was as wise as the old doctor, in her own way, but she was wrong about this. I would come to love my patients, not because they reminded me of people I love, but for themselves.

In the years since I recited it, I've thought of the Oath often and reread it now and then. My favorite line is the one about doctor-patient confidentiality, variously translated from the quasi-mystical prohibition against doctors revealing their patients' "holy secrets" to the bland and legalistic reminder to new physicians that they must "respect patients' privacy." The translation I like best prohibits the repetition of "things shameful to be spoken about," which I find intriguingly ambiguous, as it leaves unclear to whom these things, if spoken about, would be shameful.

In fact, during the early years of my career, my patients' secrets caused me no small amount of shame, mainly because I could not reliably keep my mouth shut. It's not that I was a gossip or revealed confidences out of malice; it's just that things often came up in my interactions with patients that were so moving or funny or interesting I couldn't bear not to share them. I've always been a talker. Mrs. Sylvia Krensky wrote on my otherwise unblemished first-grade report card: *Suzanne must learn to let the other children speak.* I never did. To this day I'm a chronic interrupter and conversation hog.

Not long ago my daughter and I were chatting, and she said: "Mom, you're doing that thing." "What thing?" I asked. "That thing where we're having a conversation and I can tell you're thinking: 'Here's the boring part where the other person is speaking.'" I'm aware of this tendency and I feel badly about it. In recent years, an added element compounds my shame: the fear that I may become one of those ponderous fogies so common in medicine, giving unsolicited advice to younger colleagues and endlessly reminiscing about the golden era when giants walked the halls of the hospital. I had a dream just the other night that I was attending a meeting and began to answer a question posed by the person leading it. She held her hand up to me and said, firmly: "No, let's hear from someone who hasn't spoken yet," and the others around the table nodded yes: we've heard enough from *her*.

When I was younger, my excessive talking or, as my mother called it "holding court" or as *her* mother called it "running for office"—this loquacious streak runs through the matrilineal— tended to flirtation. In his letter in support of my application for internship a dean at my medical school wrote, *Suzanne is hardly aware of her own charm and attractiveness*, which seemed to me an odd observation, at once flattering and insulting, and I begged him to take it out.

It became evident to me even during medical school that my talkativeness, which had been, for the most part until then, an asset both socially and academically, could cause me trouble in my chosen profession. When I was an intern, a patient I admitted one night alluded to his erectile dysfunction in, I thought, an amusing way. He told me: "Mr. Jones is sleeping on the job." The next morning,

when my fellow interns arrived for the day shift, I couldn't wait
to tell them about the idle Mr. Jones. I wasn't making fun of the
patient. My telling of his story had more to do with me, with my
need to show the other interns, men, that in spite of having worked
all night, I'd kept my sense of humor. That, though I was a woman,
I appreciated a good penis joke. That I belonged. The patient, it
turned out, didn't see it that way. That afternoon, when I entered
his room to check on him, he rolled over in bed and turned his back
on me. Somehow—*how?*—he'd found out. "I told you something
private," he said, glaring at me briefly before facing the wall again.
"And you betrayed me." I backed out of the door and vowed never,
ever to violate a patient's confidence again.

But it wasn't so easy. Once, a couple of years after I went into
practice, my mother and I were having lunch outdoors at a restaurant in Manhattan. We'd always had an affectionate relationship
and yet, since early adolescence I'd felt judged and criticized by my
mother: for my weight, my outspokenness, my untidiness—the very
things for which I castigated myself. That day at lunch, though,
we'd knocked off a couple of glasses of white wine apiece and any
tension between us melted away under the midday sun. I sat back in
my chair, relaxed and expansive. I told my mother that my practice
was growing, that I now had more than just hand-me-down patients
from older, well-established colleagues, that in fact, I said, leaning
forward across the starched white tablecloth, one of my new patients
was an actual celebrity. I was about to say the person's name when
my mother's lawyerly impulses kicked in. She reached out her hand
and placed it on mine. "No, sweetheart," she whispered, "*don't.*"

As the years went by, my urge to repeat interesting information, to tell a good story, never diminished—I just got better at resisting it. I've found it simpler to adopt a strict rule about never revealing anything I see and hear in the exam room or at the hospital bedside than to decide on a case-by-case basis. I never mention a father to a son, a husband to a wife. I am monklike in my continence. A patient tells me she's concerned about the drinking habits of her sister (also my patient) and I say, "Uh-huh." My husband's coworker comes in for an annual physical and asks me to convey his regards, but I don't convey them because my husband does not know, will never know, that I am this man's doctor.

Once, I was rounding in the hospital and found myself inches away from a Very Famous Person, clothed in a pale blue hospital gown, leaning on the arm of a physical therapist, looking ill and frail but still wearing that Very Famous Person shimmer; the white teeth and the perfect haircut. I quickly put my head down, as if even making eye contact would be an intrusion. Even with my eyes averted I was still certain it was that person because an email had gone out to the entire hospital staff alerting us to the fact that this person would be a patient in the hospital—a fact that had already been reported on the local and national news—and warning us that if we accessed their electronic chart for any reason other than direct patient care we risked being fired. Several times over the next days and weeks, I caught myself on the verge of telling my husband about my close non-encounter with fame. But I didn't. Whom would it harm for him to know that I'd seen this person in my hospital when the fact that they were being treated there was all over the news? Me. It would harm me. By revealing whom I'd seen I would forswear myself.

8

Lineage

By spring of my internship year I was exhausted, I'd gained ten pounds, and my periods had stopped. I assumed that months of thirty-six-hour hospital shifts fueled by coffee and vending-machine candy had finally taken their toll. But when summer arrived, my schedule eased up, and the waistband of my white uniform pants continued to tighten, I considered another diagnosis.

At my first prenatal visit the obstetrician determined that I was well into my second trimester. On the top of my chart she wrote, in large letters, *LATE REGISTRANT*, a term I'd previously only heard applied to teenage girls who arrived in the emergency room in labor, complaining of "stomachache." This inauspicious start to my pregnancy—which produced, a few months later, a small but otherwise perfect baby girl—may have shaken what little confidence I had in my ability to care for an infant. I'd been the youngest in my family, and my babysitting career had ended after one outing, when a brat plastered bubblegum in my hair. Certainly, I'd learned nothing about tending babies in medical school.

I'm not sure why I didn't ask my mother for help. She had, after all, raised children of her own and presumably knew a thing or two. Partly I think that, even though I'd turned thirty by the time I learned I was pregnant, I still wanted to show my mother that I didn't need her help, particularly in matters related to health, about which she tended to speak to me as if I were not a doctor. I seethed each time she reminded me of the importance of regular Pap smears or flu shots, or when she reported details about my father's many medical conditions in lay terms, explaining his emphysema or prostate cancer to me in the same simple language his doctors had explained these conditions to her.

Perhaps another reason I didn't consult my mother was that I'd been in school for so many years by the time I became pregnant I assumed I needed to prepare for parenthood the same way I'd prepared to become a doctor: I needed to study. Two days after my daughter's birth I waddled to the maternity ward's class, "Bathing Your Newborn," and took notes. I invented the same kind of mnemonics with which I'd crammed for anatomy and biochemistry to remember how to properly care for my daughter: *Lie Baby on her Back in Bed* (BBB, to prevent crib death). And, of course, I bought books: Benjamin Spock's *Baby and Child Care*, T. Berry Brazelton's *Touchpoints*, and Frank Caplan's *The First Twelve Months of Life*. I found these books—all by men, I just now notice—of little use. When my own baby arrived, she fascinated me. I could stare at her for hours. But I found babies in general and, especially, advice about babies dull. What did it matter how long the experts said you should let a baby cry before picking her up, or at what age she should crawl? My baby crawled when she crawled. When she cried, I picked her up. I wasn't sure I was doing it right—but also unsure that a book would help. The only thing I remember from any of those manuals is the famous first line of Dr. Spock's: *You know more than you think you do.* I wasn't confident this statement was true, but it provided some comfort. After all, if millions of parents since 1946, when Dr. Spock first published *Baby and Child Care*, had needed such reassurance, at least I wasn't alone in my uncertainty.

◆　◆　◆

"You know more than you think you do" might have been the motto of the medical residency program at Johns Hopkins Hospital as well. The "Osler Marines" as we called ourselves, had a reputation for giving interns a level of respect and independence that we—or, at least I—secretly feared we hadn't earned. After the first two weeks of July, when a junior resident stayed overnight in the hospital while we were on call, we flew solo. The educational philosophy in those days held that you would never learn to do something if you weren't forced to do it yourself. "See one, do one, teach one" was the pedagogic approach to everything from performing a lumbar puncture to managing heart failure. Residents inclined to mordant humor added: "Then *kill* one." You could call your resident at home, or even stroll up to the ICU or down to the emergency room to ask advice, but it was a point of pride not to. Thank God for the nurses. It's an untrue "truism," one I've only heard repeated by men, that nurses, most of whom are women, bear particular animosity toward female doctors. During my medical training I found that nurses were, in fact, especially supportive of us new women MDs. One night, a couple of months into my internship, I was paged by a nurse to the bedside of a patient with pulmonary edema, a condition in which fluid accumulates in the lungs and which feels like drowning. I found the patient sitting bolt-upright, gasping, sweat dripping down her face, her eyes wild with panic (me: also breathing hard, sweating, panicking). Without saying a word the nurse handed me diuretics and morphine in the proper doses and dialed up the oxygen.

Now, we tell interns "never worry alone" but then the idea was that you *should* worry alone for as long as you could. Even on the private medical wards, where patients were admitted by physicians who had cared for them for years, it was the intern's name written in black marker on a strip of masking tape stuck to the spine of the loose-leaf binder that, in the predigital era, served as the patient's hospital chart. Everyone including the ward secretaries participated in the fiction that the intern was the patient's doctor. A mere month after I graduated from medical school, if you'd called the floor and asked to speak with Ms. So-and-So's physician, you would have gotten . . . me.

In exchange for this independence we followed a set of unstated but universally understood rules:

- Do not complain
- Do not ask for help, except when a patient is about to die and you can't think of anything else to do
- Do not acknowledge exhaustion, hunger, thirst, the need to go to the bathroom and, most especially, menstrual cramps
- Display a calm demeanor, even during emergencies such as when a patient has a cardiac arrest, or when a patient curses/ spits/yells at you or when a superior dresses you down, however unfairly
- Maintain an empathic but distant relationship with patients,

calling them Mr. or Ms. and discouraging them from calling you anything but Doctor, and do not reveal personal information about yourself to patients

• Do not cry

There actually was an unofficial manual that more or less outlined these rules, a kind of Dr. Spock for residents. In 1978, eight years before I started my internship, Stephen Bergman, then a young psychiatrist writing under the pseudonym Samuel Shem, published *The House of God*. Roy Basch, the bestselling novel's protagonist, is a medical intern who struggles to maintain his humanity in the inhumane system of residency training. For poor, overworked Roy the patients are the enemy, keeping him from sleep. Women, especially sexy nurses, serve chiefly as distractions from his misery. *The House of God* has been compared to *M*A*S*H*—not the TV series featuring kindly Alan Alda, but the grittier book and film versions.

When I interviewed Bergman in 2013 for an article marking the thirty-fifth anniversary of the book's publication he told me that he'd written *The House of God* as a satire, an indictment of the harsh culture of medical training, which, by the way, he didn't feel had improved much in over three decades despite limits placed in recent years on the number of hours per week residents are permitted to work. When I was an intern, my fellow trainees and I didn't view *The House of God* as an indictment of this system, but, rather, as a guide to perpetuating it. Though I hadn't read the whole book back then and didn't, in fact, read it in its entirety until years later in preparation for my interview with Bergman, it set the tone and supplied the language for my medical training. Like Roy Basch, we called elderly demented patients GOMERs (get out of my emergency room), especially those whose many medical problems made extra work for us. When LOLs (little old ladies) fell they were GTG (gone to ground). Private, nonacademic physicians, for whom we had contempt, were GOME-docs.

Even if I had read the book back then, I think I would have *misread* it, particularly its female characters. I was so thoroughly indoctrinated that I doubt I'd have been offended by Shem's portrayal of nurses as buxom man-pleasers. I'm certain I would have seen myself a bit in Jo, the only female physician in the novel, a smart but chilly senior resident whom Roy let "lop a bit off of his schlong daily by telling him what he'd failed to do." As a senior resident myself, and especially a year later when I was a chief resident, I saw myself as tough—not schlong-lopping tough, but tough—and liked to think I was respected by the men I supervised as if I weren't a woman.

Years later I proudly described my masculine performance as a chief resident to my therapist. "I was like Helen Mirren in the British detective series *Prime Suspect*," I explained. He looked puzzled. "But," Dr. Katz asked, "wasn't the whole point of the Helen Mirren character that she was a brilliant detective *and* an attractive woman? And didn't she have an affair with one of her subordinates?" I'd forgotten that plot line entirely.

Ironically, the first person in my internship class to violate the unspoken tough-guy rules was a man. During those first few weeks in July Pete Cushing complained about being tired, confessed to feeling anxious when he was on call and needed to make decisions quickly and on his own, and expressed doubts about whether he was cut out to be a doctor. He didn't last till Christmas. After he was gone, one senior resident told us interns, jokingly, that Pete had succumbed to "Cushing's syndrome" (an actual disease). The message—the *warning*—was that Pete's behavior was so uniquely abhorrent it merited a name: his. Of course, this was not true. Any of us could have, and many of us did have, these same doubts. But it was crucial for each of us to believe that what happened to him would not happen to us.

There was to be no Koven's syndrome, I was determined about that. I wasn't consciously aware of needing to be stoic, a true Marine, *especially* because I was a woman. I think I was, then, naïve about sexism. I assumed that if I were manly enough, I'd be treated with the respect accorded to men. On call nights I was at my most virile. Though I felt a pang of dread and also self-pity when my fellow interns and the residents went home and the nurses changed shifts at seven p.m., my adrenaline soon kicked in. I jumped at my beeper, hurried from room to room drawing blood, taking histories, responding to emergencies or purported emergencies. I was very happy, in a way, and felt validated after each night on call, especially if I'd admitted many patients and gotten little or no sleep, which was frequent.

It wasn't unusual for me, like other interns then, to arrive at the hospital on a Monday morning, work without stopping until Tuesday evening, and report again for work early on Wednesday. Some months were even more punishing: twenty-four hours on, twenty-four hours off, week after week. The obscene fatigue that this schedule produced made me euphoric at times, depressed, irritable, and nauseated at others, but always obsessed with sleep. I would stop at the grocery store on my way home from the hospital and glare at the cashier, resentful that she was able to go home to her own bed at night. I envied dogs I saw in the street, because they could lie down when they chose. I also envied Alex Trebek, the host of *Jeopardy!*, which I often watched while having dinner on my nights off. I didn't care about getting the Daily Double or Final Jeopardy correct; I only longed to sleep as much as I wanted, like Alex Trebek could. Never before or since in my fortunate life have I suffered such sustained physical distress. For hours or even a few days I've been hot or cold, thirsty or hungry, uncomfortable or in pain, but I had never experienced and never would again experience anything like the tiredness I felt during those years. There's no evidence that severe sleep deprivation made me a better doctor, but I could not have survived my residency if I had not believed it would.

Attempting to stay energized when I was on call, I hit the vending machine for infusions of sugar—Snickers or stale Little Debbie cakes—on my way to the lab or blood bank or ER. I often chose the route that led through the surgical clinic, dark and deserted at night, in an unrenovated part of the hospital with linoleum flooring from the '60s that reminded me of my father's old medical office in Brooklyn. My sneaker squeak echoed in the empty clinic, adding to its delicious eeriness. Ghosts lined the walls: framed eight-by-ten black-and-white head shots of past members of the surgical staff, nearly all men, going back to the twenties. These photographs mesmerized me and made me feel less alone. So, too, did the reproductions of oil portraits of Osler and his disciples, and his disciples' disciples that hung on the walls of the medical wards. Sometimes, I paused by one of these portraits and listed, in my mind, the string of medical "begats" that ran from Osler through his trainees and successors and their trainees and successors—Drs. Barker, Janeway, Longcope, Harvey, and McKusick—to me. As a medical student I'd presented a case to Dr. McKusick shortly before his retirement, so I legitimately traced my lineage back to Osler himself. I never once paused to consider that my professional ancestry included no women.

◆   ◆   ◆

I have no recollection of my husband and me deciding to have our first baby when I was an intern and he was a resident. We had no discussions about trying to time the delivery with our preassigned vacations, futile as that effort might have been, nor a conversation about whether we could afford childcare on our meager trainees' incomes. Near the end of my internship, on a rare Sunday afternoon when we happened to be home at the same time, I looked at a calendar and counted eighty days since my last period. I went to the drugstore, bought a home pregnancy test, and peed on the plastic wand. Then, like a crazed vampire slayer, I waved the dark-blue cross back and forth in front of my husband's initially confused and then smiling face as he was speaking on the telephone.

I'm not sure now whether my pregnancy was really unintentional or whether I simply prefer this version of the story that features me as a bumbler. I inherit the tendency to present myself in this light from my mother, whose humor relied heavily on the catalogue of what she perceived as her shortcomings, large and small. Even as a child I could have enumerated them: She was a terrible speller and an awkward writer; she never learned how to ride a bike and couldn't carry a tune; she didn't outgrow her acne until she was forty and started going gray in her twenties; she didn't get into Wellesley, felt out of place at the country club, was never as good as she wanted to be at bridge or tennis or casual home entertaining, and could never stay below size 14 for long. Her garden, though she spent thousands of dollars and hours of her own labor on it, never looked, according to her, "like anything."

And yet. Beneath my mother's self-criticism thrummed self-confidence, and I would say the same of myself. In many ways, it now occurs to me, this combination of insecurity and confidence echoes how I felt about being a doctor, even from the beginning of my career: I worried endlessly—well, not endlessly, I stopped after age fifty or so—about not *knowing* enough as a doctor but I never worried about *being* a doctor.

Once I learned I was pregnant I started taking prenatal vitamins faithfully and complied with all the recommended obstetrical visits, blood tests, and ultrasounds. Still, I drifted through my last two trimesters in a kind of oblivion, not requesting any change in my work hours. I first felt my baby move early one morning as I stole a few minutes of rest on an empty patient bed in the Coronary Care Unit, where I was on call as a junior resident. Strange as it sounds, being pregnant as a resident made me feel more macho. The pride I felt in telling (and retelling) the story of first feeling my baby move while on call in the CCU was a macho pride. My swagger had a price, though. I spent the last six weeks of my pregnancy confined at home with preeclampsia, my dangerously high blood pressure no doubt caused by my long work hours. After months of wanting nothing more than sleep I was now forbidden to leave my bed. My obstetrician instructed me to lie on my left side to keep pressure off my vena cava and maximize blood flow to my baby. I rolled over and lay on my right every day from four to five p.m. so that I could watch *The Oprah Winfrey Show* on the TV that didn't fit on the other side of the room. *Oprah* was new then, though I'd been a fan of her local Baltimore show years before she went national and so I felt a special connection to her. I don't think I would have gotten through that time without Oprah's warmth and kindness, her weepy guests and her diets. At forty weeks a monitor detected fetal distress and I had an emergency c-section, delivering a healthy five-and-a-half-pound girl. Another female resident tacked my daughter's newborn photo onto the bulletin board in the room where we residents entered notes in patient charts and stole naps on a ratty couch.

I now ask myself why I was so unquestioning of a system that was fundamentally hostile to women and certainly to mothers. So complete was my denial that when I recently looked at a photograph of my residency class I was surprised to see that barely a quarter of its members were women. I'd have guessed closer to 40 or 50 percent. Medical training had been designed in the nineteenth century as a *residency*, which excluded women almost by definition: male trainees were required to live together in the hospital and in many programs not even permitted to marry until well into the twentieth century. Though Osler, the founder of the residency at Johns Hopkins, was progressive in many ways, even a proponent of women's suffrage who reportedly was kind and respectful to the few women who did study medicine under him at the insistence of the female benefactors who funded the establishment of Johns Hopkins School of Medicine in 1893, he could not easily conceive of women as doctors. He once stated: "There are three classes of human beings: men, women, and women physicians."

Perhaps I was oblivious to the sexism that existed during my residency in the 1980s, and persists in medicine today, because it was as ubiquitous as air. Like my old mentor Henry, who walked past the segregated blood bank day and night for years without thinking about it, I failed to perceive much less question the sexism that was no less a part of my medical training than doughnuts before morning rounds, pizza at noontime lectures, and coffee all night on call.

It's true, no one hit on me, unless you count my anatomy lab classmate's lame overture; no one made crude comments to me, and no one offered me career advancement in exchange for sexual favors. I did fear my virology professor Kent's unfair and possibly sexist accusation of plagiarism would hurt my chances of acceptance to medical school, but he'd quickly recanted it. Many women, especially women of color and LGBTQ medical professionals did and do experience overt harassment and abuse—but I did not. In forty years, only a handful of sexist comments have ever been directed at me at work, the worst of which was when I was told to my face by one of the men in my year that everyone knew I'd been chosen to be a chief resident as a "token."

Still, the fact that my residency program had no formal maternity-leave policy, that it never occurred to any of my superiors—or to me—that it might not be advisable for a pregnant woman to work sixteen- or even twenty-four-hour days on her feet,

that I put my life and my unborn baby's life in danger rather than
risk jeopardizing my good standing as a resident by asking for a
lighter schedule near the end of my pregnancy, all speak to how
inimical this system was to women. Also, the women in my residency, while lauded for our assertiveness and ambition, risked public rebuke for these very traits, as I learned one painful evening at
the end of my third and final year.

Every June the Department of Medicine sponsored a dinner
cruise around Baltimore Harbor for the residents and their spouses.
The highlight of this event was a slapdash show including skits and
stand-up routines in which certain residents and attendings were
roasted or given fake awards. When I was an intern two years earlier,
I'd won the award for most weight gained, though no one, including me, realized I was pregnant then. As a senior resident, I'd been
chosen to be a chief for the following year, the third woman in the
department's hundred-year history and the only married woman
or woman with a baby to be selected for this honor. It was probably naïve of me to think that I'd go unscathed during the roast, but
it was more brutal than I would have imagined. Two of my fellow
senior residents, men, stood at the microphone and, as everyone
laughed and raised their little plastic cups of wine and their bottles
of beer, skewered me for being a suck-up, for climbing the ladder
with my nose up someone's ass. I leaned against the boat railing as
we cruised back toward the dock and no one comforted me or even
spoke to me except my husband. He told me that I was a smart, out-
spoken, curly haired woman and that of *course* my male colleagues
felt they needed to try to put me in my place. The next morning,
back on the wards, I mentioned something to my chief about not

having found the boat ride too much fun and a few minutes later overheard him tell a male resident: "I think we have an acute case of hypersensitivity on the floor."

Not long ago I spoke again with Edward, my friend from residency. We hadn't been in touch for a few years and, feeling the urge to reach out that so many of us have felt during the Covid-19 pandemic, we arranged a Sunday-morning coffee date on Zoom. During our conversation we compared his experience of racism during our residency with my experience of sexism. I told him that the more I thought back to those days, the more mystified and ashamed I felt about my complicity in a system that had so little regard for me. "That's where you're wrong," said Edward. "They *loved* you. And me too. We were stars. We made them look good and they heaped praise on us. But at some level we knew how easily we might be discarded if we made a wrong step. That's why we worked so hard to be perfect."

◆ ◆ ◆

When I was a kid our next-door neighbors had a subscription to *LIFE* magazine and they saved all the back issues. That plus their endless supply of Hawaiian Punch and pretzel rods and the fact that they had a daughter my age drew me to their house for hours every week to play. One old issue of *LIFE* included a series of black-and-white photos called "Country Doctor." I particularly loved looking at one photo with the wonderfully unmelodious title: "Dr. Ernest Ceriani in a State of Exhaustion, Having a Cup of Coffee in the Hospital Kitchen at 2 AM." The image features a dark and handsome surgeon leaning heavily against a counter. He grips a cigarette in one hand and a cup of coffee in the other, presumably to stave off the fatigue that seems about to knock him down. Never mind that I wasn't a man, didn't live in the country, had no desire to be a surgeon (or to smoke). I wanted to be *him*. Just as I'd flexed my biceps and pretended to shave in front of the bathroom mirror when I was a child, when I was in medical school and my husband was an intern, sometimes when he wasn't home I would try on his white uniform pants, Oxford shirt, and departmental tie, navy blue with a pattern of tiny white shields emblazoned with *Aequanimitas*, the unflappability to which all physicians should aspire, according to Osler. Perhaps it was this fantasy that made me blind to much of the sexism around me, ready to dismiss incidents such as the boat-ride roast. Perhaps the reason I didn't rebel against the culture of my medical training was that I loved it.

And yet, when I became a chief resident myself, I didn't perpetuate that culture. Despite what I later told my therapist about how "masculine" I'd been, the persona I took on as a chief resident in the Osler Marines was more maternal than military. I supervised ward rounds and gave lectures but I also fed and hugged my interns. I wore shift dresses and pearls beneath my long white coat in unconscious imitation of my mother's 1960s civic-minded-housewife's wardrobe. In fact, my main disciplinary tool as chief was one I'd picked up from my mother: disappointment. Once, I summoned to my office an intern who'd written something disrespectful about a patient in a medical chart. He was defensive and surly—it had been a long night in the ER, he whined, and the patient was a dirtbag. I leaned forward and touched his arm. "Greg," I said, "I thought better of you."

As a chief resident I was more comfortable giving advice, intervening when interns and residents had difficult interactions with patients or with one another, and inviting my residents for dinner than delivering chalkboard lectures on hyponatremia and sepsis. I found I was skilled at "making life less awful for everyone" just as my mother had been, with her peppy demeanor, smart outfits, and beautifully presented platters. I suspected that my three male co-chiefs knew more medicine than I did. Maybe they did and maybe they didn't. And yet, I also knew that what my fellow resident told me, that I'd been selected to be chief as a token woman—as hurtful as that was, as much as I feared it might be true—*wasn't* true. At some level I felt secure in my medical knowledge and proficiency and knew that this other something I had to offer was valuable too.

My preferred style of dress and my behavior as a chief were not dissimilar to my opting to talk about *Illness as Metaphor* in my pre-med virology seminar instead of viruses: I gravitated to what felt more natural to me. What had changed in the eight years between my taking Kent's seminar and becoming a chief resident was that I felt less ashamed about my choices, less convinced I was taking the easy way out. The fact that I was, as a chief, in a position of relative power and status, that I was being validated by men, by the department chairman who'd selected me, and by the male residents I supervised—albeit some of them grudgingly at first—had more to do with this confidence than I'd like to admit. In time this confidence would become less dependent on praise and prizes and promotions—or on men. The process by which my confidence grew was the opposite of how imposter syndrome so often develops; I internalized men's approval rather than their sexism, which, in turn, helped me outgrow my need for their approval.

I didn't realize it then but in applying my motherly instincts to my role as chief resident—and worrying that I might undermine my own authority in doing so—I was participating in a conversation that had begun over a century earlier. Elizabeth Blackwell, who, in 1849, became the first female graduate of an American medical school, felt that women brought to clinical practice certain qualities that men did not possess. Though she herself never married or bore children, she believed that mothering made women at least as well suited to medicine as men. The "spiritual power of maternity," as she called it, which encouraged "the subordination of the self to others," served women well as physicians. But Blackwell and many of her contemporaries were hesitant to claim that women brought different qualities to medicine than men did since, after all, "different" could so easily be read as "inferior"—and usually was and often still is.

I also didn't know, until I came upon a copy in a used bookshop not long ago, that there was a female version of *The House of God*, a novel called *Woman Doctor* written by obstetrician and gynecologist Dr. Florence Haseltine with English professor Yvonne Yaw at around the same time as Samuel Shem's bestseller. Like Shem's novel, *Woman Doctor* is semiautobiographical. Unlike *The House of God*, though, no one's heard of *Woman Doctor*. It's out of print. My copy has a tacky '70s cover featuring a grainy photograph of a glamorous, dark-eyed, long-lashed woman in full surgical garb who looks nothing like Dr. Haseltine as she appears in her author photo. Haseltine's account of a brilliant college classmate who dropped out of "the best medical school in the country" halfway through her first year to get married and get pregnant because of "the female 'fear of success'" seems dated. Still, I found *Woman Doctor* reflected my own experience much more closely than *The House of God* had. Like Roy Basch, Phyllis Donnan, the protagonist of *Woman Doctor*, is an intern, exhausted and with little time to tend to her own needs. She describes herself as "flooded [. . .] with fatigue," wolfing down hospital cafeteria food and chugging coffee during brief breaks as she runs from task to task. But, unlike Roy, Phyllis isn't angry or self-pitying. She's moved by the suffering of her patients. The first pages of the book show her late at night, struggling to conceal her own distress while examining a woman who's just had a radical mastectomy, the disfiguring operation now no longer performed on women with breast cancer.

My true lineage, I now think, included Blackwell and Haseltine—not to mention Oprah, and my mother—at least as much as Osler.

◆ ◆ ◆

I never read another childrearing manual after the batch I perused before my first child was born. I quickly concluded something about myself as a mother that it would take me many more years to understand about myself as a doctor and then as a writer: that I can only be who I am. And that this is OK.

One day as I was driving my youngest child to the airport to catch his flight to Europe for a college semester abroad, he asked me: "Now that we're all grown-up, do you have any regrets about how you raised us?" I said, yes, two: I should have been a little stricter about the junk food, all those boxes of Cheez-Its and foil pouches of high-fructose-corn-syrup juice. And I wished I'd been a little less slavish about signing up for activities that no one really seemed to enjoy as much as hanging around the house: Cub Scouts and soccer and music lessons. My son laughed. "That's it, Mom? Cheez-Its and Cub Scouts?"

His handsome head disappeared through the security gate without turning for a last goodbye. I whispered the atheist mother's prayer I say whenever my children travel far from me, which is often now. I can think of many deficits in my mothering, but few I'd call regrets. "Regrets" implies you'd do it differently if you had the chance, and I'm not sure I could.

Each year on Mother's Day, social media is flooded with pictures: moms with babies slung to their chests and moms with teenagers towering over them; moms walking their kids down the aisle and moms in wheelchairs; moms in surgical scrubs and moms in graduation gowns. I love them all, but the ones I love best are the old black-and-white photos of moms now long dead, from before they were moms: young women with lush hair and dreamy eyes. They didn't yet know how much joy and pain children would bring; how much motherhood would change them, and how little. Or how much they already knew.

9

The Last Three Pounds

I'd been working at Mass General for six years when I decided to add a subspecialty to my primary care practice. With a demanding medical career, three kids under eight years old at home, and aging parents increasingly in need of my attention, I still thought I wasn't busy enough. The more I did, the more I felt I needed to do. My frantic multitasking depleted me, but I also found it exhilarating. As I ran from exam rooms to committee meetings to parent-teacher nights, I felt ambitious, expansive, successful. But too much of anything, no matter how enjoyable, is still too much. As the poet Samuel Hazo writes:

> *One apple satisfies.*
> *Two apples glut.*
> *Three apples*
> *cloy.*

When it came to being busy, I never stopped at one apple.

I'd known other primary care physicians who'd pursued additional training to care for patients with HIV, pregnant women with

medical complications such as diabetes and heart disease, and people struggling with addiction or homelessness. The subspecialty I
chose was one in which I felt I already had a fair amount of expertise: obesity management. Though never obese myself, I'd always
considered myself overweight and reasoned that a lifetime of dieting would surely give me special insight into the challenges faced
by those who carry the medical and psychological burden of excess
pounds. Plus, I hoped that becoming an obesity specialist would
cause me—*force* me—to finally lose weight. Who'd want to go to an
overweight obesity specialist?

My timing was propitious, I concluded, as I arrived in June 1996
at the grand ballroom of a hotel in downtown Boston for the New
Frontiers in Obesity conference. In many ways the scene was no
different from any medical conference I'd attended before or have
since. But there *was* something undeniably new at New Frontiers
in Obesity. Excitement permeated the recirculated air. Though the
American Medical Association wouldn't declare obesity a disease
until 2013, in 1996 the condition clearly had new status and urgency
among clinicians and scientists. Just four years earlier the National
Institutes of Health had released a consensus report listing the dire
consequences of obesity, including diabetes, cardiovascular disease, and several types of cancer. The report also highlighted the
alarming fact that a third of Americans were overweight or obese,
a sharp rise over the previous decade. By 1998 that rate would go
up to more than 50 percent overnight due to a change in how overweight and obesity are defined. People went to bed normal weight
and woke up fat.

In 1996 promising new treatments for obesity seemed to be

emerging. Scientists hoped that a recently discovered hormone, leptin, which acts as a natural appetite suppressant and that obese mice had been found to lack, might be synthesized and administered to humans to aid weight loss. Meanwhile, two prescription weight-loss drugs, fenfluramine and phentermine, were being newly marketed in combination as "fen-phen" and a new drug, Redux, containing dexfenfluramine, a chemical variant of fenfluramine, had just been approved by the FDA.

The speakers at New Frontiers in Obesity seemed giddy. The stigma society attaches to obese people had long extended to the doctors who treat obesity and the scientists who study it. Now physicians and researchers who'd toiled away for years in the outskirts of medical respectability found themselves in the mainstream. Several wore giant buttons reading "300,000," the number of preventable deaths per year attributed to obesity, with a red slash mark through it. Conference-goers were similarly enthusiastic. More than a few saw dollar signs. The demand for weight-loss drugs had grown dramatically—the number of prescriptions dispensed peaked at 85,000 per week. "Eventually," science journalist Gina Kolata reported, "an estimated six million Americans would take fenfluramine or dexfenfluramine, most of them women, not all of them obese." Still, most doctors felt uncomfortable recommending these drugs and so lucrative fen-phen clinics, basically prescription mills, popped up around the country to fill the void. A breakout session at New Frontiers in Obesity offering doctors tips on how to open clinics of their own was packed.

◆   ◆   ◆

Obesity has long held an uncomfortable place in medicine. Hippocrates cautioned that excess adiposity can cause early death. Osler, whose only child, a son named Revere, died of battle wounds in World War I, observed that "more people are killed by overeating . . . than by the sword." Still, even though doctors have known for centuries that obesity contributes to life-threatening medical problems, we've been reluctant to consider obesity a problem itself. As a medical student and resident I'd seen patients with conditions that clearly resulted from or were exacerbated by obesity but whose obesity I didn't address—and my superiors never chastised me for this omission. The collective unspoken attitude seemed to be that obesity was the patient's responsibility, likely because there was so little that doctors could do about it.

The 1992 NIH report on the high incidence and medical seriousness of obesity had offered discouraging news about its treatment. Despite a then $30-billion-a-year diet industry no method produced lasting results for more than a tiny percentage of the millions of Americans trying to lose weight. And yet, doctors routinely applauded patients each time they rejoined Weight Watchers or exhorted them to simply move more and eat less. There's no other medical problem whose treatment doctors consistently outsource to commercial enterprises or for which we mainly prescribe therapies that have been proven ineffective. We don't tell patients with cancer to seek cures at meetings in church basements or to try leeches, but this is more or less what we did with obesity—and mostly still do.

I went into practice in 1990 at the height of the low-fat craze, not to be confused with the low-carb crazes that preceded and followed it. I nodded approvingly as my patients handed me food journals in which they recorded snacks of pretzels, Entenmann's fat-free cake, and jellybeans. They weren't losing weight, but that didn't surprise me, not because I'd read the NIH report or because of my vast knowledge of nutrition, about which physicians receive notoriously scant training, but because I wasn't faring too well on pretzels, Entenmann's fat-free cake, and jelly beans myself.

I barely remember a time when I didn't think I needed to lose weight or when food wasn't fraught for me in some way. In fact, this idyllic era is preserved in a single memory: I'm four or five years old and our family is having lunch at the deli in the neighborhood where my mother grew up, near the Brooklyn Museum. Jake and Al's. My mother orders a tongue sandwich on rye with brown mustard. I still believe then that "tongue sandwich" is just an expression and has nothing to do with actual tongues. It's my mother's favorite and so I decide it's my favorite too. The waiter sets the sandwich in front of my mother. She removes some of the filling and gives me a quarter of the sandwich, not because I'm fat or because she thinks I shouldn't eat too much but because a quarter is all my little stomach wants.

By the time I'm six or so my brothers, as part of their endless teasing, start calling me "Big Tush," a nickname I somehow feel mocks my talkativeness and my curly hair as much my rear end. Though there's zero photographic evidence that my tush or anything else about me is big, the size of my behind becomes a long-running family joke. When my mother hugs me she pats my big tush. My grandmother gets in on the act, pinching my childish buttocks and thighs, which she calls *loshkies*, a variation on the Yiddish word for egg noodles.

I didn't start dieting until I reached puberty at age twelve. The sudden appearance of hips and breasts and libido launched me, as it has millions of young women, on a lifelong quest to lose weight. A recent study revealed that 80 percent of American girls have dieted by age ten, likely reflecting the fact that girls go through puberty earlier on average today than I did five decades ago.

Years before I hated my body, I hated my hair. My mother always described my hair as dirty blond (I heard that *I* was "dirty") and my curls as wild and unmanageable despite gallons of Hair So New detangling lotion (I heard that *I* was "wild and unmanageable"). In fifth grade I begged her to take me to a salon specializing in hair straightening for Black women. The lye solution applied to my curls was so caustic I had to wear a blindfold to prevent eye injury. When the blindfold was removed and I saw myself in the mirror I felt like a fairy princess, my greatest wish granted. For a couple of weeks, until my hair started to grow out and pricks of frizz appeared along my part line, I felt what I would later feel during brief periods when I'd lost weight and didn't recognize my own reflection as I passed a store window.

I hadn't connected my early hair hatred to my later body hatred until recently when a patient of mine, a middle-aged woman named Stephanie, told me this story. After years of trying to lose weight Stephanie decided to undergo gastric banding. She hadn't shared this decision with her mother because her mother had been nagging her to lose weight for years and Stephanie couldn't bear the prospect of her scrutiny—and approval—as she shed pounds after the operation. I understood her concern because Stephanie's mother, a slender woman named Enid, was also my patient. Whenever Enid came to see me she always asked why I wasn't doing more to make Stephanie lose weight. After Stephanie recovered from surgery and had lost about fifty pounds, she finally felt ready to face her mother. Enid, of course, noticed the change in Stephanie right away. She broke into a big smile and clapped her hands gleefully. "You lost weight!" Enid cried. "Now do something about your hair!"

I finally made peace with my curls when, in my forties, I went to a new stylist and inquired about the expensive Japanese hair straightening procedure that a friend swore by. The stylist, a lovely silver-haired gentleman named Federico, gently gripped fistfuls of hair on either side of my head and turned my face to the mirror so that I could see what he correctly surmised I'd failed to see my entire life: "You have curly hair!" said Federico. "Accept it! This is you!"

Unfortunately, no one ever said anything similar to me regarding my hips.

I remember the precise moment I first resolved to lose weight. One Saturday when I was in seventh grade I lied to my parents about where I would be spending the evening: I said Lisa's. It was actually Teddy's. As I dressed for my clandestine outing, I assessed my appearance in a pair of purple striped hip-huggers and determined to be thinner. I devised a diet that seemed sensible: four hundred calories a day, not enough to sustain a growing adolescent, or a cocker spaniel, for that matter. It took me years to figure out that my impulse to diet had more to do with shame, specifically shame about desire (see above: Teddy) than with what I actually weighed—which wasn't much.

If only things had remained so simple, or only just that complicated.

Over the next five decades:[*]

- I consulted Dr. Stillman and Dr. Atkins, and the Scarsdale Diet Doctor.
- I joined Weight Watchers again and again. And again and again. And again.
- I believed Oprah when she said she'd found the best way to lose weight and I believed her when she said she'd found an even better way.
- I drank liquid protein and SlimFast, Tab, Diet Coke and Crystal Light.
- I counted out eleven almonds and measured two tablespoons of hummus.
- I halved bananas.
- I became a vegan for three months and then stopped being a vegan during lunch one day at a restaurant in Florence, where I ordered a two-pound bistecca that I held by the bone and ate with my bare, greasy hands.
- I hired a Pilates instructor and an intuitive eating counselor and a personal trainer.
- I blotted the oil off pizza, pulled the skin from chicken, discarded the yolks of eggs.
- I walked and ran and stepped and swam and spun.

During all my years of dieting I led a secret counterlife of eating. My habit of stealthily obtaining, consuming, and destroying the

---

[*] Partial list

evidence of my hunger started early. I hid Devil Dogs in my Barbie doll's wardrobe case. My mother went to her grave not knowing—but of course she must have known—that I was responsible for the mysterious disappearance of the box of French chocolate-covered marshmallows that a guest had brought to her dinner party when I was a teenager forty years earlier. After school, as I walked home from the subway, I stopped at Jimmy's luncheonette on Cortelyou Road, bought a Sky Bar or Charleston Chew, and ditched the wrapper in a trash can on the corner. At Jimmy's I also bought and then hid a paperback copy of Erica Jong's racy feminist novel *Fear of Flying* and several boxes of Dexatrim.

Long after I'd grown up and moved away from home, when I was married, a mother, and a doctor, I still ate large amounts of food when no one was looking: bacon, egg, and cheese sandwiches from Rein's off of I-84 in Connecticut while driving to visit my parents in New York; sheet cake left over from someone's goodbye party in the break room at work; my kids' stale Halloween candy. I'd always thought of my surreptitious eating as a bad habit, the one area of my life in which I had no self-control or self-discipline. But in 2013 I had cause to reconsider this view. The fifth edition of *The Diagnostic and Statistical Manual*, a compendium of psychiatric diagnoses, released that year, included a new condition: binge eating disorder. The criteria for this condition include:

1. Recurrent and persistent episodes of binge eating
2. Binge eating episodes associated with three (or more) of the following:
   Eating much more rapidly than normal
   Eating until feeling uncomfortably full

    Eating large amounts of food when not feeling
      physically hungry

    Eating alone because of being embarrassed by how
      much one is eating

    Feeling disgusted with oneself, depressed, or very
      guilty after overeating

3. Marked distress regarding binge eating
4. Absence of regular compensatory behaviors (such as purging)

I was sure I met all these criteria, though looking back I'm less certain about whether my bingeing caused me "marked distress." "Embarrassed," yes. "Disgusted," maybe. "Depressed" and "very guilty," not really. Still, I was relieved to learn that my secret had a medical name and "embarrassed" was enough to spur me to seek professional help.

I made an appointment with a psychologist who specialized in cognitive behavioral therapy (CBT), the recommended treatment for binge eating disorder (BED). In her thirties, twenty years younger than I was, Alexis had straight blond hair and practiced in a sunny, plant-filled office next to a Chinese restaurant on the main street of a town a few miles from my home. We met three or four times, but I could never shake my first impression that Alexis wasn't smart enough to help me with my uniquely hopeless situation. But I may have been wrong. Once, Alexis asked me to recount in detail what went on in my head while I binged. I told her that I usually thought something like *Shut up! You can't stop me! I can do what I want!* Since I always binged alone, I sometimes said these words aloud. Then Alexis asked me who I was yelling at. *Who* did

I want to shut up? Without thinking, I answered: "My mother, of course."

◆ ◆ ◆

As a child I could have recited my mother's height and weight on her wedding day in 1949—five feet eight and a half inches, one hundred and thirty-two pounds—as readily as my family's home telephone number. My mother often repeated these figures wistfully, as if remembering a lost love. In her attempt to reclaim them she filled our sugar bowl with Sweet'N Low, our butter dish with Diet Mazola, and our pantry with No-Cal coffee soda, which, for a treat, she topped with a small spoon of Schrafft's ice milk. She lined the kitchen bookshelf with diet books, wedging them alongside Julia Child and *The Joy of Cooking*. I still have my mother's 1966 edition of *The Weight Watcher's Cookbook*. As a child I lingered over one illustration in particular, a sad cartoon showing a portly woman with a large nose and wavy hair blowing out the candles on a cake. The caption reads: "Your stomach doesn't know when it's your birthday! . . . Sing a lot! . . . Don't eat a lot!" The message was clear to me even then: *You must deny yourself. It's not OK to want what you want. You can't have your cake and eat it too.*

In the months before my wedding, my mother went to a weight-loss clinic in a glass-and-chrome office on West Fifty-Seventh Street. She derisively referred to the slick doctor she saw there as "The Ski Instructor" but dutifully drank the liquid meal supplements he prescribed and, conveniently, sold. She'd always been size 14 but, after a few weeks of the Ski Instructor's watery shakes she lost twenty pounds and was able to buy a lavender chiffon mother-of-the-bride dress in size 12. It still needed to be let out, which she found exasperating. When the wedding proofs came back from the photographer my mother shuffled through them shaking her head and handed me the ones in which she thought she looked fat. "Tear this one up," she commanded. "And this one. And this."

During visits to my parents when I was in medical school my mother would gather in her hands the loose flesh over her midsection and ask me half-seriously whether I thought she had an abdominal tumor. In her late seventies, she finally lost weight, as most people do. Despite all the money and effort we expend trying to alter our size and shape, the body has other ideas: Most women are leanest at eighteen, gain weight gradually through the next few decades, experience an increase in girth at menopause, and become thinner again in old age as bone density, muscle mass, and appetite diminish. The last article of clothing my mother ever bought was a St. John knit suit, size 10.

When I began to diet, my mother was thrilled. She only wanted for me what she wanted for herself: to be thinner. She recited dietary bromides to me as if they were nursery rhymes: *We must re-ed-u-cate our eating habits!* At age fourteen I assembled my Scarsdale Diet lunch of fruit salad and cottage cheese topped with exactly six pecan halves as my mother looked on smiling. She proclaimed: "*Now* you really mean business!" Her attitude toward my brothers' eating was entirely different. I once overheard her tell a friend with obvious pride that she'd caught one of them chugging milk straight from the gallon in front of the open refrigerator. "He's bulking up for football," she explained.

I don't blame my mother for any of this. Really, I don't. It would have required enormous will and imagination for her to reject the ambient pressure on women to be thin, an act even more radical than applying to law school in 1970 as a forty-three-year-old housewife.

Unlike my mother, my father, who rarely spoke about his weight, was obese. Mostly, he ate whatever he wanted, often followed by a cigarette, which he stubbed out defiantly in the rubble of his food, as if to doubly torment my mother, who worried about both his smoking and his weight. A handful of times, he went on diets to appease her. The first was shortly after they met on a blind date not long after his discharge from the army, after which he started his orthopedic surgery residency. She liked him, but she thought he was fat, and he must have sensed her hesitation. He returned to his residency in Iowa City and arranged with the owner of a restaurant near the hospital to serve him the same three meals every day: coffee for breakfast; hard-boiled eggs and fruit salad for lunch; steak and vegetables for dinner. He returned to Brooklyn six months later, svelte and bearing an engagement ring, which my mother accepted—after which he regained all the weight. I once told this story to my therapist and he said, "Ah, so you owe your very *existence* to a diet!" which didn't seem to me an adequate explanation for my own preoccupation. I must say, though, I found my father's difficulty with his weight endearing and I sensed a bond with him regarding weight and especially regarding appetite that I didn't feel with my chronically dieting mother. Once, when I was home from medical school and the two of us were strolling up Madison Avenue, my father stopped to look in the window of a bakery that sold the chocolate cake with thick mocha buttercream frosting that my mother often ordered for special occasions. He'd just returned from a grueling four-week program at Duke Medical Center. The Rice Diet, I think. He turned his face slowly from the cake toward me and grinned. "Imagine what I could eat," he sighed, "if I needed to *gain* instead of lose." I don't think I ever felt closer to him.

◆   ◆   ◆

I used to joke that if I ever knew as much about medicine as I know about dieting, I would win the Nobel Prize. It may have been a funny line, but it wasn't honest. For all the hours I spent thinking about it, for all the books I read, for all the calorie and carb gram lists I memorized, I never actually learned much. My obsession with dieting and losing weight was an inner droning, a monotonous mental tinnitus; sometimes annoying, occasionally maddening, at rare times barely noticeable, but never different, never going anywhere. Each diet started with the same promise and ended with the same disappointment, often within a single day.

One moment did feel like a crossroads. In 1995, a few months after giving birth to my third child, I made an appointment to see Denise, a dietician at Mass General to whom I'd referred several patients. I'd told her on the phone that I felt frustrated, unable to lose the extra ten pounds I'd gained over my baseline, which, I didn't mention to Denise, was normal by medical standards but too much by my own. Breastfeeding hadn't caused me to lose weight, contrary to what the magazines claimed, which should have come as no surprise since it hadn't after my two previous pregnancies either. I'd just tried another diet: Dr. Dean Ornish's *Eat More, Weigh Less*, a vegan, low-fat regimen. I did eat more—whole pizzas prepared without cheese and oil, for example—but I didn't weigh less, and I was ravenous all the time. Oprah, just a few years after wheeling sixty-seven pounds of fat across her TV-show stage in a wagon to represent the weight she'd lost on a liquid diet, was heavy again. I needed a new idea. I needed help.

Like many consultants with whom I communicate by email and telephone, I'd never actually met Denise. Later she would tell me that when she first saw me she'd wondered if she'd misheard me on the phone. Did I really need to lose weight? Was this a weight *maintenance* issue?

I waited for Denise in her office while she finished seeing a patient in the next room. On her bookshelf sat a little toy grocery basket, similar to what my kids had in their play kitchen at home, containing plastic cubes of cheese, small bunches of plastic grapes, and tennis ball–size clumps of plastic spaghetti meant to demonstrate healthy portions. I'd come to the right place. Denise was going to give me rules, give me some control, fix me. My confidence in her soared further when she walked in. She was slim and muscular. I was going to do whatever she told me to do. Denise had squeezed me in during her lunchtime and she ate while we spoke. Twenty-five years later I still remember exactly what she ate: a small container of microwaved bow-tie pasta with peas and a can of Fresca. Denise, I hoped, was going to tell me how to be her. But she didn't. She listened to my story, starting with my first diet, the purple hip huggers and Teddy, and ending with Dr. Ornish and his miserable pizza. Then she set aside the empty container, placed her hands on her knees, leaned forward and asked: "Aren't you tired of this? Why don't you just *stop*?"

Perhaps sensing my disappointment—she couldn't send me away with nothing—Denise suggested a book for me to read: *Overcoming Overeating: How to Break the Diet-Binge Cycle and Live a Healthier, More Satisfying Life*, published in 1988. The authors, Jane R. Hirschmann and Carol H. Munter, are two social workers from New York who had collaborated in the '70s with Susie Orbach, author of *Fat is a Feminist Issue*. The main message of *Overcoming Overeating* is that diets are meant to keep women oppressed, and that bingeing is a completely reasonable response to deprivation, an attempt at self-care and self-liberation. They advocate keeping the freezer stocked with gallons of ice cream and replacing even one partially eaten gallon with a fresh one while commenting nonjudgmentally, *Oh, look, I need more ice cream.*

I devoured the book and immediately ordered the companion set of cassette tapes on which Hirschmann and Munter tell story after story of women who overcame overeating by surrounding themselves with previously forbidden foods. I particularly loved the one about a large woman who for years had resisted the hot pretzels sold from sidewalk carts in Manhattan. One day she bought ten of them. She took one bite as she walked down the street, found it too salty, and dumped all the pretzels into the nearest trash can. As I listened to the tapes, the New York accents of Hirschmann and Munter briefly replaced my mother's similarly inflected voice. Instead of "*Now* you really mean business!" I heard: "You want a cookie? Eat a cookie!" The two women promised that if my freezer were full of ice cream I would calm down and then something magical would happen: the ice cream would just sit there.

Which was exactly what I wanted. *Overcoming Overeating* was merely another one of my ploys to lose weight, a reality brought home to me by the dreams I began having as I read the book and listened to the tapes. Previously, whenever I'd been on a diet, I'd wake up almost sick with relief that I hadn't actually eaten the jar of peanut butter or the entire cake I dreamed I'd eaten. Now, when I was supposed *not* to diet, I had dreams I'd gone on another diet and then woke up relieved that I hadn't "cheated."

◆ ◆ ◆

For the most part, despite being a doctor, dieting (and not dieting) is no different for me than for most women. My medical training, though, does afford me certain unique opportunities. For one thing, all day long I'm privy to other people's heights and weights. I see a patient whose numbers match mine and think: *Well, she looks pretty good*—or not. I see a patient who has lost a lot of weight and ask, with, I hope, not-too-obvious personal interest, how she did it. Not infrequently my patients comment on my weight because the intimacy of the exam room invites certain reciprocities not seen in other professional settings. Recently I saw a couple who like to schedule their annual physicals back to back. The wife, whom I saw first, remarked that I must have given up jogging, which I'd mentioned to her years ago, because I'd "put on a few." Minutes later, when I saw the husband, he marveled at how I'd managed to remain so trim.

In medical school I was offered a chance to slim down only available to insiders. My classmate Janie told me that a plastic surgeon at Hopkins was just starting to perform a new procedure called liposuction and that he was looking for female students and nurses he could practice on for free. Janie had undergone the procedure herself a few weeks earlier and though I saw no appreciable change in her physique I couldn't wait to sign up. One detail Janie shared with me about her experience sold me particularly. She said that the surgeon's staff was incredibly nice and that after the operation, when bandages had been placed over the holes in her thighs and buttocks into which the suction probe had been inserted, and she'd pulled on the girdle she'd been instructed to bring with her, they'd invited her to lie down on an exam table to rest while they served her brownies. The prospect of having both thinner thighs *and* brownies was irresistible.

There were no brownies served after my procedure, and when I went for my follow-up appointment with the surgeon, more letdown was in store. He placed my Before and After Polaroids side by side on his desk and I could detect no difference. Despite the photos, despite the fact that I'd seen with my own eyes the jars of blood-tinged fat that had been sucked out of me, Big Tush remained.

◆　◆　◆

After the New Frontiers in Obesity conference I made a discovery: even at one of the world's great academic medical centers you can easily declare yourself an expert in a condition that no one else wants to deal with. Shortly after I attended the conference I declared myself an expert in obesity. I read article after article about metabolism and hormones, including leptin, involved in the regulation of body weight and about the pharmacology of diet drugs. As I prepared to start prescribing these drugs myself, I visited an endocrinologist who'd opened a fen-phen clinic in a suburb a few miles from Boston. The clinic looked hastily furnished from an office-supply store, with generic wood-grained chairs and inspirational wall posters featuring intensely colored photos of mountaintops and sunsets captioned TEAMWORK and ASPIRE. As I sat in the waiting room I overheard two patients chatting. One woman in skinny jeans was telling another, larger woman in a loose black skirt that she was going to be amazed at how little she'd want to eat after starting the pills. "Just last night I grabbed a small handful of cherries and couldn't even finish them," said the leaner woman as the heavier woman (and I) nodded. It was too good to be true.

In 1997 the FDA pulled fenfluramine and Redux from the market after the drugs were shown to cause heart defects. I'd never had a chance to prescribe them. Leptin was a bust too. Obese mice may lack leptin but obese people, it turns out, have a surplus of the hormone and are insensitive to its effects in suppressing appetite. My first and only public appearance as an obesity expert was on a local NPR show about a woman who'd died of cardiac arrest after taking fen-phen to fit into her wedding dress.

I think I knew all along that obesity wasn't a problem that would be solved by medication. Based on my own and my patients' experiences, I'd never really believed that people overeat because they're hungry and that manipulating neurotransmitters and hormones to suppress appetite would be the key to weight loss. At the peak of my enthusiasm for obesity as a medical condition I had coffee with a psychoanalyst friend, an extremely slender woman. I waxed on at length about doctors' longstanding lack of interest in obesity and about how that would change as more effective weight-loss drugs became available. My friend sipped her coffee. "But there's another reason we've avoided dealing with our patients' fat," she said. "What's that?" I asked, reaching in my purse for my pen and notebook. She answered: "It disgusts us."

I could have stayed in obesity medicine. Doctors I respect have done so and helped people, including some of my patients, improve their health. In the past decade safer weight loss drugs and bariatric surgery techniques have enabled a small but growing number of people to lose enough weight that they no longer require insulin, antihypertensives, or cholesterol-lowering drugs. Obesity specialists have become the chief advocates within the medical profession for the rights of obese people. Obesity conferences today highlight workplace and housing discrimination based on weight, and obesity clinics, unlike most medical facilities, provide extra-large examination gowns, chairs, and blood-pressure cuffs. This advocacy isn't much appreciated by those in the current anti-diet movement, who see the medicalization of weight in any form as oppression, particularly of women. Recent books such as *Anti-Diet: Reclaim Your Time, Money, Well-Being, and Happiness* and *The F*ck It Diet: Eating Should Be Easy* echo the themes of earlier books such as *Overcoming Overeating* and *Fat Is a Feminist Issue*, but they identify a new patriarchy: doctors, whom they believe are particularly guilty of perpetuating what they call "diet culture." Their authors claim that obesity itself doesn't cause diabetes but, rather, that the stress obese people experience in being stigmatized by their physicians and by society in general leads to elevated blood sugar.

I've seen enough patients whose diabetes improved when they lost weight to be skeptical of this argument. Still, I'm sympathetic to the idea that obesity isn't strictly a medical problem. For every patient I see whose reduction in blood sugar neatly tracks with the amount of weight they've lost I see many more whose weight—like mine—is an impossibly complex manifestation of genetics, physiology, culture, and personal history; the relationship between weight and health is not straightforward. A patient tells me she can't understand why she's so unmotivated to lose weight when she has diabetes and her own mother lost a leg to that disease. But I understand. A few years ago I pitched an idea to a literary agent for a book about how complicated weight is, how much more is involved than "calories in, calories out." I'd come up with a title for this book: *The Last Three Pounds*, which is the weight of the average woman's brain. I told the agent that I'd been struggling with my weight my whole life and that most of my patients had too. I wanted to give voice to our stories. The agent listened politely and then said that no one would buy a book about weight by a doctor who offered no advice about how to lose it.

Discouraged as I am about my own longtime pursuit of weight loss, I can't become nihilistic. I'm still a medical doctor with obese patients whose weight I can't ignore. For a while, I followed the advice of doctor, writer, and Crohn's disease patient Rachel Naomi Remen, who once observed, "It is our wounds that enable us to be compassionate with the wounds of others." I shared some of my own experiences to help my patients understand the connection between their stress and their eating, their eating and their health. I started a cardiovascular-disease-prevention group for patients in my internal medicine practice. A nurse practitioner, a dietician, and I recruited patients who had two or more of the known risk factors for cardiovascular disease: male sex, smoking, obesity, hypertension, diabetes, high cholesterol, and a family history of atherosclerosis. In blocks of ten sessions we tried to help them modify those risk factors that are modifiable. The nurse practitioner reviewed their blood-pressure and blood-sugar readings. The dietician took them on a field trip to a nearby grocery store and taught them how to use nutritional labels as guides to reducing sodium and saturated fat. As the physician in the trio I was supposed to give the patients the hard data, the science that supported making these behavioral changes. But the data and the science bored me.

At each of the sessions I led, the patients and I sat around a conference table in the office of my practice. In the center of the table lay a Spartan feast, also funded by the grateful patient: plastic mini bottles of water, a Styrofoam tray of cut-up fruit, and several containers of Yoplait yogurt, which no one ever touched. At the first session of each block, after we'd gone around the table and introduced ourselves, I would make this statement: "In this program we will talk about the importance of exercise and controlling blood sugar and blood pressure, but we all know that we're here for one reason and one reason only." The participants, who had been looking down at their laps, or at me with neutral expressions, or at the Yoplait yogurts, raised their heads and leaned forward.

"We're here," I'd continue, "because we can't manage stress or anx-iety without stuffing our faces." I repeated this statement to several different groups over the next few years and not once did anyone ever disagree with me.

I left the food labels and the blood-pressure monitoring to the dietician and the nurse practitioner and worked with the group on stress management, often using guided meditation. I'd learned this technique in a continuing medical education course during which I found that while I was an impatient meditator myself, I was good at coming up with scenarios to guide others. In one, I led the group across an imaginary meadow, which, in my mind, resembled the grassy field where my sons had played in town baseball league games. I placed a small, arched wooden bridge at the edge of the meadow and led the group across it as we envisioned improving our health with each step.

In another, borrowed from the course I'd taken, I asked par-ticipants to conjure the dinner tables of their childhoods: Where was everyone sitting? What was served? Who said what? How did it feel? When we opened our eyes at the end of this meditation, I often saw tears streaming down at least one or two faces. A man of sixty with a neatly trimmed steel-gray beard, his voice cracking, once said: "I haven't thought of it in years. My father never looked up from his plate. Mother jumped up every other minute to run into the kitchen. The silences. It was all so . . . *tense*." I participated myself, traveling in my mind to the dining room in Brooklyn with the dark-blue wallpaper, the smell of roast beef, and the silver bell that my mother never rang. I, too, wanted to learn how to manage stress without stuffing my face.

In a few years the funding for the program dried up and, in truth, I'd lost my enthusiasm for it. I'd entered a diet limbo, neither believing nor disbelieving that weight matters. I came to feel that my problem was not medical, nor cosmetic nor political but ontological. What did it all *mean*? I'd have a glimmer of clarity at times: This incessant rumination about weight was my way of never being present. By focusing on my desire to lose weight I could remain in a perpetual state of becoming rather than being. Every year I spent family vacations at the beach fantasizing about how much thinner I'd be *next* summer. In college I laid out jeans and a fitted top, both two sizes too small for me, on my dorm-room bed, and admire the disembodied outlines of my future self. On our honeymoon, as my husband and I drove along the winding Grand Corniche in the French Riviera I gazed not at the Mediterranean, or at my handsome new husband, but at my thighs, which I noticed were wider than his, as we sat side by side in the car.

A few years ago, a new thought occurred to me: "What if there isn't a solution because there isn't a problem?"

Many years ago, when I'd been in practice awhile, I briefly considered giving up medicine to become a rabbi. This was a ridiculous idea because I've never been observant and my Jewish education barely progressed beyond the Hebrew alphabet. Still, I went to a weekend retreat for prospective rabbinical students at a local seminary. A current student, a woman who'd heard me introduce myself and had quickly sized up my meager qualifications, sat next to me at lunch. "Listen," she whispered, "what do you need to be a rabbi for? You're a doctor! You're already doing God's work!"

What *had* I been looking for? A less hectic, less harried oppor-

tunity to help people than medicine offered. I longed especially, I
now realize, for a break from my constant need to improve myself.
After registering for the retreat I read Abraham Joshua Heschel's
The Sabbath and was moved by the story of the pious man who sees
a broken section of fence while strolling in his vineyards on Shabbat. He makes a mental note to repair the fence during the week.
But he never does repair it because the thought of doing such work
should not have even occurred to him on Shabbat. I still yearn for
this state of presence, but I fear it too. To be fully present without
thinking about what I should be or do or weigh feels too still, too
much like death.

About three years ago I joined Weight Watchers one last time.
They'd tweaked the program again, as they must do every couple
of years because it only produces significant and lasting weight loss
for a tiny percentage of the people who try it. The latest iteration
emphasizes wellness and includes a personal coaching option. My
coach was a lovely woman about my age named Peggy Ann who
lived in Georgia. She was thoughtful, psychologically inclined, not
strictly a company spokeswoman like leaders I'd had in the past
when I'd attended meetings. But as insightful as Peggy Ann was
about the relationship between my busy life and my overeating, I
just couldn't convince myself that these insights mattered. During
our weekly fifteen-minute phone sessions I started chatting Peggy
Ann up about her grandchildren and about the weather in Georgia.
I even got her to allude, once, to the fact that she didn't like Donald
Trump. One time she repeated the dieter's platitude: *Nothing tastes
as good as being thin feels.* I said, "That's the problem, Peggy Ann:
everything tastes as good as being thin feels." And she laughed.

◆   ◆   ◆

Now I eat salad because I like salad. I eat cheeseburgers for the same reason, though less often because they're bad for the planet and for my arteries. I walk almost every day because walking helps me think and gives me a chance to be alone. I lift weights in a class at the gym across the street from the hospital because I like feeling strong and because the nurses who are regulars in the class make me laugh. And I weigh more than I ever have other than during my pregnancies. But I *feel* thinner than when I weighed much less. I look at a photo of myself as a medical student, and I feel thinner than I was then, even though I weigh forty pounds more, even though I have now, in late middle age, inherited my mother's "abdominal tumor." Because feeling thinner has never had anything to do with weight.

Patients still comment on my weight. The other day a Guatemalan-born woman told me: "Doctor, you gained weight! You look good!" So discordant were these two statements that I was sure I'd misheard my patient because of her accent and since she was wearing a mask because of Covid-19. "You look *good*," she repeated. She went on to explain that she had never weighed more than ninety-five pounds and that she wished she was "big" like her sisters. "Like *you*, doctor." I puzzled all day about whether I should be flattered or insulted or neither or both.

Just recently, I've found an unlikely ally in Zoom, to which all meetings and some of my visits with patients have relocated during the pandemic. On the one hand, videoconferencing is hard on one's self-image because you're staring at yourself all day on camera in harsh light. As I listen to my patients and colleagues speak I notice that I'm slumping down in my chair, which makes my chin look double. My hair, because I've not been able to get it cut or colored during the quarantine, adds to my slovenly appearance. But then I sit up straight and one of my chins disappears. I adjust the lighting and now my hair looks leonine. I'm a wise older woman and suddenly I feel fine about myself. It doesn't hurt that no one else looks their best on Zoom, either. I see an unmade bed in the background, a stubble on a chin. One older doctor has on his dresser a giant bottle from Costco of glucosamine chondroitin, an unproven arthritis remedy. It's as if we've all made a silent pact. The standards by which we judge one another and ourselves have been temporarily relaxed, like on the beach, where people who would never, in public, wear a tucked-in shirt or horizontal stripes parade half-naked.

A psychiatrist colleague once told me that patients with psychosis don't stop believing in their delusions, they just lose interest in them. They're still sure the CIA is bugging their home, but they've learned to ignore that intrusion. Perhaps after all these years something like this has happened to me regarding my weight. Still, when I learned recently that a young doctor named Helene needed a practice subject as she worked toward certification as a health coach, I volunteered. I was up to my old tricks, of course, but Helene saw through me. She identified after our first session that weight was not a compelling goal for me. I'd already told her I could never go on another diet again with a straight face. What did I want then? she asked. "Simply to be myself," I answered.

In our most recent session I told Helene that I'd come to realize that I've been slowly extricating myself from a voice in my head with which I've lived for over fifty years, a voice constantly critical and controlling and sometimes frankly abusive and which has never, not once, offered me a moment of pleasure. "Wow. That's some analogy," Helene observed. "It sounds like you really are in a new place with all of this. So how do you feel now? Are you afraid you'll go back to this . . . 'abuser'?"

I was walking on a trail near my house on a beautiful summer day as Helene and I spoke by phone. I'd decided my work with her was pretty much done, a decision confirmed for me by the fact that during my walk I hadn't once thought about how many steps I'd logged or how many calories I'd burned. So my answer to Helene's question surprised me. "Yes, I'm afraid!" I said, more vehemently than I'd intended. "It knows where I live! It still has the keys to my house!"

10

Mom at Bedside, Appears Calm

We carry a nylon lunch bag everywhere we go, royal blue with purple trim, containing two plastic syringes, each preloaded with 5mg of liquid Valium, plus packets of surgical lubricant and plastic gloves. At the first sign of blinking or twitching, we lay him on his left side, tug down the elastic waist of his pants, part his small buttocks, and insert the gooped-up tip. Within moments, the motion stops, as if an engine has been switched off. Then he falls into a deep sleep. When he relaxes, so do we.

He's five years old, the first time. Our babysitter takes him to a pizza place for lunch. He laughs mid-slice, blinks several times, slumps to the floor, and climbs back onto his chair. She hesitates—what was that?—and then calls 911. She pages me. I keep the message stored in my beeper, periodically daring myself to relive my first reading of it.

I meet them in the ER at the community hospital near our home, showily flashing my downtown hospital ID tag. Soon my husband rushes in, wearing the ID from his downtown hospital. All the tests are negative, they say. Bring him back if something else happens.

Something else happens. The next day, I skip work and keep him home from school. He sits happily in front of cartoons while I pace and polish, pace and fold. Maybe the babysitter overreacted, I reason. Maybe he's just a goofy kid. The moment I stop watching him, he cries, "Look, Mommy! Look what my hand can do!"

No mistaking it this time. Grand mal, big and bad, right on the gurney. Lumbar puncture. MRI. All negative. Before we go home, the neurologist asks if we have further questions. "Just one," I say. "What do we do if he does it again?" The neurologist seems surprised. His raised eyebrows silently ask, *Aren't you both doctors?* He hands us a pamphlet.

Chewable yellow triangles three times a day. Triangles to first grade and the beach and day camp and a sleepover. The other kid has cochlear implants. "Don't worry," his mother says, accepting my baggie of pills. "My kid comes with instructions too."

One day, almost exactly a year later, the school nurse calls. "It's been ten minutes and it's not stopping," she says. I'd started working part-time after my second child was a year old and I'm home when the nurse phones. I screech over in seconds, leaving one tire on the schoolyard curb. He's in the nurse's office, lying on the plastic divan reserved for kids with sore throats, bellyaches. Fakers. I know what this is called, this shaking that will not stop. I know how to treat this, in adults. But all I know now is how to hold him, jerking, foaming, soaked with urine.

In the ambulance, the foam turns bloody. I ask the ponytailed EMT whether he will die. She pretends not to hear, turns to adjust his oxygen. At the local ER, I bark instructions. "He has a neurologist downtown," I say. "He needs to be transferred." The ER attending, who has been bending over him with her lights and sticks, straightens. "I think," she says, not unkindly, "Mom needs to wait outside."

Tubed, taped, lined. Ready for transfer. There is one last thing. The ponytailed EMT hands me a specimen cup in which the source of the blood that had burst my heart open rattles. "Here, Mom," she says, smiling. "For the tooth fairy."

Back at home, forty pills a day, crushed, on spoons of Breyers cookies-and-cream. Still he blinks and shakes, shakes and drops. The weeks go by in a slow and sickening descent, landing on the carpeted floor of the playroom in our basement. We spend most of the day there because it's the only place in the house where he can't fall down the stairs. At night we tuck him tightly into *Star Wars* sheets but still find him on the floor in wet pajamas. If the Valium fails, we call 911. A fire truck arrives with the ambulance, and the firefighters, with their giant boots and helmets, crowd along with the EMTs into the small bedroom our boys share, delighting our younger son.

He is admitted. He is discharged. He is admitted and discharged again. Admitteddischargedadmitteddischargedadmitteddischarged-admitteddischarged. My husband, too tall for the fold-out chair/bed, takes the day shift. I pad in slippers through the hospital at night with the other parents. We buy one another coffee. We commiserate. I grow more at ease in this sleepless company than with anyone else—my family, my friends, my medical colleagues. I also cling to the nurses, Jen and Sarah and Kristen and "the other Jen," as we call her. One leaves my son's chart in his room, and I sneak a look. "Mom at bedside," a progress note reads. "Appears calm."

Finally, a break. The sixth or seventh MRI shows a subtle irregularity in the right temporal lobe, possibly a tiny tumor, a focus. Epilepsy is usually not curable by surgery but when there's an abnormality visible on MRI, something that might be removed surgically, the possibility of a cure is greater. We love the word "focus," a raft of hope in a vague and endless sea of anxiety. Never have parents been so happy to learn their child might have a brain tumor.

The surgery works. The medications are discontinued. I don't ask to read the pathology report, the operative note. I am startled by my lack of medical curiosity. I wish to know nothing other than that my son no longer shakes. After the staples come out, we pile into the car and take a nine-hour drive—unthinkable during the previous months—to visit my in-laws. On the way home, my husband glances at the backseat through the rearview mirror and, returning his eyes to the road, says, "He's blinking again."

A second surgery. A third. This time, we're lucky. "The luckiest unlucky parents ever," I joke.

Years pass. We renovate our kitchen and find the lunch bag with two dried-up syringes of Valium in a cabinet about to be torn down. Our emaciated boy doubles in weight and then doubles again. He graduates from high school. He graduates from college. He moves away from home.

I do not know how much he remembers. He rarely speaks of those years, except to comment on whether a barber has done a good or not-so-good job of hiding the scars.

As for me, occasionally my terror will snap to life again, as if I've been holding it by a long and slack tether. It happens when I am walking through the peaceful, leafy streets of our town, pumping my arms, working my aging heart and muscles, quieting my busy mind. A siren sounds. An ambulance appears. Though I know from reading the log in our local paper that the emergency is rarely dire— a dog bite, an asthma attack—and I know that my son is nowhere near, I still stop to see which way the ambulance is heading.

People ask, "Is it easier or harder to have a sick child when both parents are doctors?" But this is the wrong question. There is no hard, no easy. Only fear and love, panic and relief, shaking and not shaking.

Curbsiding

In my thirties, I decided I needed therapy. Though I seemed OK, more than OK—I worked as a doctor at one of the best hospitals in the world; had a husband, also a doctor, who loved me; three adorable children; and, as my mother would say, a decent head of hair—I was miserable. But instead of doing what most people would do when they think they need therapy, call their insurance company to find out which therapists are covered, ask friends for referrals, see their primary care provider, I did what most *doctors* would do, which is to say that I asked for help while pretending I didn't actually need help. I emailed Howard, a psychiatric colleague with whom I'd shared a number of patients. Subject line: *Favor?* I asked if I could speak with him. No big deal, I wrote, but I preferred to meet in person. He replied that he would drop by my office at the end of the day.

Asking for advice casually, one physician to another, has a name: "curbsiding." When you call a colleague and say: *Can I run something by you?* or: *Have you ever seen anything like this?* you're asking for a "curbside consult." The exchange is off the record, there's no bill involved, and the giver of the advice bears no responsibility for the outcome of the case. The term brings to my mind someone slowing down to crane their neck out a car window to ask for directions. I have a terrible sense of direction, and when I'm walking in my suburban neighborhood and a driver asks me how to get somewhere, I'm always afraid that they'll find I've led them astray, and circle back to yell at me.

When Howard arrived I sat surrounded by my diplomas on my office wall and Lucite-framed photos of my family on my desk. I felt safe, in control, able to tell Howard only what I wanted to tell him, which was that I was fine, had no problems really, but that there were just a few things I needed to sort out. What I didn't tell him: I feared my marriage was falling apart; I felt accused of incompetence and indifference by my patients with every phone call, drug side effect, and difficult-to-diagnose symptom; I was overwhelmed by the needs of my three young kids, one of whom had medical issues, and struggling to balance the demands of my children with those of my parents, especially my retired doctor father who, in his seventies, after a lifetime of hypochondria, was now actually sick.

My father had been hospitalized for several weeks in New York with a severe knee infection. That winter in Boca Raton one of his old orthopedic surgery cronies had backed into my father with a golf cart and when he returned to Manhattan another old crony stuck a needle into his swollen knee under less-than-sterile conditions in my parents' Upper East Side living room. *That* curbside consult had caused a bacterial infection requiring a prolonged hospitalization during which I made many trips from Boston to visit him.

I turned thirty-five that spring and, in my father's room at Mount Sinai, my mother gave me my birthday present: her mother's diamond ring, a beautifully cut round stone set in filigreed platinum, which I always pictured on my grandmother's warm, capable hands, dotting her famous rugelach with cinnamon sugar before putting them in the oven. My mother explained that she'd planned to give me the ring for my fortieth birthday but it was clear to her, she said as she nodded around the hospital room in which she'd introduced me as Our Daughter, a Doctor at Massachusetts General Hospital in Boston to my father's physicians, nurses, and even the guy who came to fix the TV, that I was now fully an adult.

Adulthood wasn't going well. I couldn't stop eating, I was drinking too much coffee, and then too much wine to counteract the effects of the coffee, and then too much coffee to pep me up after the wine. My husband and I could barely speak without fighting. I'd taken to screaming in my car during my morning and evening commutes; at my husband, my kids, my patients, my father, and especially at my mother, who had done absolutely nothing other than thank me for all the trips I'd made to my father's bedside in New York and then rewarded me with a family heirloom and a sentimental note ending with a question from a sweet childhood routine between the two of us: *How come I'm so lucky? Because I have you!*

Still, when I replayed conversations with my mother, and even when I thought about the contents of that note, I gritted my teeth so hard I feared they'd break, including later that day after she gave me my birthday present when I drove back to Boston, my grandmother's ring in a black velvet box in my purse and my mother's reminder about having the ring appraised and insured echoing in my head.

No one knew I was struggling. In fact, a doctor a few years

younger than me, a woman who had a tendency to compare herself unfavorably to me for reasons I couldn't fathom (she was smarter, more devoted to her patients, had even better hair) had taken to telling people what an amazing role model I was after a visit to my home. She marveled at how I'd simultaneously served her coffee and cookies, cuddled my daughter in my lap, offered my son, who lay on the floor in a car seat, a bottle, and swatted away our Chesapeake Bay retriever who was determined to lick milk dribbles off the baby's face—all while we gossiped about work. "You should have seen her," my younger colleague, who at that point had one child and felt frazzled, told the other women doctors in our medical group. "She was a *goddess*." A few days later, feeling the need to disabuse her of this notion, I limped the few yards from my office to hers to show her that I, the woman who had it all together, the goddess, had worn two mismatched shoes to work. And, I pointed out, not closely mismatched: a black flat and a navy heel.

To this day, over twenty years later, I still wince when I drive by the large white house in which the therapist to whom Howard referred me lived and practiced. He was a short, intense man of about sixty, an old-school analyst, whose bushy eyebrows were more expressive than most people's smiles. With him I was more forthcoming than I'd been with Howard and even than I'd been with myself up to that point. I told him about the teeth gritting and the drinking and the screaming in the car, but I also told him something I'd never told anyone before: that I'd always felt not quite like a woman. His eyebrows went up.

Having absorbed my confession, the psychiatrist told me that he thought I would benefit from therapy, perhaps even analysis, but unfortunately his schedule was full. I felt as if I'd failed an audition. Were my problems not sufficiently interesting? He explained that he'd agreed to see me only for triage, the medical term that derives from the French *trier*, "to sort," and he had, apparently sorted me into the category of people he did not want as patients. Crestfallen, I listened as he, eyebrows now bouncing furiously, told me he would do his best to find me the right therapist and that I should be prepared for a long and arduous process. "First," he explained, "you'll have to talk yourself into trouble, which might take years." I asked what happened after that. He said, smiling, "After that, you'll have to talk yourself *out* of trouble."

I began leaving work early every Monday to get to my four o'clock appointment with the psychiatrist to whom he sent me: Dr. Robert Katz, nicknamed, exclusively in my own mind, "Katzie." I thought no one in my office noticed that I had blocked out this weekly time, but years later my secretary told me that she and the other "girls at the front desk," as she called them, had speculated about whether I was having an affair, moonlighting at another hospital, or going to a yoga class. In fact, my weekly meetings with Katzie did have an illicit feeling about them. I would rush out of work at three thirty, heart pounding with fear that I would be late for my appointment and also with excitement. Sometimes as I drove the few miles from Boston to Katzie's office in his home in Cambridge I even sang a little song to myself: *Be still, be still my heart!* I told my medical school friend Tracey about this. I told Tracey everything about my meetings with Katzie, especially during the first couple of years. I'd leave her long messages, a series of several, since her voicemail had an exasperating time limit, in which I would recount, almost word for word, much of what had transpired during the fifty minutes of each of my therapy sessions. Tracey had become a psychiatrist herself and practiced in another city. She'd been urging me to "see someone" for years. To "get help." She understood the heightened sensation I experienced each Monday afternoon. She told me that when she'd started her own compulsory therapy, she'd noticed that in the presence of her therapist she could feel the air circulating on her forearms, as if she'd developed new and superior powers of perception.

My feelings for Katzie were not sexual, but they were not *not* sexual either. I loved to look at his thin wrists, and at the hair on his calves between his socks and flannel trousers, exposed when he crossed his legs. I searched for clues about his personal life: in the books in the waiting room (a dog-eared copy of Dr. Spock's *Baby and Child Care* with the giver's inscription, "as you begin the most important job of your life," made me swoon); the view through the narrow gap in the pocket doors between the waiting room and the Katz family's dining room; the small corner of backyard I could glimpse from the path that led to the side entrance for patients. The kilim pillows on the waiting room couch. The tantalizing presence of Katzie's wife, also a therapist, whose muffled voice I sometimes heard as she spoke on the phone in her office. I assigned nicknames to the patients who occupied the time slot before me and imagined how I compared with them in Katzie's estimation. Surely he found me more interesting than Bicycle Girl, the young woman who pedaled away from the house as I arrived. Or Sad Man, who replaced her after a few months. Or Mustache Guy, who took his slot a year later.

When I parked in front of Katzie's house, which stood on a

street with a slight incline, I always pulled up my emergency brake, an unnecessary act of extra caution, which indicated, I assessed, my fear of losing control with Katzie. As I told Tracey about this, I could picture her nodding in approval on the other end of the phone. "This is *good!*" she pronounced. "It's transference. Almost like falling in love, that stage where everything about the other person is fascinating, amazing. Like, 'Oh my god how incredible! We both like Chinese food!'"

I'd been an A student and now I wanted to be an A therapy patient. At first, I boasted to Tracey about insights I made in therapy and then, as I became more comfortable with Katzie, I started congratulating myself during the sessions themselves. I got pretty skilled at recognizing when an interpretation, his or mine, rang true and sometimes, at the end of a session, I would ask him, "Now honestly, Dr. Katz, aren't I the easiest (most entertaining, most charming) patient you've ever had?"

In truth, the real progress came in moments when I was *less* sure of myself. Moments when tears flowed for no reason and my questions had no easy answers. Tracey approved of these most of all. "*Now* you're getting somewhere," she'd say. And I did get somewhere. After five years Katzie and I agreed that we'd accomplished what we'd set out to do, though our goals had never been stated. There's no doubt the therapy helped. I'd become more tolerant of uncertainty, felt less concerned with what sort of woman I was. My marriage improved greatly, in part because our kids were now older and more independent. I've since half-facetiously told my younger colleagues and patients that children bring unimaginable joy and also, unfortunately, ruin your life. My father, after many more illnesses and countless rushed trips to the hospital, died. Time had moved on, a fact brought home to me one evening when I attended a meeting in the empty waiting room of my medical office to which doctors forty and under had been invited. When I received the invitation by email, subject line: THE FUTURE, I was a bit hesitant to accept since I was already a bit over forty. Was I welcome? Of course, came the reply. But at the meeting, as my younger colleagues discussed balancing parenthood with work, growing a practice and a referral network, I had the strong sense that I didn't belong there, that I had moved on to a new phase of life.

And with it came a new kind of misery, a much quieter one.

In truth, I think this other misery had been there all along, its dull beat drowned out by the incessant busyness of raising children, building a career, and helping to take care of my father. It was similar to when, a few years ago, I fell and fractured my shoulder in three places and was so focused on the pain from that injury I didn't notice I'd also broken two toes. I arrived at my first physical therapy appointment after my shoulder surgery and the therapist, a plainspoken woman named Connie, listened patiently to my story. Then Connie pointed down to my sandal-shod left foot, swollen and purple, and asked: "OK, I get that you broke your shoulder, but what the fuck is *that*?"

What *was* this other, less noticeable pain, the one that had become more intense in my forties? I coined a self-mocking phrase, my own play on the title of a novel by Milan Kundera, to describe it to myself, one I was sure couldn't make sense to anyone else: *the unbearable about-ness of being.* By "about-ness" I meant that I felt disconnected from myself, abstracted from my own life.

The feeling was not entirely new. As a child, I called it "willowy." Willowy would hit me hardest when I was being looked at, like when I stood on the granite steps of our house in Brooklyn, waiting to get picked up for a birthday party, holding a wrapped gift, wearing tights, which I despised, my unruly hair clamped in the vicious jaws of a plastic barrette. Someone's mom would pull up and I would see her and the other kids carpooling to the party staring at me and I felt not invisible but worse than invisible, a blob rather than a vapor, a shape without an identity. I felt the same when I looked in the mirror and said my name over and over again until the movement of my teeth and lips seemed disassociated from my face and the syllables of my name derailed: *zanne-sue, zanne-sue, zanne-sue*. The word "willowy" would stick in my mind and the only way to drive it out was to curse, to say under my breath: *shitfuckshitfuckshit*.

In college, "willowy" became "The Hanging Plant." There was this girl in my class at Yale named Renee Blatt. She was kind of prim and judgmental, but I can't think too badly of her because one of her judgments was that my then future husband, with whom she had taken an English course, was smart and cute and seemed to like me and that I should snap him up. Anyway, Renee was slender and always tidily dressed in kilts and Shetland sweaters. She played the harp in the Yale Symphony. Renee had the kind of femininity that I envied: small, contained, soft. The kind of femininity that I knew I, with my wild hair and wide hips and smoking and drinking and overeating and loud voice, could never achieve, but to which I aspired.

Renee's roommate was Missy Taylor, a diver from Fort Worth. Missy was a self-described "lady jock" who acknowledged openly that she hadn't gotten into Yale based on her grades and SAT scores. Though she was quite unlike studious, musical Renee, Missy had, to my eye, a similar girlish quality. Missy, like Renee, was thin, and she had perennially tanned, smooth limbs and wore diving-themed jewelry: miniature gold dolphins adorned her delicate earlobes and throat. Renee and Missy's suite, sophomore year, was very different from the one I shared with my roommates. For one thing, ours always smelled of smoke. My three roommates and I had been placed together because we were the only four girls in our dorm who smoked. So our suite stank. And none of us were very good housekeepers, so it stank even more than it might have—old pizza boxes and beer bottles frequently sat beside overflowing ashtrays on our thrift-shop coffee table. We were often drunk and sang loudly along with LPs, which rarely found their way back into their jackets. We played Fleetwood Mac and Joni Mitchell and Springsteen and Steely Dan and Stevie Wonder and Dylan over and over and over, each of us insisting that this song or that spoke to us alone. Jessie, who came out that year, argued that "Rikki Don't Lose That Number" was about coming out. Her evidence was the spelling of "Rikki." I was sure my annoying, well-off parents and privileged upbringing made me uniquely qualified to howl along with "Like a Rolling Stone."

Ahh you've gone to the finest schools all
right, Miss Lonely
But you know you only used to get juiced in it

In the suite Renee and Missy shared there was no smoke, no

mess, no loud music. They had a clean, grown-up couch. A rug. Well-tended and healthy spider plants hung from the ceiling on macramé slings. I remember once watching Renee, or maybe Missy, pinching off dead leaves and gently misting one of the hanging plants with a copper sprayer and thinking: *I will never be this adult, this competent, this together. I will never be this much of a real woman.*

It took decades, and therapy, for me to understand that to certain men—my husband, for example—the loud, messy, poorly contained me was sexier than those two fastidious girls with their hanging plants. It seems so obvious now, and yet I held then an unshakable conviction that I was not as attractive, as feminine as they were. I now see that everything I have ever felt good about— in my marriage, my parenting, my writing, and my doctoring—has been the work of the loud, curvy, curly headed girl, operating on instinct and without self-consciousness. And every wrong turn I've ever taken has been in pursuit of those hanging plants, symbols of the woman I thought I was supposed to be. Curvy Curly always wins. Always.

In medical school I confided in Tracey that I'd always feared that I didn't have a discernable identity. The way I expressed this fear was to say that I didn't have a handwriting. This might have seemed surprising given my tendency to perform, my love of the limelight. But Tracey knew what I meant. The way she put it was that I didn't know what flavor ice cream I preferred. I couldn't like chocolate just because I liked chocolate. I had to consider first whether there might be some reason vanilla was the most popular, or whether a more complex concoction—say, coffee Heath Bar or mint chip—might be better than chocolate. This became a kind of shorthand between Tracey and me. I'd tell her about something I liked, a TV show or an article of clothing or a possible choice of medical specialty, and she'd ask if it was really my "favorite flavor" or just what I thought *should* be my favorite.

In 1978, just four years before we entered medical school, Pauline Clance and Suzanne Imes, two psychologists at Georgia State University, first described "imposter phenomenon," which they defined as "an internal experience of intellectual phoniness that appears to be particularly prevalent and intense among a select sample of high achieving women." Tracey and I hadn't yet heard of this condition, but we knew we suffered from it. We called ourselves "The Asterisks," as in:

We got into Johns Hopkins*

*but there weren't many applicants to medical school that year.

During my thirties and forties, I read a lot of self-help articles and books, as my mother always had. There was some overlap in our choice of reading material—anything about weight loss, particularly. But while my mother pored over bridge and tennis and gardening books, I looked for more psychological and moral guidance. My mother, I think, felt confident that she was a good and substantive person, and equally certain that she lacked many skills that she ought to have mastered. I, on the other hand, was less obsessed with what I could and couldn't do than with who I was and was not. I had a perpetual feeling that I needed what I started calling the Answer and that someone—*someone*—had the Answer. I never fully articulated to myself the question that needed answering, but fixated on the idea that my feeling of being defective, the adult version of the feeling I'd had since earliest childhood, could be relieved if I only knew . . . what? Something someone else knew.

Once, in those years when I thought about the Answer all the time, I was walking down Harvard Street in Brookline and passed an old-fashioned stationery and toy store. It was owned and run by a woman in her nineties. Hanging in the window of the storefront was a poster listing, in digital-printer calligraphy, the old woman's secrets to a long and healthy life. The list included such advice as: *Take pride in your appearance*, *Be cheerful*, and *Don't spend more than you earn*. I needed to have a copy of this list. I *needed* it. This woman had the Answer! I walked into the store and asked if she had copies. She did. She sold them for 99 cents apiece. I bought one, folded it neatly in half, and tucked it into the loose-leaf binder that contained my first writing efforts. Even then, I must have sensed that whatever this list revealed had less to do with thrift and cheerfulness and more to do with why I, at that stage of life, had acquired it so urgently. That, one day, I would write about my need to possess that list.

◆　◆　◆

In the mid-2000s, my husband and I went to a resort in southwestern Utah, where we ate rustic spa food (elk meat, very lean) and took guided hikes up and down the massive red rock formations. The resort offered evening activities, lectures on nutrition and spirituality that we never attended. But one night there was to be a presentation on "The Secret," as featured on *Oprah*. How could I resist? I left my husband in our room and walked in the dark through the dry, eucalyptus-scented heat to the resort's main building. I entered a large meeting room, where seats had been arranged in front of a giant flat-screen television. I was the only one there. I waited five minutes, ten, fifteen. No one showed up.

Finally, I went to the reception desk and announced that I was there for "The Secret." The woman behind the desk said, "Oh!" and then she led me back into the meeting room, popped a DVD into the player on the shelf below the big TV, and excused herself. The "presentation" turned out to be a video hawking a book called *The Secret*, whose author had appeared on Oprah.

Here is the Secret: if you think about something you want hard and long enough, you get it. In one part of the video, a boy dreams of owning a red bicycle. He cuts out a picture of the bicycle he wants from a magazine and stares at it night and day. Sure enough, a man appears at the front door of the boy's home with that exact bicycle. Never mind that the man in this dramatization looked like a child molester. Here's your new bike, little boy!

Do you think the cheesiness of the DVD or the fact that I was sitting alone watching it kept me from being glued to the screen until the very end? No! I was there to learn the Secret! I needed to find out the Answer! I must confess that to this very day I occasionally picture my body thin, my home immaculate, my name in *New Yorker* font, as hard as that little boy pictured that red bicycle. I mean, you never know.

◆ ◆ ◆

I wish I could say that my sense of not-rightness, of lacking the Answer or the Secret faded as I grew older but, in fact, it actually grew much stronger for a while. Here is something I know based on my personal and professional experience: a woman's mid- to late forties are some of her most difficult years. Forty-six and forty-seven are particularly awful and should be avoided altogether if possible. Perimenopause brings irregular periods, disrupted sleep, heat intolerance, acne flares, heartburn, gas, decreased libido, mood swings, and weight gain. Worse than all of these, though, for me and for many of my patients, is a simmering rage caused not by these symptoms, which, though quite disabling for some women, are merely inconvenient for most, but by an overwhelming feeling of being in the wrong skin, in the wrong life. One patient, at forty-seven, after assuring me that she was happily married, told me that she could no longer stand the sound of her husband's voice and that she'd asked him to stop speaking in her presence.

In my late forties my anger was not directed at my husband or at any one person but was more encompassing. I felt invaded, taken over, lost. My response to this crisis was the same as it had been when I was unhappy in my thirties: I reluctantly sought consultation with a doctor. I never actually met this doctor, Christiane Northrup, but, rather, I bought her book, *The Wisdom of Menopause*. Northrup is an OB-GYN and was, then, an Oprah favorite. I still recommend *The Wisdom of Menopause* to my patients, though I advise them to skip the parts about tarot card readings. When I read Northrup's book I found it very helpful, as it provided an explanation of what was happening to me that made sense. My newly acquired anger *meant* something. What it meant, according to Dr. Northrup, was that I was ready to move on to the next phase of my life, ready to leave a certain kind of caregiving and self-sacrifice behind. Not long after reading *The Wisdom of Menopause* I entered an MFA program in nonfiction writing. I don't fully credit Dr. Northrup—nor the expensive organic yam cream she recommended as a natural estrogen replacement—for emboldening me to take this life-changing action, but I do think I was unable to move forward until I'd named what I wanted to leave behind. Poet Leslie McGrath evokes this transition so well:

> *When she sheds*
> *her last moony*
> *red potential*
> *a woman sheds*
> *also obligation*
> *(insert obligation*
> *elsewhere)*
> *fading from*
> *lure to lore.*

On the occasion of the tenth anniversary of the publication of *The Wisdom of Menopause* in 2011, Sandra Tsing Loh wrote an essay in *The Atlantic* titled "The Bitch Is Back." Her point was that menopause represents a woman's return to the self-possession of childhood—that the years of hormonal cycling are actually the "abnormal" ones. Loh writes:

If, in an 80-year life span, a female is fertile for about 25 years (let's call it ages 15 to 40), it is not menopause that triggers the mind-altering and hormone-altering variation; the hormonal "disturbance" is actually *fertility*. Fertility is The Change. It is during fertility that a female loses herself, and enters that cloud overly rich in estrogen. And of course, simply chronologically speaking, over the whole span of her life, the self-abnegation that fertility induces is not the norm—the more standard state of selfishness is.

How I wish I'd been able to read Loh's essay in my forties, to be reassured that the discomfort I felt then was not the loss of but the return to myself. And how I wish I'd been able to travel in time and reassure my mother of the same. In her late forties, she'd suffered anxiety and palpitations that were, in retrospect, undoubtedly related to menopause. Her symptoms became particularly severe one day when she was playing tennis at the country club on Long Island to which my parents belonged. She worked full time at a Wall Street law firm then and had led a successful petition to get the club to change its policy barring women from the tennis courts during weekends. The board had presumed, inaccurately, that women didn't work and could just as easily play during the week when their husbands could not. One hot Saturday my mother nearly passed out during a singles match. Her heart raced and she felt anxious. A few days later she saw a cardiologist, who ordered an echocardiogram, then a fairly new test, and told her she had mitral valve prolapse. MVP was a common diagnosis in the 1980s. Doctors believed it was associated with anxiety and panic disorders, especially in women. Up to 20 percent of women were thought to have this syndrome. MVP was the "hysteria" of that era—appearing, not insignificantly, at around the same time as the women's movement was gaining ground.

The association between MVP and anxiety has since been questioned, if not debunked entirely. In a 2008 review article titled "Does the Association Between Mitral Valve Prolapse and Panic Disorder Really Exist?," researchers looked at forty published studies and concluded that the association is weak at best. The abstract of another paper, "Mitral Valve Prolapse: From Syndrome to Disease (1987)," ends thusly (italics are mine):

> Although several studies have reported an increased frequency of MVP in patients with anxiety disorders, recent studies suggest that the conditions are not linked. *Iatrogenic cardiac neurosis* is common in both groups of patients.

"Iatrogenic cardiac neurosis." In plain English: patients made crazy by being told they had heart disease.

This was my mother. From that day onward, fresh on the heels of her victory over the all-male board of the country club, not to mention the fact of her high-powered job, but sobered by whatever had stricken her on the tennis court, she identified herself as a person with both a cardiac and a psychiatric problem. She carried Cardizem and Xanax in a pill sorter in her purse. She dutifully took antibiotics before every dental cleaning, to prevent infection of her defective heart valve by bacteria that can seep into the bloodstream from the gums. For the remainder of her life she believed two conflicting facts: that her heart condition was psychosomatic, and that her anxiety was caused by a leaky heart valve. Years later, when cardiac imaging had advanced, an echocardiogram showed that she'd never had a prolapsed mitral valve in the first place.

I wonder now about how readily my mother accepted her diagnoses of "heart condition" and "panic disorder" just as she was coming into her own professionally. I ask myself if I am retrospectively overinterpreting how much the era when my mother's menopause occurred affected its course. To what extent does the individual exemplify her times? To what extent is she shaped by them? The experience of illness is conditioned by the time and place in which we live. A strep throat was a very different thing in Louisa May Alcott's time than now: the bedside vigil and the dreaded but wholly expected grief versus the bottle of chalky pink amoxicillin picked up at CVS along with shampoo and lightbulbs, a cranky child in tow.

If my mother had not gone to law school at forty-three and had not been playing tennis on the "men's courts" in the early 1980s, would she ever have had a "heart condition" or been "anxious" at all? Was her menopause really any different from my own menopause as Dr. Northrop had explained it to me? The experience of the body is never only about the body.

◆   ◆   ◆

A month before I turned fifty, I attended a dinner party at the home of my old medical school friend Janie. Now, Janie, even back when we were in our twenties, *she* had the Answer. Janie was three years younger than me—she'd gone to medical school straight from college—and, like me, had two older brothers. As an only daughter she might have been expected to be especially close to her mother, but she wasn't. Janie once told me over breakfast in the hospital cafeteria that she knew by the time she was five years old that her mother was an unreliable guide to life, that she possessed no particular wisdom on which Janie could rely. Janie was the only one of my classmates who never panicked before exams. Once, she asked if I felt like going to a movie and I said, "But Janie, it's a school night," and Janie asked me: "What are you? Eight?"

At Janie's dinner party I was seated next to a friendly couple, a few years older than me. The wife had an easy, intimate manner and stylishly unkempt hair. Funky jewelry. Her husband was younger, shaggy but handsome. After a few pleasantries the woman told me the story of their courtship. She'd been divorced many years earlier and had had no interest in remarrying. Then, in her late fifties, she decided she would marry again. She announced to all her friends that she was getting married. They asked who the lucky guy was, and she said she didn't know yet. She may not have known it, but she was following the advice of the author of *The Secret*. Soon after she made this announcement, a friend told her that she'd met a man who seemed like a good candidate to be this woman's husband. The only hitch was that he was dating someone. "Doesn't matter," said the woman. "Introduce me."

A party was arranged to which the man, his girlfriend, and my dinner companion were invited. She wore a paint-stained sweatshirt and jeans to the party. She brought along her mother, who had dementia and was living with her. "I wanted him to see me exactly as I was," she explained. Of course, they fell in love. Of course, he left his girlfriend and married her.

This was a woman worth listening to. This was a woman in possession of the Answer. I told her a little about my life: about my medical practice; about my own mother, now widowed and sick; my marriage, my writing aspirations. "How old are you?" she asked, leaning in to look at my face intently, as if reading my fortune there.

"Almost fifty," I said.

"Well, buckle up," she said. "*Everything* is about to change."

As it turned out, she was right, but not in the way I think she meant. I had the feeling at the time that this woman accurately sensed my restlessness but had mistaken its cause. I think she was predicting that I would do something drastic, perhaps quit my job or leave my husband. I did let go of something, but it was something inside me, a nearly lifelong search for . . . I never did figure out what, but whatever it was I was done with it. I knew this for sure when a patient of mine, a woman in her nineties, sent me a card for my fiftieth birthday. Though I'd never shared anything personal with this patient she'd somehow understood what I needed. A drawing of a rose adorned the front of the card. Inside, in curly pink script, was this quote from Gertrude Stein:

> *There ain't no answer.*
> *There ain't gonna be any answer.*
> *There never has been an answer.*
> *That's the answer.*

An Inherited Condition

Early one afternoon in March 2005, a lung specialist at Mass General called to tell me that he'd just wheeled a patient I'd referred from his office to the emergency room. The woman, seventy-seven years old and recently widowed, showed signs of heart failure and appeared to be having an acute myocardial infarction. My colleague delivered this news tentatively, as if to avoid seeming judgmental about my having missed such an obvious diagnosis. The other reason for his tact: the patient was my mother.

I finished speaking with the specialist and hung up the phone. I looked down at the crumbs accumulated between my computer keys from too many hastily consumed lunches, at the stack of unread medical journals on the floor beneath my desk, out my office window at the gold dome of the State House on Beacon Hill glowing coldly in the early spring sunshine. My face tingled. My face always tingles when I'm sure I've made a terrible mistake that will result in dreadful consequences. It tingled when, as a sixteen-year-old, I accidentally set fire to my bed with a snuck cigarette and also when, years later, I glanced at the rearview mirror while driving down the highway and saw that my son, then a toddler, who'd somehow gotten unbuckled from his car seat and crawled onto the floor behind me, was missing.

My mother had flown up to Boston from her home in Florida a week earlier to receive chemotherapy for a chronic form of leukemia that she'd had for years and which hadn't seemed too serious—her oncologist in Boca Raton had informed her cheerfully that she'd no doubt die of something else first—but which had recently become more aggressive, causing her spleen and lymph nodes to enlarge. The day after her first infusion, my mother complained of shortness of breath, worse whenever she lay down. She told me she was just anxious about the chemo, but, after a couple of days, when Xanax and my reassurance failed to relieve her, I arranged for her to see the specialist. Even then, I wasn't too alarmed. I saw my own patients while my oldest brother, who also lived near Boston, brought her to the appointment.

That previous fall, my usually energetic mother had called from Florida to tell me that she was tired. Not just tired, she insisted, *exhausted*. A year earlier she'd begun begging out of social engagements and had even given up her beloved weekly tennis game after the other women in her foursome complained that she no longer ran to the net from the baseline. My mother said she was just as glad—she could spend more time with my father, who had become mostly homebound. Later, a cardiologist colleague would tell me that women unaware of their coronary disease often find reasons to slow down, unconsciously accommodating their decreased ability to exert themselves. After my father died, my mother said she didn't feel like taking tennis up again. I told her it was only natural that she felt depleted given all she'd been through. My father had

been ill for two decades during which my mother had been his primary caregiver. They'd been happily married for fifty-five years and
she was grieving deeply. Plus, while her oncologists were optimistic
about the prognosis of my mother's leukemia even in its new, more
serious form, the prospect of chemotherapy must have been daunting for her. How could she *not* be exhausted? My mother seemed
irritated by what she saw as my dismissal of her concern. Arguing
her case like the lawyer she'd once been, she pointed out that she'd
never experienced fatigue like this before and that something must
be very wrong with her, something that was being missed. I was
concerned, too, but not about my mother's physical health. What
ailed her mainly, I assumed, was a broken heart.

"Alas," as Elizabeth Hardwick writes in her 1979 novel, *Sleepless
Nights*, "the heart is not a metaphor, or at least not always a metaphor." Not long after my mother arrived in the emergency room of
my hospital, a cardiac catheterization showed near total blockage of
her left anterior descending coronary artery. Atherosclerosis, not
widowhood, had caused my mother's lassitude. Because the particular blockage my mother had is so often fatal and so commonly and
mistakenly thought of as occurring only in men, it's known as "the
widow-maker."

I put down the phone and, in an instant, a cascade of seemingly
unrelated facts that had accrued over many months snapped into
place, forming a picture as clear to me as it must have been to my
colleague when he tried to lay my mother flat on his exam table and
she resisted him, leaning forward, gasping for air, her neck veins
bulging, her fluid-filled lungs crackling. Diagnosis is about pattern

recognition, and this one could have been identified by a first-year medical student or a devoted viewer of TV medical dramas: the fatigue I'd attributed to my mother's years of caring for my father and then to her grief over his death; the nagging cough she'd had for months and which Claritin and countless Halls Lemon MenthoLyptus drops hadn't suppressed; the left shoulder pain that persisted despite weekly physical therapy sessions; and now shortness of breath. A textbook case. How could I have missed it?

When something goes wrong in a person's medical care, doctors try to understand why it went wrong, whose fault it was, and how to prevent similar errors from being made in the future. These analyses are often conducted in public, at Morbidity and Mortality conferences. As a medical student, I loved attending "M&M"s, though the pleasure they offered was of a negative variety: that of *not* being the person who'd screwed up. One surgeon at the hospital where I trained was famous for asking young doctors in the hot seat why they hadn't just finished the job and thrown the patient out the window. The internists were more restrained. They tended to focus less on blame and more on what could be learned from a mistake that, it was repeatedly and, even then I knew, insincerely emphasized, *anyone* could have made.

In truth, I was more engaged by the human drama taking place in front of me than by what I might learn. Would the intern who'd made the error cry? Would he hate the surgeon who had berated him? Go on to become an abuser himself at M&Ms in the future? These were the sorts of questions that interested me. Tracey, my best friend in medical school, and I shared a fascination with what we called "the *National Enquirer* aspects of medicine," the psycho-social and speculative rather than the more scientific and data-oriented elements of our chosen profession.

One of my earliest memories involves the other kind of M&M's, the candy, though it may not be entirely unrelated. Essie, our housekeeper and my babysitter, and I are walking down Flatbush Avenue, a few blocks from home. I'm very young, not yet in school like my brothers, and Essie is carrying me in her arms. It's autumn or spring, sunny and cool, and I'm wearing a light-brown leatherette jacket with white fleece cuffs. Essie holds me close. She smells like burped Pepsi, Dixie Peach hair pomade, and laundry starch, which she eats regularly, bite-sized chunks of Argo from a rectangular blue box as if they were Junior Mints. Also endless ice cubes, which she keeps in a mayonnaise jar that sits on the wide end of the ironing board she sets up in front of the television when she watches soap operas, which she calls her "stories." Years later, in medical school, I'll learn about pica, the curious phenomenon where people who suffer from iron deficiency crave ice, clay, dirt—and laundry starch. My memory of what had seemed a funny quirk will seem less funny and I'll wonder what else I hadn't understood about the woman who helped raise me. Essie was about my mother's age and she, too, must have been losing blood every month as my mother did, sometimes in great splotches on the sheets that Essie snatched away from my parents' bed without comment.

I have a few M&M's in my right breast pocket and I squirm in Essie's arms to get at them. But the pocket is small, the jacket material is stiff, and my hands are cold, and as I withdraw my fingers the M&M's fly to the ground. One by one, red, orange, yellow, dark brown, light brown, green, they hit the gray pavement. I start to cry. Essie is gruff but kind. She tells me we'll buy more, but not now. It's getting late. I keep crying, inconsolable not because I want the candy, not because I can't have more right away, but because I want the M&M's not to have fallen in the first place. Because I want to undo what I have done.

◆   ◆   ◆

In the days and months after my mother's heart attack I conducted my own private M&M. I considered the possible reasons why I'd failed to recognize what, in retrospect, seemed so apparent. My first thought was that I'd missed the diagnosis of my mother's heart disease because I'm bad at cardiology. In truth, the heart never was my best organ. Cardiologists sometimes jokingly refer to themselves as either "plumbers" or "electricians," depending on whether they subspecialize in the heart's muscle, valves, and arteries or in its electrical conducting system. Neither play to my strengths. Though I'm entirely capable of treating my patients' hypertension, identifying their heart murmurs, and responding appropriately to their complaints of chest pain, I'm more comfortable with hormones and chemical imbalances, blood disorders, infections, and inflammatory processes whose ebbs and flows, deficits and overabundances more easily form stories in my mind. Cardiologists would point out that, in fact, the patient's story is one of the most important tools they use to diagnose heart disease. Still, I'm not the first to note this irony: though the heart has symbolized emotion in art and literature for hundreds of years, with its pump, pipes, valves, and electri-cal currents it is the most machine-like of body parts.

The idea that I'd misdiagnosed my mother due to my incompe-tence was too painful for me to dwell on for long. I quickly moved on to another theory: that my mother's diagnosis had eluded me for the same reason it had eluded her internist in Florida during the many months she'd complained to him about fatigue and left-shoulder pain: she was a woman. Coronary disease is notoriously more difficult to detect in women for several reasons. Possibly because they have smaller hearts and arteries than men do, women tend to have more diverse and subtle symptoms than the crushing mid-chest pressure with which the condition so often announces itself in men. Women with coronary disease are more likely to expe-rience what have been called "atypical symptoms": neck and shoul-der pain, fatigue, and nausea. Women, particularly women of color, are less likely to be admitted to the hospital when they come to the emergency room with angina or myocardial infarction, more likely to have a falsely negative exercise stress test (as my mother had a few months before her heart attack), and less likely to be offered interventions such as coronary artery stenting and bypass surgery.

It's only in the past several years that doctors have begun to acknowledge that labeling the symptoms of members of half the population as "atypical" is inherently sexist. In a landmark 1990 essay in the *New England Journal of Medicine*, Dr. Bernadine Healy, a Johns Hopkins cardiologist who became the first woman to head the National Institutes of Health, dubbed this phenomenon "Yentl syndrome" after the main character in the Isaac Bashevis Singer story and Barbra Streisand film, a young woman who aspires to be a scholar and who must disguise herself as a man in order to be taken seriously. Dr. Healy was at Hopkins when I was a medical student and taught our class how to read EKGs. A petite and glamorous blonde she seemed to me, then, a rare specimen: a woman respected even by men who generally didn't seem to respect women, especially attractive women. I remember as an intern I showed a confusing electrocardiogram to a senior resident, a burly guy named Dave. "You should really ask Bernadine Healy about this one," Dave advised me. "Her understanding of this stuff is like no one else's. It's *beautiful*." I was struck by how Dr. Healy had awed him and how that awe had nothing to do with how she looked.

Despite efforts to raise awareness about coronary artery disease in women, such as the American Heart Association's *Go Red for Women* campaign, women have absorbed the spurious message that heart disease is primarily a men's problem. Though coronary atherosclerosis is the number-one killer of women in the world, we fear breast cancer, which is far less common and less lethal, more. Lack of fear may cause women to ignore even the most egregious symptoms. My patient Violet dropped dead while dancing at a cousin's wedding. She'd been having chest pain all evening, her daughter told me later, but figured she'd just overindulged in the buffet and besides, she didn't want to spoil the party.

My mother, too, never imagined that she would have a heart attack—but she feared my father would. He was, after all, an obese smoker who favored the fat-laden foods on which he was raised—schmaltz sandwiches were his daily afterschool snack—and he worked very long hours as a surgeon. My mother referred to my father's health, specifically his arteries, as her "sword of Damocles."

She worried about his diet, his smoking, his lack of exercise, and his stress level, certainly more than he did. She never came home without half-expecting she'd find him dead. My parents' marriage fit a narrative first promoted in postwar medical journals and picked up by the popular press: men, particularly successful men, are prone to heart attacks, which their wives are responsible for preventing by providing a healthy diet and a calm home. A 1966 syndicated newspaper article was published under these various titles: "Don't Doom Your Man, Keep Him Ticking" (*Hartford Courant*); "Heart Experts Advise Wives" (*Austin Statesman*); and my favorite: "Heart Attacks Claim 1,400 Each Day—Want to Kill Husband? Try Atherosclerosis!" (*Youngstown* [Ohio] *Vindicator*).

I became quite taken for a while with the notion that my mother was a typically "atypical" female heart patient and sought confirmation from a renowned cardiologist who'd done groundbreaking research on the diagnosis of coronary disease. I contacted him because I planned to write an article revisiting Healy's essay using my mother's story, or rather, my failure to correctly interpret my mother's story, to illustrate that Yentl syndrome is still prevalent. "Isn't this a perfect example of what Healy was writing about?" I asked the cardiologist. "I mean, here I am, a primary care doctor at Mass General, a practitioner of women's health, and for eighteen months I didn't realize that my own mother was having angina." His answer surprised me. "No," the cardiologist said. "What it's a perfect example of is that doctors shouldn't take care of their own families."

◆ ◆ ◆

No laws prohibit physicians from providing medical care for our relatives, though it's considered unwise to do so. The American Medical Association's Code of Ethics states: "Physicians generally should not treat themselves or members of their immediate families." The rationale for this recommendation is obvious. Medical judgment requires a degree of objectivity that doctors can't be expected to have regarding ourselves and our loved ones, and this lack of objectivity can lead to harm. Indeed, every doctor I've told about my mother's heart attack seems to have his or her own tale of bungling a relative's diagnosis or treatment. Doctors interpret "generally" in the Code of Ethics in various ways, though. Some of my colleagues keep otoscopes at home to look in their kids' ears and then prescribe antibiotics if they see signs of otitis. Others take a more circumspect approach, as my husband and I did when our children were young. We never once auscultated the loud heart murmur with which one of our children was born and we deferred the management of our son's epilepsy entirely to his neurologist. On the other hand, we reached for liquid Tylenol rather than calling the pediatrician whenever one of our kids had a fever. We knew not as parents but as physicians that kids with fevers are usually fine the next day.

Perhaps I failed to see what was happening to my mother because the mild but persistent friction that existed between us signaled deep hostility on my part and I subconsciously wished her ill; at some level maybe I wanted to, as the bullying surgeon in medical school had put it, "throw her out the window." Or maybe I was in denial since atherosclerosis is to some extent hereditary; if my mother had the condition, it would put me at risk. And then there was the observation that my mother herself had occasionally made: Daughters can't bear to think of their mothers as weak or vulnerable. The story my mother used to make this point concerned the differing reactions my brothers and I had had when she told us that, in her late sixties, she was going to start driving again after a long hiatus. My father's illnesses had made driving unsafe for him and, after sitting in the passenger seat for decades since her carpooling days, my mother now needed to get behind the wheel. "I'll teach you, Mom," my oldest brother said, "or we'll find you a driving school." My other brother said, "Why aggravate yourself, Mom? Let's hire a car service." I, on the other hand, told my mother, "You know how to drive, so just drive." I was reminded of this exchange recently when I read Alice Munro's short story, "Save the Reaper." It features a young woman living away from home for the first time who enjoys playing a game with her female friends that she calls "What did you hate most about your mother?" The friends' answers mainly involve their mothers' bodily imperfections: their corsets, fat arms, and corns.

◆   ◆   ◆

Doctors take a fairly narrow view of what we call "family history." When we ask patients which diseases their relatives had, we're looking for genetic disorders like muscular dystrophy and hemochromatosis and more common conditions often passed from one generation to the next: diabetes, aortic aneurysms, and atherosclerosis; cancers of the breast, colon, ovary, and prostate; depression and alcohol-use disorder. We're less interested in diagnoses that don't run in families and may not even bother recording those that have afflicted people close to the patient but not related to him or her by blood: a spouse, stepparent, or adopted sibling. Except not all family illnesses that influence a person's health are hereditary in the usually understood sense. Growing up with a chronically ill parent or sibling or in a family in which there has been trauma may impact a person's well-being and attitudes about health profoundly.

Another aspect of family history that doctors rarely take into account is what I think of as the *culture* of illness in which a person grows up. I've had patients whose childhoods were overshadowed by their parents' extreme anxiety about illness and others whose illnesses were ignored, sometimes to the point of neglect. These early experiences can't help but shape a person's health in adulthood. This is no less true for doctors. In *Your Medical Mind: How to Decide What Is Right for You*, Dr. Jerome Groopman and his wife, Dr. Pamela Hartzband, describe their respective families' cultures of illness. Groopman's father died young of a myocardial infarction. This tragedy made Groopman become what he calls a medical "maximalist." The specter of premature death inclined Groopman to visit doctors more liberally than he might have otherwise and to opt for medication when doctors suggested it. He chose to practice oncology, which involves aggressive treatments such as bone-marrow transplant. Hartzband, on the other hand, came from a family of "minimalists" who believed in the healing power of fresh air, exercise, and nutritious food and who thought that doctors, as Hartzband's mother once informed her physician-daughter, "don't know everything." Hartzband is less quick than her husband to seek medical care for herself and she chose to specialize in endocrinology, in which there are few emergencies and therapeutics are rarely interventional.

The fact that my father was both a doctor *and* a hypochondriac made our family's culture of illness hard to define. When it came to other people's symptoms, my father exhibited a physician's sangfroid. My mother used to joke that if my father ever showed any interest in one of her aches or pains she'd know it was time to call Riverside Memorial Chapel. His own symptoms, in contrast, were cause for alarm, canceled plans, and trips to the hospital. As a child I found the episodes when my father became ill frightening. I think they resulted in my becoming a minimalist myself, and likely inspired my future professional fascination with psychosomatic symptoms. On the few occasions when I sought attention by feigning sickness I intuited that my best bet was a joint injury. My orthopedist father always had splints and ace bandages at the ready for a sore finger or a turned ankle.

The main effect on me of my father's illness behavior was that, almost from the beginning of my career, I found my dual roles of doctor and daughter uncomfortable. At the end of my first year in medical school I proudly brought to my parents' home in Connecticut my new black bag, monogrammed with my initials in gold and filled with medical equipment. I displayed my new tools as my parents and I sat around the living room one morning after breakfast. My mother insisted, with enthusiasm: "Take Daddy's blood pressure!" I wrapped the cuff around my father's thick upper arm, placed the diaphragm of my stethoscope over his brachial artery with my left hand, and pumped the rubber bulb with my right hand, all while listening for the pulse. It's harder than it looks. I couldn't hear my father's heartbeat as I released the air in the bulb, and so I tried again. And again. And again. Each time I pumped the bulb harder, making the cuff around my father's arm tighter. "Stop!" My mother cried. "You'll give him a stroke!" I still wince at this memory, as if the cuff were tightening around my own arm.

As my expertise grew, I became more, not less, uneasy when my mother enlisted me as a consultant regarding my father's many maladies. The odd mixture of reverence and mistrust with which she viewed doctors extended to me. I always felt she was somewhat skeptical of my medical advice. On the other hand, she always thanked me profusely for my help and apologized for burdening me by asking for it. When she had medical issues herself, I think she saw me as both her defense against illness and, equally dangerous in her eyes, any member of the medical profession to whom she was not related. Once, whether as a compliment or a small dig, I could not tell, my mother sent me a "Jewish haiku," one of many humorous items passed around on the Internet among my parents' retiree circle:

> *Beyond Valium*
> *Peace is knowing*
> *One's child is an internist*

As my parents aged, I found myself torn between being their child and being their caregiver, as so many people do when their parents decline. My being a doctor added an extra layer of complication. Often, I didn't know if I was doing more harm than good. There were several times when I stepped in to deflect an unnecessary procedure or to remind a specialist that a planned treatment had already been tried and proven ineffective. On the other hand, I think I contributed to an increased fragmentation of their already fragmented medical care. My parents had primary care doctors in Connecticut and in Florida, plus various specialists in both places and in Boston. Many of these physicians communicated with me rather than with each other. And my involvement in my parents' care always put me at risk of being seen by their doctors as intrusive. Geriatrician and writer Louise Aronson describes this dilemma eloquently in an essay about taking her elderly doctor-father to an emergency room after he collapsed at home. Aronson suspects that her father might be hemorrhaging from his gastrointestinal tract but she can't convince any of the doctors in the ER to perform a rectal exam. Finally, with her dad's blessing, she does the job herself. She withdraws a bloody gloved finger, which she displays to the ER staff. "In retrospect," Aronson writes, "what is most interesting is how much more comfortable I felt performing an intimate procedure on my father than demanding the attention of the professionals assigned to care for him."

◆   ◆   ◆

I accept that lack of objectivity led me to miss the signs of my mother's heart disease, but what did that mean, exactly? Certainly, I was emotionally invested. I loved my mother. I was also irritated by her. And I chafed at my role in her care. But I now think that my lack of objectivity had less to do with emotion than with the fact that I was too caught up in my mother's story to believe that it would turn out any other way than how she herself had imagined it. I didn't recognize my mother's heart disease because it simply wasn't what she thought was supposed to happen to her.

In May 2004, when, after years of illness and disability, my father's death finally seemed imminent, my mother still found the prospect of it inconceivable. On the evening he was admitted to the intensive care unit for what would be the last time, she slapped the Formica counter in front of the nurses' station with her palm several times sharply and informed the doctor on duty, "I expect my husband to be better when I get back here in the morning." A month later, when we returned from the cemetery in Queens to the house in Connecticut, my mother lowered herself onto a living-room chair, looked around at the half-century's worth of books, antiques, and Oriental rugs that she and my father had collected, plus the arsenal of green oxygen tanks, red plastic needle-disposal bins, and other medical detritus of his final years, and said, to no one in particular: "Well, now I can buy the regular strawberry jam. Not sugar-free."

During the next few days, as we sat for hours over many cups of coffee—black for her, with milk for me—we considered her options. My mother was a young seventy-six. Perhaps she'd get involved in local politics, finally see Prague, maybe even return to practicing law. Unlike my father, she'd had no major health problems other than her chronic leukemia, which was monitored every few months with blood tests and had not yet caused any symptoms. My mother often commented that when you consider everything that could go wrong with the human body it's amazing that anything goes right—and for her things mostly had gone right. The only medications she took were a quarter of a quarter milligram tablet of Xanax three times a day for anxiety, Cardizem for the mitral valve prolapse diagnosed in her fifties, and TUMS for everything else. She'd shrunk a bit from her glamorous five feet eight and a half inches—an inch and a half taller than me—but she still had fairly smooth olive skin, chicly highlighted auburn hair, and an eagle eye for discounted couture. Not long after my father died, my mother confessed to me that a Boca man who'd just lost his wife had asked her to dinner and that she'd all but laughed in his face.

At first she approached her newly solitary status with optimism. My mother believed in self-improvement. More than believed: it propelled her like an engine. Every August, flying home from the European trip my parents made annually while my brothers and I were in camp, my mother pulled out a yellow legal pad and made lists: menus of nutritious family meals, possible dinner-party guests, outfits to freshen her wardrobe for the fall season. Once, a friend of hers moved from one Manhattan apartment to another and was so determined to make a new start that she packed up and gave away everything she owned. "She didn't take so much as a *spoon*," my mother marveled, each of the many times she repeated the story to me.

Widowhood seemed, at least initially, like her new project. I think she was inspired by her own mother, who'd lost her husband when she was only fifty-five. My grandmother often commented that people give widows exactly six weeks of sympathy, after which what she called the "Noah's ark parade of couples" moves on. Determined to be neither an object of pity nor to remarry, my grandmother took over my grandfather's business and turned a profit that allowed her to live independently and fashionably for the next thirty-five years.

Though my mother was widowed much later in life than her mother had been, she still saw herself as capable of reinventing herself after my father died. She seemed determined to be, like her mother, a woman on her own, independent, admired, a welcome unpaired guest, someone who could be counted on to entertain. Not depressing, clingy, obsessed with her own ailments. Not one of *those*. My mother spent the summer after my father died defiantly alone in the Connecticut house at the end of a dark country road, a place I'd be afraid to stay by myself. She was embraced there by a circle of younger women friends who drove up from the city on weekends, members of a book group she'd joined years earlier. Now she congratulated herself on her foresight. At least in the summer, my mother would have a ready-made social circle of women who still worked, drove, and had interesting things to say.

Back in Florida that fall, the ambiance was less invigorating, but my mother still seemed intent on forging ahead with her new life. She signed up for bridge lessons, bought a subscription to the Miami City Ballet, and filled her appointment book with lunch and dinner dates. At home or when running errands she still dressed in pleated khaki shorts and neatly tucked-in T-shirts from the Gap, and when she went out with friends she wore brightly colored linens with dramatic but tasteful costume jewelry. In a guest-room closet of her Boca home, smelling of mildew despite lavender sachets and cans of Damp Rid, hung the suits and silk blouses my mother had worn as a lawyer, as if she might one day travel backward in time and need them again.

In October my mother went on a cruise to the Caribbean with another widow. She came back miserable, defeated. The ship had been tacky and the chief attraction of the ports was duty-free shopping for liquor and cigarettes, neither of which interested her. In the past, with my father, she'd sailed the Baltic and Mediterranean on a small luxury line featuring evening lectures on art and history by noted scholars. "Your father spoiled me," she announced to me sadly. It turned out my mother didn't know what to do next, didn't know who to be next. Sickness filled the void left by my father's death. A patient was who she'd become next. "It wasn't supposed to be like this," my mother told me. "I was supposed to be the merry widow."

I knew my mother was lonely. Though she had many friends, she tended to be guarded with them, unwilling to share her grief. She once told me that, especially when she was a younger woman, her friends said that she was cold. "You never tell us anything," they complained. She said that my father was the only one she needed to tell anything to. Then, when he became old and sick, I became the person she told things to, a fact for which she apologized, again and again. I felt guilty for not making more time for her and for not trying harder to disguise my impatience with her increasingly frequent calls. I've since developed a standard line to assuage the guilt of my patients caring for elderly parents. "Listen," I tell them, "you could duct tape your mom to your body and still not feel like you're giving her enough attention."

Not long after she returned from the cruise, her oncologist in Florida told my mother that her abdominal lymph nodes were enlarged along with her spleen, indicating that her chronic leukemia had progressed to lymphoma, as it does in a small percentage of cases. He advised a course of chemotherapy. My mother, in relating this recommendation to me, focused on how close the oncologist's office was to her house in Boca and how easy the parking was. I said, "Mom, it doesn't matter if there's free parking, you are *not* getting chemo in some guy's office in a strip mall on Glades Road." I repeated this conversation to my brothers by phone, proudly. I, alone, could shield my mother from substandard medical care, not that I had any reason to doubt the oncologist's competence. I told her that I wanted her to come to Boston for a second opinion, which I would arrange. "You'll stay awhile," I said. And, sounding just like her, I added: "We'll make it a visit."

◆ ◆ ◆

We decided that my mother would remain up north for the duration of the chemotherapy. She settled in part-time with me and my family and part-time with my oldest brother and his family, in another Boston suburb. "Joint custody," we joked. My brother and my sister-in-law would seat her by the fireplace in their living room, play an Ella Fitzgerald or Frank Sinatra CD, and pour her Champagne. They, unlike my husband and me, had an actual guest room with a TV and DVD player next to which my brother stacked Julia Roberts and Meg Ryan films. My sister-in-law kept a vase filled with fresh flowers on my mother's nightstand.

I, on the other hand, had no place for my mother other than a room with a twin bed and bookshelves lined with Harry Potter books and plastic Little League trophies, which my younger son had vacated, happily decamping to the basement. After the first couple of nights she spent with us my mother said she felt so weak she could barely climb the stairs and asked to sleep on our living-room couch, which our Chesapeake Bay retriever usually occupied. In the morning I held my mother's underwear, into which she stepped one leg at a time, leaning heavily on my shoulder. The dog sniffed and my mother bemoaned the indignity of her position, paraphrasing Bette Davis: "Old age is not for the faint of heart."

The first chemo session went smoothly. Still, as I sat with her in the infusion unit at Mass General, I couldn't help but feel that the gradual reversal of our roles, which had begun years earlier, had finally reached its sad completion. When I was a child my mother had stayed by my bedside when I had chicken pox and German measles and also when, as a teenager, I had cramps and tearful angst. Now I sat for hours with her, a visitor in my own hospital. Though I wore my ID badge and a stethoscope slung around my neck, simply by sitting with my mother I became invisible to my colleagues. It was as though I had stepped behind an unseen scrim. Some did look us in the eye, smiled, asked us how we were doing and actually listened to our answers. But many either ignored us as they went about their efficient business or treated us with a kind of stiff cheer. If they recognized me, they seemed embarrassed. I imagined that what embarrassed them was seeing me, only a few inches from my usual place among them, yet—*over there*. When I brought my mother back to my house after the infusion I gritted my teeth as I listened to her tell one friend after another on the phone that she had no idea what kind of chemo she was getting—"My daughter would know"—only that it was "the kind where you don't lose your hair."

The next day my mother said that she'd had some trouble breathing overnight but that she'd taken some extra Xanax, which had helped. She also complained that her left shoulder was hurting more than ever. The physical therapy she'd been getting in Boca hadn't provided any relief. "Maybe," I said, "it's from sleeping on my couch." "Your couch is perfectly comfortable," my mother assured me. I took her to my acupuncturist. Yes, I had one, though I don't really believe in acupuncture. Jason had a couple of rooms in the yoga studio not far from my house where I took classes irregularly. He sold probiotics, packets of Super Green to make power shakes, and brown vials of "tinctures." The place was quiet and peaceful, and Jason gave a good massage. That's why I started going to him. Sometimes my lower back was so painful to the touch that he couldn't work on it so he suggested inserting a few needles first and that did the trick. I didn't believe in any of it—the needles, the tinctures, the anatomical diagrams of energy flow—and yet I always left feeling better. My mother was agreeable. She liked massages too.

Jason led us into a dimly lit room and instructed my mother to take her top off and lie down. She asked me to stay with her. She became restless and uncomfortable lying flat and I fluffed up the pillow. She lay back down again and then sprang up and asked me where I'd put her pocketbook. She didn't trust Jason—was it his earring? "Just my shoulder," she instructed him sharply. "Don't touch anything else." Afterward, when we were back in the car, my mother agreed that he did, indeed, give a good massage, and that her shoulder felt a little better.

Late that night, when my husband and I were in bed, my mother appeared in our room barefoot, in her nightgown, like a child seeking comfort after a nightmare. "I can't breathe," she said. "I feel anxious." I led her back to the couch and got her a glass of water. I gave her more Xanax. In the morning I called the lung specialist. "I just don't know how to put this together," I told him. "She seems anxious, and maybe that's why she gets so short of breath sometimes, but I just can't sort it out." "Of course you can't," he said. "She's not your patient. She's your mother."

◆ ◆ ◆

In the weeks and months after my mother's heart attack, I found it hard to believe that it had actually happened. I struggled to make it real for myself. I recalled articles I'd read about the high incidence of myocardial infarction among those who care for chronically ill family members and among new widows. I reminded myself of my mother's diet—the decades of Philadelphia cream cheese in silver packages with blue writing; cheese omelets and BLTs; hamburgers and steaks and prime rib and liver topped with bacon; and, my mother's favorite, tongue sandwiches with Swiss cheese and Russian dressing. I pictured the cloud of smoke from my father's cigarettes that had enveloped my mother for decades. Why *wouldn't* she have had a heart attack?

A few years later, I requested the records of my mother's 2005 hospital admission from the company contracted by Mass General to store charts from the pre-digital era. After several weeks they finally appeared in my mailbox at home: a five-inch-thick stack of papers encased in one of those fiber-impregnated mailing envelopes, flimsy yet strong, and too large for its contents. My first thought, lifting the heavy parcel shifting awkwardly in its loose white wrapper was of a corpse in a body bag. I carried it inside, set it on my desk, and there it sat, unopened, for days. When I finally tore into the envelope and flipped through page after xeroxed page of laboratory results, EKG tracings, and variably legible handwritten notes I came upon this, written by her Mass General oncologist after my mother's first visit with him:

She says she is fatigued but is engaged when interesting people are present.

This made me smile. I knew he was quoting my mother accurately here. *When interesting people are present* is just the kind of thing she would have said.

One part of my mother's record intrigued me, especially: the diagram of her coronary arteries drawn by the cardiologist who had performed her catheterization soon after she arrived in the emergency room. It showed the blockage in her left anterior descending artery—the "widow-maker"—and a number of smaller blockages. I contacted Dennis, who'd been a year behind me in residency and who'd become one of the foremost authorities in the world on cardiac catheterization. I emailed him a copy of the diagram and, over the phone, Dennis reviewed it with me patiently. I interrupted him several times to ask whether my mother may have had an atypical form of coronary disease, one that might easily have gone undetected for months and more likely to be seen in a woman, perhaps? He said that she did not. Finally I just came right out with it: "Dennis," I asked, "did I kill my mother?" He laughed. Then he said, "Wait . . . what?" as if he hadn't heard me correctly. "Did you kill your *mother*?" I told him about the months of fatigue and left shoulder pain, her persistent cough, the days she lived in my house, complaining of how short of breath she became when she lay flat. And Dennis said: "No. Jeez. C'mon. She was old and sick and she had coronary atherosclerosis, the most common cause of death in the world." He made it sound as if I'd blamed myself for the sun going down.

When someone you love suffers, you've failed to protect them. This may seem irrational and unfair, but, in the largest sense, it's true. And if you have medical training and you don't prevent someone you love from becoming ill and dying, you feel an even greater sense of failure. Why couldn't I do for my mother what I'd done for other people's mothers? Why couldn't I have done better for her?

◆ ◆ ◆

Minutes after the lung specialist phoned to tell me he thought my mother was having a myocardial infarction I arrived in the emergency room and made my way to the bay to which she had been assigned. The bed, stained with blood and littered with spent tubing and crumpled wrappers, was empty. My face tingled. *I killed her. I killed her. I killed my mother.* I walked back out into the corridor, looking frantically for someone, something, I didn't know whom or for what. Bright lights and loud buzzers and bells, medical noise to which I'd so long ago become inured, now felt lancinating, accusatory. Beep. Beep. Beep. *I killed her. I killed her. I killed my mother.*

Except. There she was, being wheeled briskly down the hall to X-ray, pale as the thin white flannel sheet draped over her shoulders, sweat beading on her upper lip and forehead, her mouth pursed to suck in every last bit of air. Her chicly styled auburn hair was, as always, perfectly in place. My mother saw me. She held her hands out to me. "Stop!" she commanded the attendant wheeling her. "Wait!" she said. "Here's my daughter!"

The Disease of the Little Paper

Toward the end of his life, my father tried to engage me in conversations about our shared profession. He presided over these sessions from an armchair, his legs tucked under a blanket against the air-conditioned Florida chill to which my parents retired.

"Seen any great cases?" he'd ask. This question set my teeth on edge. Even well into middle age as I was then, it didn't take much to fan the embers of my adolescent anger.

I'd explain—again—that I was a general internist, not a specialist as he had been, and derived my professional satisfaction from long and close relationships with patients and not from making obscure diagnoses.

He would give me a pitying look and shrug. Then he'd tell me some anecdote in which I heard him imply that he was more resourceful, wiser, and more devoted to and beloved by his patients than I could ever hope to be. About how, during the war, he recycled penicillin from patients' urine and injected it into other patients. About how, in the 1980s, during a housekeepers' strike, he'd mopped floors and folded sheets and towels in the laundry room of the hospital where he was chief of staff.

The reminiscence I bristled at most was about ladies—always they were "ladies"—with something he called *la maladie du petit papier*: the disease of the little paper. They would come to his office and withdraw from their purses tiny pieces of paper that unfolded into large sheets on which they'd written long lists of medical complaints.

"You know what I did then?" my father asked. I did, but I let him tell me again anyway. "I'd listen to each symptom carefully and say 'yes' or 'I see'—that's all. And when a lady finally reached the end of her list, she would say, 'Oh, Doctor, I feel so much better!' The point is, all those ladies needed was someone to listen."

After my father died, I researched some of the things he'd mentioned to me. Data collection was crucial to my mourning process. I longed for evidence of my father other than my own memory of him. He tended to embellish facts and confabulate anecdotes. When my brothers or my mother or, more often I, challenged the veracity of one of his whoppers he'd say, "Go look it up." Now, after his death, I *was* looking it up. I wanted—irrationally, I know—proof that my father had existed.

An article in *Time* magazine, dated September 11, 1944, reported a novel extraction method whereby 30 percent of the penicillin injected into one patient could be reclaimed from the urine and injected into another patient. Doctors at a military hospital on Staten Island, facing a shortage of the wonder drug, were using this technique in enlisted men with gonorrhea.

An article in the *New York Times* in 1984 mentioned my father's hospital as one of several in the city where housekeepers and other workers went on strike.

I found *la maladie du petit papier* too. It's defined in an online medical dictionary as a condition in which "an exhaustive list of purported ailments—[is] carried around by a neurotic patient, often accompanied by extensive documentation of each bowel movement or sip of water." The term, probably coined in the clinic of Jean-Martin Charcot at the Salpêtrière in the late nineteenth century, has never been complimentary. A disciple of Charcot described one Jewish list-maker with particular scorn: "In a voluminous batch of filthy scraps of papers that never leaves him, he shows us prescriptions from all the universities of Europe and signed by the most illustrious names." Osler was more restrained but no less dismissive. He observed, "A patient with a written list of symptoms— neurasthenia." In recent years, one doctor updated the diagnosis to "*la maladie du grand printout*," a nod to the indispensability of the Internet to the modern hypochondriac.

In 1985 internist John F. Burnum challenged the notion that the disease of the little paper is a disease at all. He reported the results of an informal study he conducted in his own practice. Of 900 patients he saw in a four-month period, 72 (8 percent) brought in lists of concerns. Burnum observed no higher incidence of mental illness and no lower incidence of physical illness in his list-making patients than in the non–list makers. He concluded that patients who make lists aren't neurotic, but simply "seeking clarity, order, information, and control."

Of course I was familiar, from my own practice, with the phenomenon of patients making lists, but I'd never known it had a name. I confess that these lists sometimes irritate me, as they do many doctors. Especially irksome is the sight of my last name without my title, scrawled at the top of a list—evidence that to my patient I am often merely another stop in a series of tedious errands guided by similar lists headed "Groceries" or "To-Do." I steal an upside-down glance, in hopes that the list will be short, or at least that we'll have covered most of the items by the time the little piece of paper makes its appearance. Each checkmark floods me with relief: "Prescriptions, you filled them . . . that mole on my thigh, you looked at it . . . we talked about that weird dizzy thing. . . ."

Why should these little pieces of paper bother me? I know that often patients, sensibly, bring lists to make the most of hard-to-schedule and ever-shorter visits with their doctors—indeed, in recent years they've been encouraged to do so, often by doctors ourselves. I'm aware of the studies that show the mere act of jotting symptoms down can ameliorate them. As a writer, I surely understand the urge to put pen to paper.

I wonder if I resent these lists because they threaten me. The "control" that Burnum thought patients reasonably seek is wrested, in part, from the doctor. When a patient pulls out that little piece of paper, I feel a shift in the exam room: the patient taking charge of the agenda, my schedule running late, the reins of the visit loosening in my hands.

I'm ashamed of my resentment, which is as unjustified as it is unbecoming. I know these lists aren't really threats to me. They're not about me at all. They are, like all writing, forms of self-expression. I remember the mathematician who handed me spreadsheets of his blood pressures with the mean and standard deviation calculated; the flamboyantly dressed woman who favored hot-pink clothing and penned her lists in ink to match; the savvy businessman, many years ago, who clicked through his list on an early mobile device. And, a fact I have never before acknowledged while silently groaning at my patients' lists: I'm a list maker myself.

For years now I've never been without a ledger of to-dos or, really, *should*-dos: phone calls I don't want to make, emails I don't want to answer, errands I don't want to run. I used to keep an index card tucked in my purse, then I switched to an iPhone app. But I found deleting completed tasks from an electronic list less satisfying than checking them off manually, so now I'm back to paper. I keep my lists in freebie notebooks from literary festivals and medical conferences. My current book has a cheerful silver and purple cover emblazoned with the logo of a local hospice.

I acquired my list-making habit rather late—in medical school. From elementary through high school at the beginning of each year we were instructed to purchase a small memo book, top spiral bound, in which to keep track of homework assignments. After the first hopeful days of September my memo book invariably deteriorated, sloppy and incomplete. Later, in college, I sometimes dawdled over my studies by scrawling lists that reflected both immediate and long-range concerns. I recall one, late in my junior year, when I started panicking about my post-graduate plans, which read:

Buy Tab and cigarettes
Apply for fellowship
Lose weight
Decide about career, etc.

It was during medical school and residency that I became a habitual list maker. Like my peers, I was never on the wards without a clipboard to which was affixed a sheet of progress-note paper on which, in those primitive early computer days, I wrote each patient's name in ink along with all the tasks—draw blood, order x-rays, etc.—that needed to be done for them, with a little box next to each task, waiting to be checked. I also jotted down puzzling symptoms and rare diseases with the intention of reading about them later, but I was always too tired "later" and so I rarely did. Medical trainees still create such lists, most often electronically.

List-making is an essential part of the medical profession, central to how doctors think. Doctors deal not so much in facts as in possibilities. For each symptom, we make a list of plausible explanations, alternate scenarios, like in the Japanese film *Rashomon*, where a story is told from several perspectives. Except in differential diagnosis, as this mode of thinking is called, each doctor alone comes up with many versions of the same story.

I first learned differential diagnosis in my third year of medical school. In the first two years, in lecture halls and laboratories, we studied the normal structure and function of the human body and the seemingly infinite ways these can go awry. Then, on the hospital wards and in the clinics, we began seeing patients with symptoms—"complaints" we were taught to call them, though this hardly seemed fair, as if abdominal pain or a headache were merely gripes, such as you might make about poor restaurant service or lost luggage—and made long lists of their possible causes.

SHORTNESS OF BREATH:
- Asthma
- Blood clot
- Pneumonia
- Anxiety
- Angina
- Heart failure
- Myocardial infarction

Maybe we resent our patients' list-making because we feel they're usurping our role, trespassing on our territory.

It turns out that my father was right: often, even when I have no explanation for the headache, upset stomach, or itch documented on the back of an envelope or punched into an iPhone, a patient feels better just having presented me with his or her recording of it. Perhaps naming our demons and saying their names aloud helps make them less frightening. Perhaps the shorthand of the list somehow abbreviates the anxiety associated with its entries.

Or maybe lists bring still deeper comfort. Concerns set in ink are made concrete, less likely to be ignored. Those little pieces of paper are declarations: *I'm human, and my suffering is real.* Susan Sontag, a self-described compulsive list maker herself, might have agreed. She once wrote that in writing lists, "I confer value, I create value, I even create—or guarantee—existence."

Strange that writing this, so many years after my father's death, makes me miss him more, yet also lessens the pain of missing him. Sometimes a lady really does just need someone to listen.

14

The Noncompliant Patient,
Reconsidered

The needles on a white pine in my yard had turned brown so I consulted Jack, an arborist, to see what might be done. "Bad news," Jack said. The tree was infected with a fatal and contagious blight. He advised taking it down, along with its neighbors on either side. Though the other two trees looked healthy they, too, would soon be blighted. It would be best to do the job all at once and quickly, before the infection spread even farther.

Though I trust Jack, I was reluctant to follow his advice. Instead, I stalled by peppering him with questions: Were the trees in any real danger of toppling over? What if the dead-appearing tree recovered? What if the other trees didn't get infected after all? Would there really be any harm in waiting a few months and seeing what happened?

If Jack had been a physician he might have labeled me "noncompliant," the term used to describe patients who don't do what we think they should. Like certain other medical jargon—"deny" comes to mind, as in "The patient denied alcohol use" (implying that they might be hiding something)—"noncompliant" contains a seed of judgment. In other contexts, "noncompliant" means rigid or stubborn.

The high prevalence of medical noncompliance, however, suggests that it must be explained by more than sheer obstinacy. The Centers for Disease Control and Prevention estimates that in 2018–19 fewer than half of all American adults received the recommended vaccination for influenza and the number of Americans who have had screening for colon, breast, and cervical cancer failed to meet targets set by the government's Healthy People 2020 initiative. Beyond the United States, the 2017 Future Health Index, a survey of 33,000 healthcare professionals and patients across five continents, reported that a high percentage of patients didn't even recall their physicians counseling them to lose weight and stop smoking.

When I first went into practice as a primary care doctor I saw my role as paternalistic—an odd stance for a young woman, in retrospect. I took pleasure in knowing that the Latin root of doctor is *docere*—to teach—and assumed that if a patient didn't do what I thought they should do either they were recalcitrant or I hadn't communicated my instructions effectively. I remember a woman named Daisy who often skipped her prescribed insulin doses and was admitted repeatedly for diabetic ketoacidosis, or DKA, a condition in which high blood sugar can lead to coma and death. I asked her to enlist a family member or an aide to help administer the medication, but she refused. At every discharge, the medical staff asked Daisy who would be helping her with her insulin and she'd reply: "My own self." We were flummoxed. How could someone make a decision so self-destructive, so ill-advised, so plainly wrong? We referred Daisy to a social worker and a therapist but never got to the root of why she was so intent on managing her own diabetes when she was incapable of doing it safely.

In a 2017 blog in *NEJM Journal Watch*, an emergency medicine physician describes a patient much like Daisy. Despite repeated admissions for DKA, the woman missed appointments and insulin doses and ate sweets. Why would someone act so blatantly against her own self-interest? The author provides a list of possible answers—in effect, a differential diagnosis of noncompliance—including "premature discharge," "low health literacy," and "financial difficulties." Then, the author considers a more disturbing possibility: that self-harm may actually be the patient's goal. She quotes an intriguing 1984 article observing that patients admitted to the hospital repeatedly with DKA resemble the family in William Faulkner's early novel *Sartoris*, inclined to poor judgment in their relationships and also to reckless driving resulting in numerous car crashes: ill-fated simply because they are "hell-bent on self-destruction."

Slow suicide may indeed be the intention of certain noncompliant patients. Fear of pain and complications or side effects and the high cost of prescription medication and inadequate insurance coverage, not to mention skepticism about science and mistrust of doctors, are, no doubt, much more common. Yet when I've probed deeply into a patient's reasons for rejecting medical advice, I've found that they are highly individual, deeply rooted in a life story, and not so neatly classified.

Take, for example, my patient Edgar, who refused to take antihypertensives despite the fact that he had dangerously high blood pressure and, as I reminded him frequently, several risk factors for cardiovascular disease including a father who died young of a heart attack. Edgar, an intelligent and accomplished man, wasn't self-destructive. He simply had his own illogical logic regarding blood-pressure medication: Yes, his father died young of a heart attack. And his father had taken pills for high blood pressure. So, according to Edgar, he could avoid his father's fate by avoiding his father's pills.

Then there was Maurice, who refused to wear oxygen despite his chronic hypoxemia. When I first met Maurice, his behavior puzzled and frustrated me. How could someone with an oxygen saturation in the low eighties (normal is near 100 percent), someone with blue lips and fingers, someone who often seemed visibly short of breath, refuse oxygen? At every visit I talked while Maurice shook his head. "No, no, no," he said. "No oxygen."

Then one day I asked Maurice to tell me more about his life, about what oxygen meant to him. It turned out that he'd been chronically ill as a child but very proud and independent, an athlete, determined not to become an invalid. Wearing oxygen, to him, represented surrender in a very old battle. Plus, Maurice was a handsome, well-dressed man, and green plastic tubing and metal tanks didn't fit his self-image. Ultimately he agreed to use oxygen, but only in the privacy of his home. It wasn't ideal, medically, but it was what he could abide. I reflected later that without calling it such, Maurice and I had participated in the relatively new model of shared decision-making in which patient preferences are taken as much into account as doctors' recommendations.

Like Edgar and Maurice, there was more to my "noncompliance" regarding the white pine trees than met the eye, or Jack's eye, anyway. To him, the problem, and its solution, were obvious. He likely thought my main concern was the cost of taking down the trees. I did balk at the expense, but mostly I just loved the trees and couldn't bear to lose them. I feared severing the connection I feel to the young mother I once was, holding my now-grown babies while looking at the trees' perfect, horizontally oriented limbs. Contemplating their loss, I could relate to Henry David Thoreau, who, a hundred and seventy years earlier, living not far from where I live now, wrote about mourning the loss of a tree just like mine:

> A plant which it has taken two centuries to perfect, rising by slow stages into the heavens, has this afternoon ceased to exist . . . Why does not the village bell sound a knell?

In the end, Jack and I agreed that the tree in the middle, the dead one, should come down, but that we would wait and see how the other two fared. It wasn't exactly what either of us wanted, but it was a plan both of us could live with. Like healthy trees facing a strong wind, we'd each bent a little. We'd each complied.

15

The Hateful Patient, Revisited

For many years I was this woman's doctor and she was my patient. The relationship had not been easy. Her list of complaints about me was long and she recited it often: I prescribed too many drugs, but not the ones she needed. My office was inconveniently located, but the doctors nearer to her home were even more incompetent than I was. I didn't spend enough time with her (even though our visits routinely lasted three times longer than scheduled), but it didn't matter, because I couldn't help her anyway. Every time we met, an old joke came to mind—the one about the man who whines, "The food in this restaurant is terrible, and the portions are so small!"

One day, something, I don't know what—it may have been exasperation or even curiosity—made me interrupt my patient's accusatory litany to ask: "Is there *anything* I can do to make you happy?"

Maybe it was because she had mellowed a little over time. Now that she was old and very sick, her negativity had lost some of its edge. Maybe it was because we both knew she wouldn't live much longer. Maybe it was because my mother, who was about this woman's age and who colored her hair nearly the same auburn shade, had also been ill and I'd felt as powerless to relieve her suffering as my patient's.

Had my professional forbearance softened into empathy? Or could it be that what I felt for the old woman, widowed, in a wheelchair, tethered to an oxygen tank, was pity?

Whatever it was that prompted my question, her surprising answer popped out as if it had been on the tip of my patient's sharp tongue all the years I'd known her. She said: "Just tell me that you love me."

I didn't know how to respond. I didn't love her. I didn't even like her.

In 1978, psychiatrist James E. Groves published a now-classic article in the *New England Journal of Medicine*: "Taking Care of the Hateful Patient." "Hateful patients," Groves noted, "are not those with whom the physician has an occasional personality clash." Rather, they're the patients whose names evoke cold dread every time they appear on a doctor's schedule or in his or her phone messages. That would certainly describe this patient, whose calls and visits never failed to induce in me a silent groan. Groves argued that if a physician owns up to his or her negative feelings about a patient, and specifically characterizes those feelings, treatment becomes more effective.

For example, Groves wrote, if a patient repeatedly makes a doctor angry, the patient is likely a "demander," whose unreasonable expectations simply need to be redirected into a desire for good medical care. A patient whom a doctor finds depressing may be a chronic "help rejecter," who needs reassurance that the doctor won't abandon him or her once a symptom abates. Two other categories of hateful patients Groves identified are "clingers" and "self-destructive deniers."

I didn't read Groves's article until I'd been practicing medicine for several years, but if I had read it earlier I doubt it would have helped me much with my patient. For one thing, she wasn't really hateful. I didn't hate her any more than I loved her. Also, she didn't fit neatly into any of Groves's categories. She could be clinging, demanding, help-rejecting, and in denial, sometimes all at once. And she could also be, I had to admit, inspiring. As with most people, my patient's flaws were the flip side of her virtues; the same orneriness that made her so unpleasant to me had seen her through several life-threatening illnesses. I sometimes wondered if she'd survived the odds against her out of sheer spite.

In fact, for all her hostility toward me, this woman was a remarkably good patient. She kept appointments, took her medications faithfully, and, even when ill, tried her best to maintain a consistent exercise routine and healthy diet.

Did it really matter, then, what I felt about her? Groves concluded that ultimately a doctor's feelings toward a patient are only important insofar as those feelings affect the doctor's behavior. I always believed that though I had negative feelings toward this patient, my behavior toward her was appropriate, that I'd played the good doctor to her good patient despite the tension that clouded our every exchange.

Still, that day when I found myself unable to tell the woman that I loved her, I wondered what I *did* feel for her. There was no simple answer. She evoked in me feelings of guilt, protectiveness, admiration, annoyance, helplessness, responsibility, inadequacy, defensiveness, frustration, and even a kind of affection.

Once, another doctor saw her in my absence and commented on what a pain she was. I became as defensive as you might when someone criticizes a close relative you've criticized liberally yourself. She was a pain, yes. But she was *my* pain.

The woman lived only a few months after that day. During that time, our relationship improved. She became less prickly with me and I stopped dreading her calls and visits. I can't say that I came to love the woman, but her question did force me to acknowledge my complicated feelings toward her, to let my guard down with her, to stop resisting her.

That day she asked me to tell her that I loved her, I couldn't think of anything to say. Lacking words, I leaned in to hug the woman, first moving aside the metal part of the stethoscope slung around my neck so it wouldn't get trapped between us and press painfully into her bony chest. It was an awkward hug, not entirely sincere on my part—and probably not entirely satisfactory to her. But the distance between us had been partially bridged, and we both knew it.

16

The Doctor's New Dilemma

The woman sits perched on the end of my exam table, leaning forward, blond curls tumbling over her eyes, her precarious posture mirroring her fragile emotional state. Though the symptom she describes is relatively minor—some diarrhea on and off—she appears distraught. She grips the table as if doing so will hold back her tears.

A psychiatrist colleague tells me that such moments, when there's a clear mismatch between what a patient says and the intensity of feeling with which he or she says it, are especially ripe for probing. But the psychiatrist sees patients for forty-five minutes. I have fifteen, several of which have already passed, in which to address and document the woman's chief symptom: loose stool. I find myself in a quandary: Do I ask the patient why she's so upset, or do I order a culture, prescribe antidiarrheal medication, type my note, and send her on her way?

In 1906, George Bernard Shaw's *The Doctor's Dilemma* first appeared on the London stage. The play concerns a physician, Sir Colenso Ridgeon, who's discovered a cure for tuberculosis. Ridgeon's dilemma is that he has a limited supply of the medication and a small staff to administer it. He can treat only ten patients at a time and so must decide whose life is most worth saving. Other conundrums Shaw highlights in the play's lengthy prologue are how to prevent doctors from being motivated by financial gain and how to rid the medical profession of charlatans.

In recent years, Shaw's turn-of-the-twentieth-century drama about the ethics and economics of healthcare has been seen as prescient, prefiguring the establishment of the National Health Service in Britain and the Affordable Care Act in the United States. Even with these developments, modern Colenso Ridgeons still grapple with limited resources, inequality in access to healthcare, and unscrupulous or incompetent colleagues.

The dilemma I face most often as a primary care doctor, however, is not one that Shaw anticipated. The commodities I struggle to ration are my own time and energy. Almost every day I see a patient like the woman with diarrhea and I find myself at a crossroads: Do I ask her what's really bothering her and risk a time-consuming interaction? Or do I accept what she's saying at face value and risk missing a chance to truly help her?

Often, the situation is not so dramatic. Say I walk into an exam room and find a patient waiting for me, reading a book. Do I ask what book she's reading? If it's one I've read myself, do I ask whether she, like me, enjoyed it but found it a bit longer than it needed to be? We might debate that point, and then she might start telling me about other novels her book group has read, and pretty soon we'd be having—horrors!—a *conversation*. Precious minutes wasted on useless chitchat.

But is chitchat really useless? Such conversations can gener-

ate the trust that, studies have suggested, may improve health outcomes, such as control of blood pressure and relief of pain—the
trust that is essential to healing. Once, when I was covering for a
colleague, I saw an older woman I'd never met before. I pride myself
on being able to put patients at ease, being able to establish rapport
with almost anyone, but this woman would have none of it. She
expressed skepticism about everything I said. Finally, she pulled a
pen out of her purse to write down my diagnosis, clearly intending
to look it up later and marvel at my foolishness in proposing it.

"What a beautiful pen!" I blurted out. And it was: a lovely tor-
toiseshell implement with a shiny gold nib. The woman's wariness
evaporated. She told me that fountain pens were a great passion of
hers. She collected and traded them. She'd been to pen shows and
pen shops all over the world. I told her that I liked fountain pens,
too, that in fact my husband had just bought me one for my birthday, at a shop in Dublin. Of course she knew the shop. "What make
of pen?" she inquired. I confessed I didn't remember, so she asked
me to describe it. Thick . . . natural wood shaft, chrome cap . . . "A
Faber-Castell!" she pronounced, beaming. "That's it!" I shouted,
my grin matching hers. She put her pen away without recording my
diagnosis. She believed in me.

◆   ◆   ◆

At my hospital, I often meet with groups of doctors and nurses to
discuss works of literature relevant to clinical practice. Before these
meetings, I always ask whether there's a particular theme they'd
like to address, and the answer, alas, is always the same: burnout.

For several groups, I've selected "Communion," an essay published in 1995 in *Annals of Internal Medicine* in which Richard Weinberg, a gastroenterologist, recounts his interaction with a young woman who suffers from chronic abdominal pain. At first, Weinberg finds it difficult to reach the woman, who seems hidden beneath layers of baggy clothing, vague symptoms, and stacks of results of tests ordered by exasperated doctors. The turning point comes when Weinberg, an avid cook, asks the woman, who works in her family's bakery, about pastry-making. As the woman expounds on the art of producing a perfect Napoleon, Weinberg observes, "For the first time her eyes came alive."

This moment of connection leads, over time, to the woman's confiding in Weinberg a painful secret. In regular meetings, which Weinberg schedules at the end of his clinic sessions, they sit and talk. Weinberg is uncomfortable playing the role of therapist, but the patient will speak only with him. Gradually, she emerges from her shell, and her symptoms resolve.

At first it's not obvious how "Communion" relates to modern medical practice. In 1995, relatively free from the shackles of the computer screen that now demands so much of doctors' attention, the main obstacle Weinberg faces in engaging the troubled young woman is his own willingness to do so. His leisurely conversations with her seem as quaint to us now as black bags and glass hypodermics.

Still, the moment when Weinberg takes the plunge, when he asks the woman about pastry, is very familiar. It's a moment every clinician has inhabited and, all too often, pulled back from—a threshold we fear crossing. We imagine ourselves, now, in Weinberg's place, and recognize a double bind, a new doctor's dilemma: if we ask about the pastry, we fall hopelessly behind in administrative tasks and feel more burned out. If we don't ask about the pastry, we avoid the kind of intimacy that not only helps the patient, but also nourishes us and keeps us from feeling burned out.

The woman with the blond curls can keep back her tears no longer. She gestures to her midsection and sobs, "I can't hold on to anything!" I'm struck by her choice of words, by the metaphorical power of her cry. In the past, she's told me of her difficulty maintaining relationships, of her loneliness. I've recommended therapy, but she's declined. I consider suggesting that her diarrhea might be an eloquent manifestation of her psychological pain. But twenty-five minutes have passed in a visit for which fifteen minutes were allotted, and there just isn't time to open that door.

I order the stool cultures, prescribe an antidiarrheal drug and some dietary modifications, briefly mention psychotherapy again, and leave the room. Then I sit at my workstation to document and bill for our encounter, perched at the edge of my seat, on the verge of despair.

17

Off the Charts

Looking straight ahead as I sit at my desk, my view is dominated by a large computer screen. There I examine my patients' electronic records; track their blood pressures and electrolyte levels, peruse their pathology, locate the fax numbers of their pharmacies. If I shift my gaze slightly to the left, however, a different kind of information appears. Tacked to a bulletin board are photographs of several of my patients, all healthy and grinning. All dead now.

I used to tuck my late patients' funeral-mass cards and memorial-service programs away in a file in my desk drawer. Now I post them where I can see them. A younger colleague commented recently that my little gallery seems rather morbid. I told her it's quite the opposite. I find the photographs cheering, reminders of my patients not as patients, but as people, of their lives beyond what I recorded in their medical charts. There's Alice, once again playing the beloved piano she had to give up when her arthritis became so severe. Gina's thick black hair, lost during chemo, gleams once more. And how witty and debonair Bill was before dementia set in!

Margaret's picture isn't on my bulletin board yet and, though she's now past eighty, I don't think it will be soon. Margaret disagrees. She tells me she's dying. She's been telling me this for ten years. I'm not quite sure how to document her self-prognostication. Margaret's been depressed—if that's the right word for it—since her husband died a decade ago. She and Paul had weathered much together, including the death of their only child, a son killed in a car accident in his twenties. Every night, before they fell asleep, Margaret and Paul embraced and said how lucky they were to be married to each other. They were inseparable. But then Paul developed cancer and they were separated.

Mourning Paul, Margaret seems at times to march through the orderly progression of grief-related emotions psychiatrist Elisabeth Kübler-Ross described and which I'd memorized in medical school: denial, anger, bargaining, depression . . . But sometimes she skips around, moving from "I can't believe he's gone!" to "I'm just happy I had him as long as I did" and then back to "I can't believe he's gone!" within the same sentence. One thing is consistent, though: Margaret never arrives at Kübler-Ross's final stage, the one that's supposed to come after depression: acceptance.

Many months after Paul's death, Margaret still cried frequently and slept poorly. I shared with her my concern that she'd passed from "normal" grief to depression. I suggested a trial of antidepressants, which was entirely reasonable according to standard medical practice and entirely preposterous according to Margaret. "Will a pill bring back my husband?" she asked. I was reminded of something my mother, not at all inclined to self-pity, said to me near the end of her life when I asked what I could do for her: "Bring me back my husband, my friends, my career, my health—*that's* what you could do."

Over the years Margaret's malaise worsened as her aortic stenosis progressed. Following the teaching that a patient with aortic
stenosis should be referred for valve replacement the day *before* he or
she starts having symptoms, I mentioned surgery. Margaret refused
to consider it. I agreed to monitor her, though not by the usual criteria. A retired teacher, Margaret volunteered in an elementary school
twice a week, helping students with their reading. She loved being
with "my kids," as she called them, but began to beg off when she felt
too tired. I've found it more useful to gauge Margaret's valve disease
by asking whether she'd skipped any sessions at the school than about
dizziness, syncope, or shortness of breath, classic symptoms of aortic
stenosis about which I knew she'd be reluctant to tell me. But there is
no flow sheet on which to chart "showed up for volunteering."

Margaret's mood has continued to elude categorization and
quantitation. Every visit follows the same pattern: Margaret tells me
how unhappy she is, then lights up when she talks about "her" kids
or asks about mine. The depression screen that Medicare requires
all patients to complete annually is rendered invalid between when
she fills it out, on arrival to the exam room, and when I review it,
as we chat.

One day, not long ago, Margaret's neighbor Ellen called my
office. Ellen, who helps Margaret with her groceries and errands,
said she was really worried. Margaret was talking more and more
about how she wished she were dead, about how there was no reason
for her to be alive. The nurse who triaged this call was alarmed too.
Should Ellen bring Margaret to an emergency room? That would
be a prudent recommendation for someone talking about suicide.
No, I said. This was Margaret.

She came in and I asked what was wrong. "It's Paul," she said. "Paul?" I asked. Margaret told me that an expensive roof repair had finally convinced her that she needed to sell her house. Despite Ellen's assistance, she simply couldn't manage it anymore. And the prospect of selling the home in which she had lived with Paul made her feel like she was losing him all over again. We talked for a long time about the difference between losing the house and losing Paul. I told her about an essay by the poet Donald Hall, who, in his eighties and anticipating his own death, felt a resurgence of grief for his late wife, the poet Jane Kenyon, who had died many years earlier. Hall's grief was compounded by the realization that his wife would not be there to comfort him at the end of his life as he had been able to comfort her. I wondered aloud if Margaret might be experiencing a similar resurgence of grief for Paul as she faced her own mortality. Not for the first time I felt that literature had served me at least as well as science in helping a patient. Margaret seemed moved by my words and, at the end of our visit, she agreed at last to try an antidepressant.

◆　◆　◆

When Emma died a few years ago, at ninety-two, a small crowd gathered for her funeral. She'd never married or had children and wasn't close to her extended family, but her warmth, honesty, and wit had attracted many younger friends, including me.

Emma and I met frequently to gossip, talk about books and politics, and trade stories about our lives. She came to my house for dinner several times, and my husband and kids joined me at her ninetieth birthday party. When, at ninety-two, Emma moved reluctantly into a nursing home, I brought her the bagels and lox she craved—rich, salty treats her doctor had long discouraged her from eating.

I was that doctor.

For fifteen years Emma was both my patient and my friend. Most of the time these two roles coexisted comfortably. Occasionally they conflicted (see bagels and lox above). More often than not they were mutually reinforcing.

I can't prove it, but I'm convinced that her frequent trips to my office, during which we talked at least as much about presidential campaigns, skirt lengths, and bestsellers as about her arthritis and digestive difficulties, helped prevent Emma from being hospitalized as older people, particularly those who live alone, so often are.

When I first went into practice, I had rather firm notions of the proper boundaries between doctors and patients. I wore a starched white coat and revealed little about my personal life. I never called patients by their first names and felt insulted if they called me by mine. An older colleague found my rigidity amusing. He worked in shirtsleeves and his patients called him Jim. He played golf with many of them. "You'll loosen up in time," he told me.

Looking back, I think I feared that as a young female physician I wouldn't be taken seriously unless I maintained an austere facade. My role models were those legendary physicians of the nineteenth and early twentieth centuries whose oil portraits had lined the walls of the hospital in which I trained. Dr. James Jackson summed up their philosophy in 1855, writing that a doctor should maintain a calm and neutral attitude with patients, "abstain from all levity," and, most important, "never exact attention to himself."

The prescribed separation between a doctor's clinical and personal selves is now often called "professionalism." Recently, this term has been challenged as possibly sexist, racist, and homophobic. Clearly certain doctors' personal selves are more potentially objectionable than others. A 2020 study published in the *Journal of Vascular Surgery* noted a high percentage of young physicians exhibiting "unprofessional behavior" on their personal social-media accounts. "Unprofessional behavior" included drinking alcoholic beverages, expressing political and religious convictions, participating in social activism, and wearing bikinis. The article led to an impromptu Twitter campaign, #medbikini, in which female physicians posted photos of themselves in swimwear. #Medbikini caused the authors of the study to retract their article, but it raised another set of questions about which physicians are welcome to reveal aspects of their personal lives publicly. Most of the doctors who posted photos with the medbikini hashtag were white, thin, and, based on the lush settings in which the photos were taken, able to afford expensive vacations. My own favorite wasn't photographed in a luxury resort but, rather, in an emergency room. It shows a woman physician in a red bikini standing over a gurney on which a patient with gory wounds lies bleeding. The physician had been surfing nearby when she rescued the victim of a boating accident.

As my colleague Jim predicted, I found my initially rigid standards nearly impossible to meet over time. After all, a doctor is not simply a repository of information but a human being with a personality, a sense of humor, and a point of view. Even patients' seemingly straightforward medical questions—"Should I try to have a baby at forty?" "Should I take a cholesterol-lowering drug?"—demand more than medical answers. Yes, I can offer statistics about rates of infertility or birth defects and data about the benefits and side effects of statins. But so often the real question patients are asking is: "What would *you* do if you were me?" It is, at least in part, a personal question that implies and nourishes a personal relationship.

But how personal should that relationship be? Like all primary care doctors, I ask patients about their families. In turn they may, quite naturally, ask me about mine. How did I deal with my kids going off to college? My parents' aging and failing? A two-career marriage? I'm more open with my patients about my personal life than some of my colleagues are. An ophthalmologist friend once told me, half-jokingly, that the best part of his specialty is: "The patients keep *their* clothes on and I keep *my* clothes on." Still, I do draw the line on certain questions; once, when I was reviewing birth control options with a patient she said: "Oh, I don't know which one to choose, Doctor—what do *you* use?" Over the years I've found myself answering more and more openly, feeling that, ultimately, these questions aren't about me but, rather, mirror concerns my patients have about their own lives.

I grew up among doctors whose professional and personal lives were more intertwined than most doctors' lives are today. My parents' entire social circle consisted of my father's medical colleagues and their wives. My pediatrician came to our home to examine me when I was sick and often stayed for coffee. Our next-door neighbor practiced internal medicine from an office in his house. When his daughter and I ran in from playing in the yard and opened the refrigerator looking for a snack, we saw vials of insulin and penicillin lined up next to the chocolate milk.

In the generations since, I've noticed a paradox: As doctors' personal lives have become more segregated from their work lives, the interaction between physicians and patients has become less distant. While the days of the home office, house call, and 24/7 solo practitioner are mostly past, my patients often view me as a partner in, rather than a director of, their medical care. They treat me more familiarly than my father's patients treated him.

To acknowledge this shift, there was a movement a few years ago in which doctors were encouraged to refer to patients as "clients." This term, which psychotherapists often use, is meant to imply a respectful, collaborative relationship in which the medical professional doesn't hold disproportionate power. But the term never caught on with physicians. Perhaps we didn't want to relinquish that power. Or perhaps "client" connotes a party in a business transaction, which doesn't capture how we see our patients—or ourselves. In at least one study, patients asked about the term "client" said they'd rather be called patients.

So if we're not business associates and not exactly friends, what is the proper relationship between a doctor and a patient?

In recent years much has been published, pro and con, in medical journals about whether physicians should socialize with patients or accept gifts or requests from patients to be "friends" or followers on social-networking sites. Physician-writer Jay Baruch summarized our ambivalence in the pithy title of one of his essays: "Hug or Ugh?"

In 1855 Dr. James Jackson offered this guidance: "The patient is the central object in the sick-room, or should be so." Looking back on my relationship with Emma, I realize that as mutually affectionate as our friendship was, her health and comfort were always its purpose, or should have been. Even though I was the one who had advised her not to eat salt, I was convinced that satisfying Emma's craving for lox would benefit her.

◆   ◆   ◆

While walking through the halls of the hospital where I work, I recently overheard a conversation. A pediatrician was speaking with the mother of a boy who looked about twelve. When the adults finally finished talking, the kid piped up. He jerked his thumb toward his mom and asked the doctor: "Can't you *please* tell her not to make me go to my father's house this weekend?" The pediatrician smiled awkwardly. "Well now," he said, backing away, "I believe that's a bit out of my bailiwick."

I cringed at the pediatrician's prissy deflection—*bailiwick?*—and also because his discomfort reminded me of my own. Patients often ask me about matters not within my expertise. One woman wants to know if she should stay with a husband who refuses treatment for addiction. Another seeks permission to skip a few days visiting her mother in the nursing home without feeling guilty. A third asks me to review with her the pros and cons of sending her daughter to private high school. While I possess no special knowledge about marriage, filial duty, or secondary education, I routinely offer opinions on these subjects, and I feel certain that doing so is as much a part of my role as a primary care physician as prescribing medication for high blood pressure, though I'm at a loss to articulate exactly why.

In the past few decades, many patients and physicians have come to the conclusion that evidence-based treatments by specialists (and sub- and sub-subspecialists) don't necessarily supply what people need to heal. Physicians and nurses now routinely team up with mental-health professionals, alternative practitioners, social workers, and chaplains to offer holistic care. I participate in such teams and value them, but I'm not sure that even holistic medicine fully acknowledges the difficult-to-measure therapeutic effects of empathy, attentiveness, humor, intuitive reasoning, the ability to inspire hope, and other qualities sometimes called "soft skills" (or, more appreciatively, "the art of medicine") and which are as useful in my practice as antibiotics and MRIs, if not more so. Similarly, when I've been a patient myself, or when someone I love has fallen ill, I've been struck by the importance of these qualities to healing. In fact, I've been meaning to write an essay titled "The Power of the Intangible in Medicine," but I've felt daunted by how hard it would be, by definition, to put so vague a concept into words.

A week after I prescribed an antidepressant for Margaret, the long-grieving widow, her neighbor called to report that she was feeling much better. "It's a miracle," she said. "A total turnaround." I expressed some surprise. Usually antidepressants don't work so quickly. I told Ellen I was pleased that Margaret had had such a good response to the medication. Ellen laughed. "Oh, you mean that prescription you wrote? You know how Margaret is. She never filled it." It's possible that simply receiving the prescription had a placebo effect. Or it may be that telling me about how sad she felt had made Margaret feel less sad.

◆   ◆   ◆

If I turn still further to the left, from the photographs of my deceased patients on my bulletin board to the window ledge, I see yet another collection of images, framed ones. There I am, beaming, at my daughter's wedding; my children shriek with joy on a long-ago day at the beach; a revered mentor, years since passed on, smiles reassuringly. It occurs to me that I can no more divide myself neatly into doctor and person than I can divide my patients into patients and people. That I always feel I do my best work when I play the boundary, when I bring myself as a person to the patient as a person. When I go off the charts a little.

Back to the conversation I overheard in the hallway: No doubt the pediatrician would have addressed the boy's plea not to visit his father if he suspected child abuse. That concern would fall squarely in the physician's "bailiwick"—he'd be legally bound to report it to the police. Perhaps he did later question the boy and his parents, suspect abuse, and file a report. But I'd argue that even if he were at no risk of abuse in his father's home, the boy's desire not to go there required medical attention. I can anticipate the counterarguments of my colleagues—indeed, I've made them myself: *But there's only so much time in a day. You have to triage. You have to maintain appropriate boundaries.* All true, and yet this, too, is true: when I talk with my patients about issues not strictly medical, I feel most like a doctor.

18

Head and Shoulder

A few weeks after starting my first job as a primary care internist, I made an appointment to see a psychiatrist. Not as a patient. Not exactly.

The psychiatrist I called had a special interest in "difficult" patients. I asked if I might drop by his office to chat about strategies I could employ in dealing with such patients. If my colleague had billed me for the visit, he'd probably have entered my diagnosis as "adjustment disorder." The truth, which I suspect he quickly discerned, was that the problem wasn't my patients; it was me. I was having difficulty adjusting to my new practice.

I'd just completed a year of chief residency at Johns Hopkins Hospital. My patients there were poor and sick. At the end of the year, I sorted through the index cards I'd filled out on each admission and tallied the most common diagnoses: bacterial endocarditis, diabetic ketoacidosis, sickle cell anemia crisis. Serious stuff. Fifty percent of my patients under forty were infected with HIV, which was at that time almost always fatal.

In my new practice at Mass General most of my patients were like me: young women, middle- or upper-middle-class, educated, and healthy. They frequently came to their visits armed with Internet printouts and lists of questions. *Should I try acupuncture? What about an MRI—just to be sure? Why isn't my hair as thick as it used to be? Which vitamins and supplements are best? Can you screen me for . . . everything?*

I knew that these patients, the so-called worried well, no less than the very ill patients I'd once taken care of, were worthy of my compassion and reassurance, but I found myself struggling to provide it. Didn't these people understand how lucky they were? The gap between what I knew I should feel and what I actually felt distressed me.

Many years have gone by, and I've come to know my patients, to like them, and often to love them. As they've grown older, many of them have developed those very diseases about which they'd worried when they were younger. When healthy, they still bring in printouts and lists, but these no longer bother me. I now recognize them as expressions of anxiety about mortality—also serious stuff.

But until just recently I still found it hard to empathize fully with the most extreme versions of the worried well: patients who have undiagnosable symptoms from head to toe and meet the criteria for somatic symptom disorder, but whom we'd referred to among ourselves, disrespectfully, when I was a resident as "crocks," "squirrels," or "head cases."

One such patient of mine is Claire. A charming and intelligent woman in her sixties, she's visited me several times a year for two decades, always with a new problem, usually undiagnosable, often untreatable. Evaluating Claire's many symptoms has felt like trying to make a king-size bed with a queen-size sheet. No sooner does her dizziness ease than a limp develops. When the limp resolves, a headache pops up. And on and on.

I have my own idea about why Claire has so many physical symptoms. She often mentions a son with whom she has a painful relationship. Claire feels he doesn't care enough about her. I've wondered whether Claire's symptoms are her way of attempting to attract her son's attention. I've also wondered whether, over the years, I've played stand-in for her son, each new symptom a test of my "affection."

And to make matters more complicated, during many of the years I've cared for Claire, my own aged parents were failing. They frequently called me, their daughter the doctor, with one medical crisis or another—and sometimes I was unable to reassure them.

So for a long time, Claire and I had a complex and—at least for me—uncomfortable relationship in which I felt she saw me, with each negative x-ray and ineffective medication, as an endlessly disappointing child, while I cast her as the disapproving parent. Not surprisingly, I didn't enjoy her many visits. I acted toward Claire in a friendly and professional manner, but I withheld myself from her, afraid that if I let down my emotional guard I'd be swallowed up by her voracious neediness.

Then, not long ago, an event changed the dynamic of my relationship with Claire, unexpectedly and profoundly. One rainy spring morning, I slipped on my front porch while rushing to work and landed on my outstretched right palm. A shoulder can be injured in several different ways and in one fall I'd managed to injure mine in all of them: I fractured my humerus and glenoid bones, tore my rotator cuff, and dislocated my shoulder joint. My recovery from surgery was difficult, not only because of pain and immobility—which were severe and lasted many weeks—but because of the psychological effects my injury had on me. I ruminated over how my long period of disability would affect my career and family. I regaled the clinicians caring for me with detailed descriptions of the subtly different and frequently changing types of pain I experienced. Sometimes, I told them, a certain pain medication worked very well, and sometimes not at all, and sometimes it caused intolerable side effects. I began to fear that I sounded to them like . . . a "crock," a "squirrel," a "head case"—and then I obsessed about that. On a follow up visit to the orthopedic surgeon, a nurse nonchalantly handed me the glossy photos taken during my operation, "for your records." They showed the tidy system of metal hooks and synthetic rope—royal blue woven with white—that still holds me together. I started crying. The nurse looked at me questioningly but I was afraid she would think I was crazy if I told her the thought that had brought me to tears: *I will never be fully human again.*

Over the years, I'd often told medical students that every illness is psychosomatic—involving both the mind and body—but it wasn't until I injured my shoulder that I fully understood how true that is.

After two months, I returned to work. The first patient I saw on my first day back was—you guessed it—Claire. She knew about my accident because, with my permission, my secretary had told my patients about it when she'd called them to reschedule appointments canceled during my medical leave.

When I entered the examination room Claire stood up and gestured back and forth between my shoulder and her abdomen—the body part that happened to be bothering her that day. "Well, well," Claire said, "we're quite a pair, aren't we?"

Her suggestion that our situations were in any way analogous, would, only weeks earlier, have made me cringe. But I did not cringe. I smiled warmly and genuinely at Claire. I saw her, for the very first time, not as a difficult patient, but as a person, wounded and in pain, as I had been. After more than twenty years in practice, the distinction between "real" and "imaginary" illness had finally lost its meaning for me.

I said, "We sure are, Claire. Quite a pair!

19

Sequelae

My mother didn't die of her heart attack. She lived nearly four more years, during which she suffered a series of strokes caused by small blood clots that formed in her weakened heart, traveled to her brain, and stole her away bit by bit. The strokes were "sequelae": new manifestations of an old condition that appear like ghosts, sometimes many years after that condition has been stabilized or even cured. Shingles is a good example: a childhood bout of chicken pox resolves, but the virus remains dormant in the nerves and erupts painfully one day on the face or chest or leg of an eighty-year-old. Post-polio syndrome is another: though the Salk and Sabin vaccines eradicated polio—no new cases have been seen in the United States since 1979—up to half of those who had the disease as children are now at risk of developing debilitating weakness and tender joints in old age. Sequelae are, by definition, surprising, cruel.

My mother's first stroke occurred just three months after she was released from Mass General in late March 2005. She returned home from Boston to Connecticut frail and in need of round-the-clock care. She hired a kind and capable woman named Anna, who moved into the spare bedroom of the condo my mother had bought after selling the home she'd shared with my father. Anna drove my mother to cardiac rehab at the local medical center and to the bank, dry cleaners, beauty parlor, and the monthly book club my mother loved so much. Most days the two women had lunch together at a diner. Surprisingly, my mother's white blood count remained normal after the one round of chemotherapy she'd had for her chronic leukemia days before her heart attack. She seemed to be getting "back to baseline," according to her doctors, though my brothers and I thought she had aged markedly in the few months since my father's death, and that she would never be what she had once been.

One Tuesday afternoon in early May 2005, my mother called me at work. By then, she'd settled back into her routine of phoning at precisely eight o'clock in the morning on Wednesdays, Fridays, and Sundays, when she knew I was neither in my office nor busy with the kids. I could tell by the timing of her call that something was wrong.

"What's the matter?" I asked.

"I can't read."

"What do you mean you can't read? You mean you can't concentrate? Or you just don't feel like reading?"

"No, neither. I *want* to read. But all the tails are missing."

"The tails?"

"Yes. You know, the little tails that hang down from the *y*'s and the *g*'s and the *j*'s? They've all been all cut off. But not the tails that go up. Not the ones on the *b*'s and the *d*'s. Those are still there."

As I listened to my mother describe this new symptom, I pictured her pressing one eye closed and then the other, trying to reattach the tails. A neurologist localized the problem to the occipital region of her brain near the calcarine fissure and pronounced it "a tiny deficit," but to my mother it was not tiny at all. She would never read again.

More subtle strokes likely followed. Going through her checkbook, I noted a change in her handwriting in the summer of 2007. My mother kept one of those large desktop ledgers. The names of the payees began to wander upward or downwards on the stubs, and some were completely illegible. It was around this time that a friend of hers, an old busybody, called me to report that my mother had put down a hundred-dollar bill to tip a waitress for a sandwich and a cup of coffee.

On April 7, 2008, at 5:52 p.m., I received a voice message that remains stored on my phone today, over a decade later. My mother, who'd returned to Florida, sounds very much like herself, her voice a cheerful singsong. She stretches out her usual greeting, *Hi, Sue!* into extra syllables, inflecting upward, as she always had. Only she, my father, and one of my brothers have ever called me Sue, and the name pulls me back to childhood.

Hi-yi, Su-ue! I called to say hello. You know I'm in the hospital [I didn't]. *I ... um ... I'm not quite sure why ... I think I had ... um ... some problems with my ... uh ... with my ... uh ... I don't remember which one. But anyway, it seems to me that I'm fine. I'm just waiting to have some dinner soon. And ... um ... I have ... um ... I wanted to send a message with my ... um ... but I can't figure out how to do that. So if you have a chance, call me. I'm really OK. Bye!*

It took my mother one minute and fourteen seconds to get through this. There are long pauses, during which the local TV news and Anna's voice can be heard in the background. Listening to it now I feel such . . . what is the right word? Empathy? Guilt? Sadness? She was trying to sound upbeat, to fight against the panic she must have felt not being able to find the words she wanted to say. The most fluent sentences are the last ones: *So, if you have a chance, call me. I'm really OK. Bye!*

I first played this message as I was driving home from Kripalu, a yoga retreat in Lenox, Massachusetts, not far from Canyon Ranch, the spa where my parents had once gone years earlier. My mother had dragged my father to Canyon Ranch, ever determined to improve his health—that is, make him lose weight—and had come home armed with printouts of exercise routines and recipes and a new mantra, which she repeated incessantly to me, a physician for two decades by this point: "Salt is *death*." At Kripalu I'd signed up for a detox cleanse and had been eating vegetables, tofu, yogurt, and legumes for three days. No sugar, caffeine, or grains. Not even fruit. On the second day, in withdrawal from coffee, I developed a migraine and had to excuse myself from the sharing circle to throw up. But by the time I played my mother's disturbing message I felt remarkably well: light and clearheaded. I'd privately rolled my eyes throughout my stay at Kripalu and yet all that kelp and tofu and meditation seemed to have had a calming effect on me.

I arrived in Boca Raton the next day to find that my mother, while still her animated and charming self, had lost her memory. She'd forgotten that I was a doctor and that I was married. Everything was news, which she received with a lively curiosity. "Really?"

she marveled. "I have *seven* grandchildren? Oh my! That's a *lot*, isn't it?"

I once had a patient who told me that she'd always been at odds with her mother, and that when the older woman became demented the daughter was thrust into a caregiving role, intimate with her mom in a way she'd never been before. "It drove me crazy that she couldn't remember how much we'd fought, how we basically didn't even *like* each other," my patient told me. For me, it wasn't like this. I reacted to my mother's sudden cognitive decline with horror but also acceptance, even a kind of relief. Along with my mother's memory, the tension which had existed between us since I was an adolescent seemed to have slipped away.

When, in consultation with my brothers, I arranged for her lawyer and her stockbroker to visit the house to assign me power of attorney on an emergency basis, my mother retained the fact that someone was coming to visit, and that this had something to do with her financial affairs—she loved visitors and loved working on her financial affairs—but she couldn't remember anything else. Over and over that morning she asked: *Who's coming? Why are they coming? When are they coming? Who's coming? Why? When? Who? Why? When?* The repetition of these questions didn't annoy me in the slightest. Just after my arrival, I left my mother with Anna and hit Whole Foods to stock up on organic, vegan, sugar-free supplies. I stuck with this ascetic diet throughout my stay and remained serene, floating above the catastrophe.

Once during my four- or five-day visit, Anna found a note about a dinner engagement scrawled on my mother's calendar. We couldn't make out the name. With comical equanimity, my mother prepared for her mystery date. At six p.m. she sat in the overstuffed forest-green club chair in her living room, dressed, perfumed, and hair done, with Anna's assistance, holding her black patent Fendi clutch, purchased years earlier in Florence and just big enough to hold a credit card, an Elizabeth Arden lipstick in Neoclassical Coral, and the TUMS, Halls MenthoLyptus cough drops, and linen handkerchief my mother never left home without. Amazed at how untroubled she was, I asked: "You really don't know who's coming?" She replied, jauntily, "No, but we'll find out, won't we?" This insouciance was most uncharacteristic of my decidedly unspontaneous mother whom someone once asked, jokingly, if she was the lady who had invented Post-its. When the bell rang and we opened the door, there stood an old college classmate of my father's, along with his wife. They'd planned to take my mother to a restaurant. I pulled them aside and explained the situation, asking them not to let her go to the ladies' room unattended. They nodded, as if this were a routine request, which, for people of a certain age, perhaps it is.

◆ ◆ ◆

When I returned home to Boston, leaving my mother with Anna, my oldest brother and I met with a social worker who specialized in geriatric care. This is how my brother dealt with his sadness and rage about my mother's decline: he made a few calls and found a social worker who specialized in geriatric care. He brought a legal pad. He was ready to hear about options: assisted living, home care, equipment rental. But the first thing the social worker said was:

"Don't forget that, no matter how old you are, the relationship between a mother and a child is the most primitive and basic relationship." And, right there at the conference table, my brother and I started crying.

That summer, as she was recovering from the stroke that affected her memory, I visited my mother in Connecticut. I proposed an outing—just the two of us, without Anna—to a nearby garden center. As is often the case when someone has dementia, either due to strokes, Alzheimer's disease, or some other condition, my mother's personality and tastes remained intact even as her memory failed. In proposing this outing I had in mind that my mother loved gardening, loved being with me alone—which had become rare, with Anna always by her side—and loved, perhaps most of all, having a mission, a problem that needed solving. The problem, I explained to her, was that rabbits were nibbling my own, far-inferior-to-my-mother's-old-garden garden. That spring I'd woken up one morning to find my tulips and daffodils decapitated and, just a week earlier, any evidence of my admittedly half-hearted attempts to grow arugula had vanished. All that remained were sparse patches of green gnawed within an inch of the dirt. I'd heard there was a special, nontoxic spray called Liquid Fence that smelled bad to bunnies but was undetectable to humans, a concoction of rotten egg, garlic, and cinnamon. So my mother and I set out through the windy and hilly backroads of Litchfield County in search of it.

The owner of the garden center warmly greeted my mother, who had for years been her very good customer, and produced a rusted metal folding chair that she placed on the gravel in the aisle between rough wooden tables loaded with flagging herbs, vegetable plants, and perennials priced at midsummer markdown. It had just rained, and the owner rubbed the seat dry with her sleeve just as my mother lowered herself onto it while leaning on me. The sun had come out and shone in my mother's eyes, and I worried she'd be uncomfortable squinting, sitting on the rickety chair set unevenly in the gravel. But before I could ask, my mother announced that she was "very, very happy."

We were driving back to the condo to which she'd moved a year after my father died, a bottle of Liquid Fence and a few arugula plants in the trunk, when something compelled me to ask my mother if she might like to swing by her old house, the one she'd shared with my father during weekends and summers from 1982 until his death in 2004. The moment after I suggested this detour, I wished I hadn't. For one thing, I realized that visiting the old house might make my mother miss my father more; miss her old tennis-playing, gardening, book-clubbing summer life. It might make her sad. It might make *me* sad. And for another thing, I didn't have any idea how to get there.

My sense of direction is so terrible that I've often wondered whether I have an undiagnosed neurological deficit myself. Once, years earlier, I'd taken a walk down the long driveway at the house in Connecticut and on my way back bent down briefly to inspect a flower and when I stood up and looked around, I became disoriented. My mother was staking her dahlias several yards away and smiled. "Lost?" she asked me, amused. Yes, I had literally gotten lost in my own—well, *her* own, backyard.

I didn't have a prayer of navigating the route from the gar-

den center to my parents' old house, but it turned out I didn't need
to. My mother, nearly eighty-one, frail and cognitively impaired,
directed me, without a single mistake, through the rights, lefts, and
switchbacks that landed us, a few minutes later, at the end of her
old driveway. "Are you sure you want to see it?' I asked. She was.
We approached slowly, just until the house was in view, and then
I switched off the engine. My mother looked around at the herb
garden she'd planted, at the blood-red coral belles with which she'd
lined the path to the house, at the elm and apple trees in full leaf,
and said nothing.

Several yards away, in the kitchen window, a man appeared, and
then another man, both visible only from the waist up. They didn't
seem to have seen us and my mother hadn't seen them. Neither man
wore a shirt. They might have been naked entirely, for all I knew. I
turned the ignition back on and started backing down the driveway,
something I'd never done before. Related, I think, to my atrocious
sense of direction is an extreme dislike of moving backwards in cars
and trains, but I was in a rush. I told my mother we should get out
of there. "Yes, let's," she said. "This is upsetting me."

We drove back to the condo in silence. I somehow found my
way without my mother's guidance. I wanted to chat about the men
in the window, presumably the new owners, to ask my mother if
she recalled their names. She'd told me, when she sold the house to
them, that one was "a big deal in media." But I stayed quiet out of
respect for her grief. And there was another reason too. Almost as
soon as I'd backed to the end of the driveway, I'd begun to question
what I'd seen. Were there really two bare-chested men in my mother's old kitchen window, the window she'd looked out while washing

countless dishes, filling endless pots with water to boil corn? Or had I invented this tantalizing detail? Was I writing the story of the end of my mother's life even then?

◆ ◆ ◆

That late spring and summer of 2008 my mother gained back some of her memory. She recovered the fact that I was a doctor as well as the names of her grandchildren and she was thrilled about the arrival of her first great-grandchild in May. But in November she had another stroke, which left her speech slurred and her right side paralyzed. She sent Anna to Macy's to buy sweatsuits in bright colors, and Velcro sneakers for easy on and off. She wore plastic braces on her right arm and leg and went to physical therapy. Her antique French mahogany-and-bronze headboard, which she and my father had bought for their first apartment, was relegated to the garage and a hospital bed took its place. As always, my mother tried to remain positive, but I could see her resolve beginning to falter. I think that the ugliness of illness, the dismantling of the beautiful and orderly décor with which she'd always surrounded herself, must have distressed my mother at least as much as her disability.

In December, a few weeks after the stroke that left her partially paralyzed, my brothers' families and mine met on the west coast of Florida for Christmas vacation. One day my teenage daughter and I, along with my sisters-in-law and nieces, drove across the state to Boca. For our ladies' luncheon, my mother sat with some effort at the head of the table. She'd instructed Anna to lay out sandwiches from the supermarket deli on a silver platter and to put ice for the

Diet Cokes in a crystal bucket. But she told me for the first time, after she'd retreated to her hospital bed to rest and we were alone for a few minutes: "I don't know if I can go on, Sue. I don't know if I want to."

My friend Marty, an older colleague who had mentored me when I first went into practice, is now in his eighties. He retired at seventy-five, working full-time until the end. He still reads the major medical journals cover-to-cover every week, takes Spanish lessons, and goes for long walks to keep his grafted coronary arteries clear. So I'm surprised to hear him say, when he comes to my house for coffee one recent summer afternoon, that he's given up on self-improvement. "This is what it means to be old," he tells me as we sit on my living-room couch, watching the squares of sun shining through the skylights travel across the floor. "I'm no longer aspirational."

My mother, the lifelong self-improvement enthusiast, perennial maker of lists, did remain aspirational after her heart attack. The screen saver she'd put on her desktop computer during the difficult years when my father was sick read, in wavy neon letters, BE KIND TO YOURSELF, but even that had seemed to me more of an exhortation to self-improvement than self-acceptance. After her heart attack she'd gamely gone through cardiac rehab; she'd bought and renovated the condo in Connecticut; she'd continued to work the phones and keep in touch with her many younger friends. But after the strokes my mother could not go on. She would not reemerge again.

———

Science and Kindness

Once there was a specialist at my hospital as well known for his unpleasant personality as for his brilliant diagnoses. The few patients I referred to him told me that while they were happy with how he handled their medical issues they weren't so happy with him. He was rude and brusque. He kept them waiting and he didn't return their phone calls. One patient mentioned that she'd overheard him speak sharply to a nurse and that this had made her uncomfortable. Another said that he wouldn't have chosen this specialist as a friend, but that he had to admit he was a great doctor.

Or was he?

"Medicine is an alliance of science and kindness," writes physician and essayist Gavin Francis. I agree, but I find the nature of that alliance hard to define. Is one component more important than the other? I had occasion to think about this question a while ago when I received an email from Rahmiya, a second-year medical student at a university in the north of England. Rahmiya had read an article I'd written about medical training and thought I might be able to help her with a decision. She explained that she'd failed a comprehensive exam covering pathophysiology, pharmacology, and other scientific subjects. Now she'd been given a choice of either retaking the exam or repeating the year. She was inclined to repeat the year because while she'd only missed passing her exam by a few points, she felt that it would be dishonest to merely "scrape by," as she put it, in completing what she believed was the core of the medical school curriculum. Rahmiya went on to report that her instructors routinely commented on her exceptional ability to communicate with patients and to earn their trust. This feedback pleased her, but Rahmiya believed her interpersonal skills, no matter how excellent, could in no way compensate for her less-than-stellar scientific acumen. I wrote back and told Rahmiya that I wasn't sure I knew enough about the British system of medical education to assist her with this decision, but I was certain that it's harder to learn how to communicate well with patients than to learn pathophysiology and pharmacology.

Patients agree. For many years my colleague Dr. Kate Treadway has run a course called "Introduction to the Profession" for first-year students at Harvard Medical School. Within days of their arrival, students are sent to speak with hospitalized patients. They can ask the patients anything, but there's one question they're required to ask: *What advice would you give me as I begin my career?* Kate tells me that year after year patients invariably give the same answer: *I just want you to listen to me.* Students worry about knowing enough. Patients worry about them caring enough.

The idea that in medicine competence and compassion are separable is surprisingly new. Until a hundred years ago, historian Regina Morantz-Sanchez explains, physicians drew less distinction between the art and the science of medicine. In fact, she notes, physicians in the late nineteenth century "understood the word 'science' differently than we do today." Medical science, in the years before the development of social work, nutrition, psychology, and other disciplines, took a broad view of health and thus of the role of the doctor. Morantz-Sanchez quotes Professor Henry Hartshorne, delivering the 1872 commencement address at the Women's Medical College of Pennsylvania:

> It is not always the most logical, but often the most discerning physician who succeeds best at the bedside. Medicine is, indeed, a science, but its practice is an art. Those who bring the quick eye, the receptive ear, and delicate touch, intensified, all of them, by a warm sympathetic temperament . . . may use the learning of laborious accumulators, often better than they themselves could do.

Male medical students in this era heard similar lessons from their professors. This often-quoted credo has been attributed to both Hippocrates and Osler: *It is much more important to know what sort of patient has a disease than what sort of disease a patient has.*

As scientific knowledge and technology advanced in the late nineteenth and early twentieth centuries, what it meant to be a doctor changed. Michel Foucault's insight about this change is well summarized by psychiatrist and medical historian Abraham Nussbaum:

> Foucault described the moment when physicians combined dissection with clinical practice as the "great break in the history of Western medicine." Instead of seeing themselves as people desig-

nated by society to attend to people who are suffering, they began to think of themselves as scientists. We now understand ourselves as people who observe and measure the body, hypothesize about its function and dysfunction, and then prove and disprove the resulting theories. When physicians began understanding themselves as scientists they developed antibiotics, anesthesia, and asepsis. With these disruptive and innovative technologies, they transformed what it means to care for the ill. They also transformed themselves.

As the art and science of medicine grew apart, the identification of each with opposite genders evolved. Scientific knowledge and technical competence came to be more associated with men (doctors), while compassionate care was mainly the purview of women (nurses and other non-physician medical professionals). This perceived gender split gained traction throughout the twentieth century even as more and more women became physicians. I've unwittingly perpetuated the stereotype of the empathic but scientifically unimpressive female clinician myself. For many years I described my work as a primary care doctor in self-effacing terms: "I'm just a therapist who does Pap smears." I readily repeated the derogatory term I'd heard to describe primary care, the practice of which involves much mental-health treatment and routine gynecology: *psychovaginal medicine*.

I'd been taught early on that the art and science of medicine are separate and unequal. In my first year of medical school the few sessions in which we learned about the doctor-patient relationship were relegated to Friday afternoons. One week we watched a film about an abrasive doctor who sees the error of his ways when he develops a malignancy and is shocked at how callously he's treated by his colleagues. The takeaway from the film's Scrooge-on-Christmas-morning epiphany—be nice to your patients *before* you get cancer—may have been lost on a roomful of students in our twenties. I've always seen myself as someone who especially values the art of medicine, but I've only recently realized the extent to which I'd been trained to devalue this art. Not long ago I led a discussion session attended by nurses, doctors, and other hospital staff. We'd read "Communion," the essay by Richard Weinberg about the woman with chronic, undiagnosed abdominal pain and obvious emotional distress who comes bearing a thick stack of medical records to the office of a busy gastroenterologist. "How do we feel when we encounter such a needy patient?" I asked the group. It was a rhetorical question, I thought, with an obvious answer: *not so good*. Indeed, several doctors groaned. But the nurses didn't groan. "I don't feel that way at all," one said. "In nursing school we learn that it's our job to take care of people, not just to figure out what's wrong with them."

In recent years, it's been recognized increasingly that patients who feel that their doctors care about them and relate well to them are more likely to express satisfaction with their medical care, take medications as prescribed, experience less pain and anxiety, have better control of conditions like diabetes and asthma, and are less likely to initiate malpractice suits. Accordingly, doctors are now questioning whether the rift between the art and science of medicine has grown too wide and are looking for ways to bridge it.

◆　◆　◆

In the 1980s, when I was in medical school, we spoke of "bedside manner." You don't hear that term so much anymore. Perhaps it sounds patronizing, since it emphasizes that the patient is lying down and the doctor is, literally, above him or her. Or maybe it's that "manner" sounds too much like "mannered," as in artificial. That said, my role models back then, the doctors with the best bedside manners, appeared very sincere. They seemed to me like priests, or college professors. I remember their immaculate hands, their chart notes penned in leisurely strokes of fountain ink, the folded rubber limbs of their stethoscopes peeking out from the pockets of their tweed jackets. They pored over sick bodies as if studying ancient texts.

Anatole Broyard, late book critic for *The New York Times*, seems to have shared my fantasy of the physician as a kind of literary scholar. While he was dying of prostate cancer, Broyard wrote a memoir, *Intoxicated by My Illness*. In one table-turning chapter, "The Patient Examines the Doctor," Broyard writes:

> What *do* I want in a doctor? I would say that I want one who is a close reader of illness and a good critic of medicine. [. . .] I see no reason or need for my doctor to love me—nor would I expect him to suffer with me. [. . .] I just wish he would brood on my situation for perhaps five minutes.

Now brooding is not enough. Doctors are supposed to "suffer with" our patients, to feel what they feel. The word most often used to describe this requisite is "empathy." It's a relatively new word, first introduced a century ago by a German psychologist and translated from *Einfühlung*, "feeling-in." Empathy seems to have replaced "sympathy," which has become associated with condolence, "pity," which sounds condescending, and "being nice" which connotes bland and ineffectual. Today, "empathy"—or, rather, the lack of it—is supposedly everywhere. Columnists decry the "empathy gap" between rich and poor, millennials purportedly lack empathy, and sociopathic criminals are thought to possess an "empathy switch," which they can flick off at will to avoid the inconvenience of being affected by their victims' suffering.

Hundreds of articles about empathy have appeared in medical journals in the past few years. In addition to research demonstrating how physicians' empathy benefits patients, several studies show that during medical school, internship, and residency, young doctors actually become less empathic. In the process of learning how to care for sick people, students unlearn how to care *about* them. Partly because of these studies, the results of which are reported in papers with distressing titles like: "Is There a Hardening of the Heart During Medical School?," today's doctors-to-be are encouraged, often required, to participate in activities meant to boost empathy. These include reading groups, reflective writing, museum visits, and role-play. In some improvisations, medical students pretend to be patients: they confine themselves to wheelchairs for a day, or they walk into hospitals with fictitious identities and symptoms and throw themselves on the mercy of the busy ER staff. At one medical school, male students lie down on exam tables with their pants on, place their feet in stirrups, and spread their legs.

A few years ago I volunteered to serve as faculty for an exercise in which students played doctors. It was called "Giving Bad

News." I wore headphones and sat on one side of a two-way mirror. On the other, a student informed a patient that cancer had invaded her spine—that the back pain she'd chalked up to muscle strain, or a touch of arthritis, wasn't so innocuous. Except that the patient wasn't really a patient. She was a retiree who'd been trained as a "standardized patient," to play the part and, along with me, to provide feedback to the student afterward. After watching a videotape of his or her performance, each student completed a self-evaluation form that included items such as "Builds a Relationship," "Understands the Patient's Perspective," and "Provides Closure."

I was a little skeptical about "Giving Bad News." I balked at the notion that empathy could be scripted, rehearsed—graded! But by the end of the afternoon, I'd been won over. The students who had watched an instructional video before the role-play were, in fact, more likely to ask the standardized patient about her social supports and to offer pain medication, and less likely to interrupt her. Most impressive to me, I noticed that students, who were, no doubt, empathic people in real life, didn't necessarily know how to *act* empathically. One young man, who had seemed, when we'd chatted before the session, quite earnest and sweet, bungled his delivery of the bad news. "So, Doctor, what does this mean?" implored the tearful woman playing the part of the patient. "Uh, it means you have about six months to live," answered the student. *Cut!* I wanted to shout across the glass. But the woman allowed the scene to continue. Afterward, she gently told the student that his coldness had upset her. He apologized and seemed genuinely contrite. I believed that he would, in the future, be more careful.

I've struggled to understand what I witnessed that day. I think the student became more empathic, but I'm not sure just what that means. "Empathy," physician and writer Danielle Ofri writes, "is one of those odd concepts that is so central to human interaction, so obviously a requirement in medicine, something we know when we see, yet so difficult for many to precisely define." Elusive as it is, in medicine we seem to have the urge—not surprisingly—to understand empathy as something quantifiable and physical, like a muscle that can be strengthened or fatigued, or a substance that can be replenished or depleted.

In recent years, scientists have indeed concluded that empathy is a physiological state. Doctors who feel true empathy in simulated encounters with patients experience measurable alterations in their heart rhythms and microscopic changes in the amount of sweat on their skin. Oxytocin, the "empathy hormone" that women release during labor and delivery, and which causes them to bond with their infants (to obvious evolutionary advantage), seems to be involved also in sex, friendship, and other social interactions that tend to work out better when people care about one another. Brain imaging shows that the areas of the cerebral cortex that light up when we're hurt also light up when we see another person hurting—that we really can, as Bill Clinton once claimed, feel someone else's pain.

Empathy may be as simple as remembering to say the right thing or, as the medical student I observed in "Giving Bad News" failed to do, remembering not to say the wrong one. When I've discussed the concept of empathy with colleagues, a question that comes up is whether *saying* the right thing counts as empathy if you're not *feeling* the right thing. For example, if you're telling someone they have cancer in the kindest and most sensitive way but thinking about what the hospital cafeteria is serving for lunch today, are you being truly empathic? In response to this question a senior physician once told me: "Well, early in the day I'm saying *and* feeling what I should, but by five o'clock sometimes I'm only *saying* what I should."

Empathy often takes the form of simply paying attention, making a patient feel seen. My patients seem genuinely pleased and surprised when I remember their grandchildren's names or the fact that they've changed jobs or hiked the Appalachian Trail. Conversely, when I've been a patient myself, I've doubted a physician's empathy when I read my medical chart and seen the details of my case, even insignificant ones, recorded inaccurately. But not everyone wishes to be seen. A psychiatrist once told me, with alarming frankness, that "interpretation is hostile." I think he was saying that not everyone *wants* their pain revealed and recorded. There's a fine line between interpretation and hostility, between relating to someone else's experience and appropriating it, between travel and transgression, inquiry and voyeurism. Yet another form of empathy, then, is recognizing empathy's limits. Leslie Jamison, author of *The Empathy Exams*, a collection of essays on the subject, notes that some of the medical students who interviewed her when she worked as a standardized patient "seem to understand that empathy is always perched precariously between gift and invasion."

Sometimes competence and caring are one and the same. Recently, I exchanged emails with the neurosurgeon who successfully treated my son's epilepsy years ago. He expressed concern about the lack of empathy displayed by some of his fellow subspecialists: "How focused we become in our little areas, and how easy it is to lose sight of the daily fears and concerns of our patients," he wrote. Though this surgeon was indeed very kind, I replied that the skill he'd displayed in operating on my son and curing his seizures had been empathy enough.

The phrase "bearing witness" also comes up a lot in relation to empathy. I do think that remaining present in the face of another person's suffering can be a fine form of empathy, though the presence of the clinician is unique. I recently had two experiences that caused me to reflect on how so. The first concerned a patient of mine whose eye needed to be removed when he was diagnosed with ocular melanoma. He'd later be fitted with a glass prosthesis, but two days after the surgery, when he arrived at my office, only a bandage covered his empty socket. He was worried that his incision might be infected, he'd told me on the phone. He really wanted me to check it out. A postoperative complication would be the ophthalmologist's responsibility, but something made me tell the patient to come in. I peeled back the tape bordering the clean white bandage and saw the pink hole where his eye had been. There was no sign of infection, which didn't surprise me. I replaced his dressing, and the patient left, reassured.

Afterward I wondered if my patient had been worried about an infection or something else: the possibility that the removal of his eye had made him too frightful to look at. An ophthalmologist could have assuaged him about the first concern, but as someone who'd known him for years, known him long before he'd lost his eye, I could help him with the second. And yet my being a doctor mattered too. I wasn't simply someone, like his wife, who'd known him for a long time. I was a medical professional, trained not to avert my gaze from his disfigurement, the right person to view what he could not yet stand to face himself.

A similar thought occurred to me during a reflective writing session I facilitated for a group of residents. I asked them each to describe a situation in which they'd felt like a real doctor. One young woman told the story of a patient of hers in recovery from substance-use disorder. He'd been injecting heroin for years but had stopped several months earlier and was now steadily employed as a butcher's apprentice. Not long after starting his new job he'd come to the emergency room with high fevers and was found to have a new heart murmur. An echocardiogram indicated that he likely had bacterial endocarditis, a condition in which bacteria in the bloodstream infect the heart valves. A common source of infection is the use of unsterile needles, by which bacteria can enter the body. The staff in the ER and on the hospital ward where the patient was admitted assumed that the patient was using drugs again, but the resident believed her patient when he insisted that he hadn't relapsed. When the blood-culture results came back, his claim was validated. The cultures grew *Erysipelothrix rhusiopathiae*, a bacterium carried by tainted meat or fish. It had likely entered a small cut in the butcher's hands as he trimmed sirloin and ground chuck.

When it was time to discharge the patient from the hospital, the resident stood up for him again. He would need several weeks of intravenous antibiotics for which a special catheter is usually inserted and left in the patient's arm. Medication can then be administered at home, often by a family member. But the team was reluctant to send someone with a history of using heroin home with such a catheter. They believed that would be too much of a temptation for him. The resident said she'd take responsibility for his use of the catheter. And she did. She told our group, "I followed his case closely for months to see how things went, and he did fine. He recovered well from the infection, and remained in remission from his drug use too."

It was a great story, I said. But did she really need to be a doctor to care for this patient as she had, to advocate for him so fiercely? The resident paused and thought a moment. "Yes," she said, nodding. If she hadn't had any professional expertise in addiction and endocarditis, the patient wouldn't have trusted her, nor she the patient. And their mutual trust was the basis of the medical decision. The late beloved Mass General physician Dr. Morton Swartz once said: *Patients don't care what you know until they know that you care.*

◆ ◆ ◆

I'm thinking again of that medical student in "Giving Bad News." I wonder if the real act of empathy I witnessed that day was performed by the woman who played the standardized patient; but *after* the scene had been played. Whether the care with which she led the student to see the pain he was capable of causing is what moved both him and me. Perhaps, when it comes down to it, role-modeling is at least as valuable as role-playing.

Now late in my own medical career, I find that many of the young doctors with whom I interact already display the empathy I'd want them to emulate. Just the other day, I watched an intern, exhausted and harried, tenderly stroke a dying woman's hair. I felt my heart swell with an almost maternal pride.

I felt a similar pride when, three years after she first contacted me, I heard from the British medical student Rahmiya again. She'd decided to repeat a year of medical school. But her thinking had changed. "Medicine isn't a trade-off between communication skills and clinical knowledge, but rather a merging of the two," she wrote. "I still believe that I should take every opportunity to grow my knowledge base, but now I recognize this shouldn't be at the expense of appreciating the communication skills I've already developed."

Rahmiya confessed that she'd been hesitant to communicate with me again until she had, as she put it, "substantial news." Now she did: She'd graduated from medical school and had accepted a position at a hospital in London. She was a doctor.

Bury Me in Something Warm

Late one night at the end of January 2009, a few weeks after the stroke left her paralyzed on one side, my mother became short of breath and her home health aide, Anna, called 911. The community hospital in Boca Raton where her primary care doctor practiced and to which she'd been admitted in the past was full and so she was taken to another hospital two towns away. There, a chest x-ray showed pneumonia and, when her breathing became more labored, my mother was intubated and connected to a ventilator. Despite her heart disease, her cancer, her strokes, and her age, neither I nor my mother's doctors had ever discussed with her whether she would want such aggressive treatment. Only about a third of Americans have any kind of advance directive. My parents did. My mother's indicated simply that my brothers and I were to make medical decisions for her should she become incapacitated. We'd never had "the conversation." Even after my father's protracted final ICU stay, my mother didn't say to me, as many patients have after witnessing a family member die a slow death in the hospital, that she would never want this for herself. In consenting to the intubation over the phone I relied on one piece of data: the fact of my mother's optimism.

I flew in from Boston the morning after my mother was admitted to the ICU and rented a car that had audio GPS, a bit novel then. The GPS lady's voice sounded judgmental, as if she knew about my terrible sense of direction. The palm-lined parking lot at Boca Community Hospital had what seemed an excessive number of spots marked RESERVED FOR CLERGY, which made me smile. On the lobby wall was a giant bronze oak tree–shaped plaque honoring the hospital's donors. The most generous got branches, and then the honor (and the font of the donor's name) reduced successively in size from twig to leaf to fallen acorn. This, too, made me smile. Even before I reached the elevator, I was gathering amusing things to tell my mother.

The woman at the reception desk said I couldn't see her right away. She directed me to the ICU waiting room, where I sat for what seemed like a very long time on a vinyl couch the color of dirty Silly Putty. I wore a tan cotton sweater. Florida in January. Warm outside, cold inside. "It's an air-conditioned life," my mother always said. I had no smartphone. There was no TV. Why had I brought no books or magazines? I always purchased *O, the Oprah Magazine* in the airport for good luck before a flight. Still do. But then, I was empty-handed. I read and reread a copy of some geriatric publication, *Prevention*, I think. but I'm not sure. I wish I'd taken notes, recorded these small details. I would enroll in an MFA program in nonfiction writing a year later, but, perhaps because my mother had been sick for so long by this point, I had no sense just then that anything worth writing about was taking place. At the end of *Patrimony*, his memoir about his father's death from a brain tumor, Philip Roth recalls a dream in which his dead father scolds him for burying him in a shroud. "I should have been buried in a suit," his dream father says. "You did the wrong thing." Then Roth writes:

> In the morning I realized he had been alluding to this book which, in the unseemliness of my profession, I had been writing all through his illness and dying.

I just reread this passage to make the point that Roth was taking notes at his father's deathbed, and that I wish I'd done the same at my mother's. Except, Roth didn't say he was taking notes. He said he was *writing*. The rich detail that makes *Patrimony* such a wonderful memoir may not, in fact, have had anything to do with taking notes, but with memory. The last line of the book, which I do not have to look up, is: "You must not forget anything."

I have forgotten some of what happened next, but I remember enough.

The visiting hours in the ICU were very rigid. Grim hordes of family members gathered three times a day in front of the automatic doors and were shooed out again three times a day an hour later unless a patient was about to die. Looking for my mother's room I felt the same apprehension she used to describe feeling during her many visits to my father in various hospitals for various ailments over the years: "You can't get there fast enough," she used to say, "and you can't get there slow enough." You approach the room not knowing whether you're about to be relieved or punched in the gut.

As a professional courtesy, my mother's physician made an exception for me, and I wandered in and out as I pleased. Dr. Alderman was about my age, and somewhat oddly proportioned, with a compact body, tiny hands, and a large, handsome head. He wore plaid shirts with short sleeves that accentuated the childlike dimensions of his upper extremities. I might have developed a little crush on him.

Anna and I took turns at my mother's bedside. Time, or my memory of time, became formless, punctuated only by a handful of small events.

Once, as we were exchanging places, Anna told me that she'd heard of a little restaurant, a stand, really, in Fort Lauderdale that had authentic Jamaican food, and I sent her there with some cash. She returned three hours later with a cold, sodden mess of turmeric-stained chicken and rice in a Styrofoam box.

Once, Anna pulled tweezers out of her purse, bent over the hospital bed rail, and attacked the white hairs gathering on my mother's chin which the bright lights of the ICU had mercilessly revealed. "Your mother won't ever forgive me if I don't clean her up," Anna said.

Once, Hillary Clinton, who'd lost the Democratic presidential nomination to Barack Obama, appeared on the soundless, wall-mounted television, and I told Anna it was too bad my mother had been denied the pleasure of seeing a woman become president.

Once, Anna told me that she and my mother had entertained themselves at the Boca house by googling my mother's old boy-friends. "We told each other secrets," Anna said. "We laughed like girls." I resisted the powerful urge to ask: *Tell me. Tell me my mother's secrets.*

After my mother had been in the hospital nearly a week, Dr. Alderman informed me that he had good news: her chest x-ray had cleared and she'd begun breathing on her own. He'd ordered her tube pulled out and the ventilator turned off. But there was bad news, too: my mother hadn't woken up. A CAT scan of her brain showed no new strokes, no bleeding, no explanation for why her eyes remained closed. Her unresponsiveness seemed, I could not help but feel, like some kind of protest.

In the days that followed, my mother remained unconscious and I became desperate for Dr. Alderman to know her as someone other than a body lying in an ICU bed. During his brief twice-a-day visits I told him about her late-in-life legal career, about my parents' travels and their art collection. I've thought about why it felt so important to me to tell him these things. Was I trying to impress him? To make sure he knew my mother wasn't your typical Boca yenta (which she would have hated)? Or was I making sure he knew who she was, or had once been, so that he would care more about her and try harder to save her? Perhaps I was simply flirting with him.

It occurs to me now that my impulse may have had less to do with my mother than with me. From the earliest days of my medical career I'd held a deep, intuitive feeling, almost a sympathetic pain for patients whose illnesses made them unrecognizable, sometimes even to themselves. Perhaps because I'd experienced my own identity as fragile, my old fear of not having a handwriting, I saw myself in these patients.

When I was taking pre-med courses after graduating from college, I worked part-time as an assistant in the lab of an oncologist and often accompanied him on his hospital rounds. The cancer wards were hot and steamy. Or I may have had that impression because we had to wear surgical masks since so many of the patients were immunosuppressed. I felt claustrophobic, my face trapped in my own moist breath.

Joseph was one of the patients. He was about forty, and bald and pale from chemotherapy. Joseph had an Italian last name and a New Jersey accent. I learned that he was a dermatologist who'd come to Johns Hopkins for a bone-marrow transplant, in the 1980s a relatively new procedure. On the ledge by his unopenable window sat photos of Joseph with a full head of dark curly hair: in his doctor's white coat, standing at a podium giving a lecture; and another in which he was grinning in a tuxedo, his arm around his wife who wore a sparkly evening gown.

One morning on rounds, I read, upside down and surreptitiously, a handwritten letter Joseph had received from a friend, or maybe a medical colleague. The letter lay on his bedside table. It said:

We are all so shocked by what has happened to you.

I don't remember physics or chemistry or anything about the oncology research in which I assisted. But I remember Joseph, the dermatologist from New Jersey. I remember the photo of him in a tuxedo, the letter that expressed, tactlessly but honestly, what Joseph himself must have felt. *So shocked.*

◆ ◆ ◆

After several more days my mother remained comatose and Dr. Alderman suggested that it might be time to consider hospice. As parents age, daughters often assume responsibility for their care-giving as sons recede guiltily and unhelpfully into the background, but this was not how it was with our family. During my father's final years, I'd overseen his medical care and communicated with his doctors, my brothers had handled financial and logistical matters, and all three of us along with our spouses had taken turns keeping vigil at his bedside. Now that my mother was nearing the end of her life, we repeated this pattern. My husband and my brother from the West Coast had been present when my father died and it appeared that this time I would be "it" in our morbid game of musical chairs. I sat outside the hospital on a bench in the sun, talking over the decision about moving my mother to a hospice with my brothers on the phone. As we spoke, I surveyed the hibiscus and impatiens bursting with color around a large fountain spraying luxuriantly in the manicured hospital lawn. Much of that part of south Florida looks like a golf course, and my memories of both of my parents' deaths are fixed amid carefully landscaped vitality.

A silent, slow-moving ambulance carried my mother from the ICU to a nearby hospice on a hot day in early February. I followed in my rental car guided by the bossy GPS lady. The hospice, just a few miles away, was the opposite of the ICU in every way: quiet and dimly lit. No rules. No visiting hours. Families dropped in and out, day and night. Why not?

My mother's room had sliding doors that opened onto a terrace whose rails were threaded with dark-purple bougainvillea that had no scent. I wheeled her bed out there, moving it every hour or so to keep one step ahead of the direct sun. The man on the adjacent terrace looked like he might have been in his thirties, but pallor and wasting had given him the ageless look of the dying. He smoked incessantly and his smoke drifted our way, but I didn't have the heart to object.

I suppose I could get the records and find out exactly how many days I sat there with my mother, who lay mute with her eyes closed; not asleep or even in a coma but in some state for which there is no medical term, a state uniquely her own. Whatever the records revealed, though, I would be surprised, because the suspended state my mother had entered engulfed me as well. It might have been one day; it might have been ten. When it came, her death would be a mystery, but not a mystery anyone felt compelled to solve. As I review the medical histories of both of my parents I'm struck by how much of what happened to them as they aged and declined was unexplainable and untreatable, as if a strong undertow, pulling them toward death, ran beneath all our—my—frantic efforts. Beneath the ambulance rides and the antidepressants and the chemo and the home health aides there ran a current unopposed in the opposite direction, a direction in which, ultimately, they wanted to go.

On Friday afternoon, February 13, a volunteer came by with a tray of sliced challah and miniature plastic cups filled with grape juice. I dotted my mother's lips with the juice. Her mouth opened slightly and her tongue received the tiniest amount of purple liquid. I imagined that she smiled as I recited the kiddush, the blessing over the Sabbath wine.

The next evening, I wandered around a mall during my dinner break. At J.Crew I bought a cardigan in a bright shade of pink unflattering to me. But I recalled that my mother, when she'd visited my father during his many hospitalizations, always wore bright colors, no matter the season. It was her job then and my job now to bring cheer. In front of a kiosk in the mall, unsold heart-shaped Mylar valentine balloons that had lost most of their helium bobbed weakly, their strings slack on the floor. Not then, but later—years later—I would note the coincidence: the flaccid heart-shaped balloons, my mother's flaccid heart.

On the way back to the hospice I stopped at a deli and bought myself a chef's salad topped with thick slices of ham and cheese and quartered hard-boiled eggs. Russian dressing, my mother's favorite. I had not yet inferred any risk to my own arteries from my mother's. When I arrived at seven thirty Anna and a nurse I hadn't met yet, a squat frosted blonde, were rearranging my mother's bedding. Nothing in their demeanor as they chatted signaled anything amiss. But as I approached the bed, I could see that my mother's breathing had changed. It had become slower and deeper—"agonal" is the medical term—and her breath had taken on a heavy, animal smell. With each inspiration her whole body seemed to retract into the mattress and with each breath out her whole body seemed to rise from the bed. "So, this is it?" I asked myself aloud, setting down the plastic bag containing my salad. Anna's face froze mid-smile.

I sat on the left side of my mother's bed and put my arms around her. As a very young child I used to wake up early, run down the hall from my room to my parents,' and crawl into my mother's side of my parents' bed. Nestled next to my mother, our cheeks pressed together, I would time my breath with hers to avoid drawing in her sour exhalations. I did the same now, breathing more and more slowly to stay in synch with my mother's dwindling pace. Every few seconds I would draw back to look at her. I told myself I needed to memorize my mother's body, to scan it one last time. I surveyed her auburn hair and white roots. She'd been in the hospital for a month without a trip to the beauty parlor (she never called it a "salon"). I opened her eyes gently with my fingers to examine their unusual hazel color. I pulled up the sheet and uncovered her homely bun-ioned and manicured feet. I smiled to think that her Morton's toe was slung over its neighbor like a sloppy drunk. I thought about writing in an essay: *Her toe slung over its neighbor like a sloppy drunk.*

I knew my mother would have detested the blond night nurse who moved so slowly, grudgingly, even. "Send me a peppy one," she'd said when she called the agency that had sent Anna. I couldn't let my mother die on her watch. "Please. Leave. Thank you," I told the nurse in a voice somehow both firm and frantic. I sounded exactly like my mother, who, at that moment, stopped breathing.

◆ ◆ ◆

Soon I would commiserate with other middle-aged orphans. The condolence notes I received all mentioned how hard it is to lose a mother, "no matter how old you are" and I started using that line in condolence notes myself. But the truth was that, as soon as my mother died, I had a light and hopeful feeling, as if I were at the very beginning of something, even if that something was my own old age. In fact, I was at the beginning of more than just old age, though I didn't know that then. In a year I would start an MFA program in nonfiction and begin writing professionally as well as incorporating literature into my medical work. I was, when my mother died, on the verge of becoming a person she would never know.

In her memoir, *Hold Still*, photographer Sally Mann writes:

> This postmortem readjustment is one that many of us have had to make when our parents die. The parental door against which we have spent a lifetime pushing finally gives way, and we lurch forward, unprepared and disbelieving, into the rest of our lives.

I love the image of the parental door giving way and, indeed, when my parents died any residual anger or ambivalence I'd felt toward them when they were alive did seem to dissipate. But the image that came to me in the days after my mother's death was not of a door but of a book, long and messily labored over, that had finally been written. A book bound by front and back covers, complex but complete, meant to be read and reread, like James Joyce's *Ulysses*, which my father tackled annually and a battered cloth-bound copy of which he kept by his bedside, held together with rubber bands.

Anna and I left the room and I called my brothers and my husband. The blond nurse summoned us back a few minutes later to see my mother, neatly tucked under fresh sheets, hair combed, tiny and sweet as a sleeping child. I didn't linger, because I no longer felt her there. Besides, I had to rush back to my mother's house to gather her clothes, per her written request. She'd recorded some years earlier, on a yellow legal pad and in the same handwriting I knew from so many to-do lists and menu plans and report-card signatures, instructions in the event of her death. She'd designated who would get the clock made by my father's grandfather, the clockmaker; the buddhas and the Picasso lithograph and the Majorca pearls. At the end, she'd written: *Bury me in something warm, maybe my black and white St. John suit.*

That made me smile. So *her.*

At the bottom of the page she'd declared: *I have to stop now. This is getting too emotional.* The first time I read this, years before her death, when my mother first showed it to me, I was annoyed. I felt that the emotion wasn't real. That even in this somber document she was performing. Now I know that that my mother's need to announce her emotion in a way that had seemed to me artificial was genuine, that the need was part of the emotion itself. That, yet again, I had misdiagnosed my mother's heart.

22

Extension

Ten days after my mother died, I led the second session of "Literature and Medicine: Humanities at the Heart of Healthcare." I'd agreed to lead the new program at Mass General months earlier, when my mother had recovered most of the memory she'd lost after her first stroke and had seemed medically stable. "Lit Med," sponsored by a nonprofit devoted to bringing the humanities into workplaces, provided modest funding for a facilitator and food so that members of the hospital staff could meet once a month to discuss works of literature over dinner. We gathered at the hospital in a fluorescent-lit conference room and dined, usually on pizza catered by the hospital cafeteria. From the first meeting I noticed that despite the harsh lights, uncomfortable chairs, and less-than-sumptuous fare, the nurses, doctors, administrators, and other healthcare workers who participated seemed relaxed and expansive, as if the horizons of our professional lives had broadened, even if only for two hours. Each month we'd discuss novels, short stories, plays, essays, and poems related in some way to a medically relevant theme that, like the readings, I would choose. The inaugural session, in January, had been devoted to "The Patient's Experience."

We analyzed Audre Lorde's *The Cancer Journals*; "In Bed," Joan Didion's essay about her migraines; and Anatole Broyard's *Intoxicated by My Illness*. For the February meeting, held three days after my mother's funeral, the theme I'd selected weeks in advance was "Patients' Families and Friends: Advocates, Witnesses, and Secondary Sufferers."

I remember nothing about this session. Still, I'm quite certain that the texts we spoke about that night, Jonathan Franzen's essay about his father's Alzheimer's disease ("My Father's Brain") and Amy Hempel's short story about two friends, one of whom is dying of cancer ("In the Cemetery Where Al Jolson Is Buried") were salves for my fresh grief. I'm also sure that I would have shared the news of my mother's death with the group and that others would have shared their own and their patients' stories of loss and that we would have reflected on how the readings mirrored and illuminated these experiences and that these conversations made each of us feel less alone. I know this must have happened that night in February 2009 because Lit Med has been meeting regularly ever since then and month after month, year after year, this is more or less what happens.

The chief of Mass General's division of internal medicine, my boss, had first suggested I lead Lit Med when we'd met for my annual career conference. These conferences are required and are usually pro forma—a review of professional goals, promotion status, and so forth. But this time my updates were more personal. I told the chief about the master's degree I'd just completed in literature and creative writing at Harvard Extension School, the university's continuing education program, and about how I hoped to earn an MFA degree in nonfiction writing one day. I also recounted the previous decade during which my son had epilepsy and underwent several operations; my father died after years of chronic illnesses; and my mother suffered a heart attack and then a stroke. I think he sensed, correctly, that I needed something. He told me about the new literature and medicine group and asked me whether I thought my master's degree might qualify me to facilitate it.

I hadn't anticipated that this degree would lead to anything—indeed I was informed by my professors at Extension that the degree wasn't "terminal," a word I'd never heard before in this context but which I inferred meant something different in academia than it does in medicine. A terminal degree allows a graduate to teach at the college level, which I had no interest in doing. From 2001 to 2008 I took one course per semester, at great expense and considerable inconvenience, but I wasn't really sure why I was doing it. I knew I wasn't taking these courses purely for enjoyment or to keep my mind agile, as many students in adult-education classes do. I had no idea why I felt compelled to stay up late at night after work writing papers about the Victorian novel and Greek tragedy and nineteenth-century American intellectual history, plus churning out short stories for workshops in fiction-writing, for which I had little aptitude. My husband still teases me about a particularly inauspicious effort featuring a young woman named Melissa who is befriended by a Hasidic woman while shopping for a wig before undergoing chemotherapy and who becomes enamored of observant Judaism. When, two years after completing my masters, I finally did enroll in an MFA program, I showed him my essays and he joked: "Where's Melissa? Bring back Melissa!"

It only occurs to me now that rushing out of work in order to find a parking space in Harvard Square, grab dinner, and take my seat in a lecture hall or seminar room felt not dissimilar to how I'd felt racing from work to my therapist's office, which, like the Extension School, happened to be in Cambridge. It also just occurs to me now that I'd started taking courses at Extension barely a year after ending therapy.

◆ ◆ ◆

When my husband was an intern one of his fellow interns became more and more unhappy as the year progressed. By spring his disaffection was so great he started reading a novel during morning rounds. He'd lean against the wall of the hospital ward as patients' cases were being presented and slowly turn the pages. The novel he read was *Of Human Bondage* by Somerset Maugham. We actually discussed that novel a few years ago in Lit Med. It concerns a young man who aspires to be an artist but has no talent and so he decides to become a doctor. After a passionate but disastrous relationship with a manipulative woman derails his medical education he ends up as a salesman in a department store. I'm not sure which aspect of this story appealed to the unhappy intern: the hero's torrid affair, his escape from medicine, or the aptness of the book's title to what the intern perceived as his own situation. But I am sure of this: the intern knew that reading fiction on rounds was a subversive act, an unmistakable way of signaling his displeasure.

This wouldn't be true anymore, not really. Interns may not read 700-page novels on rounds, but a short poem is not infrequently shared and medical humanities and narrative medicine programs have sprung up at many American medical schools and hospitals. But twenty years ago, when I started taking literature and writing courses at Extension, I, like the unhappy intern, felt rebellious, as if I were getting away with something. I thought I should be spending any free time I had caring for my patients—not to mention my own family—and not rushing to lectures about Aeschylus. Chekhov, a practicing doctor during his short but prolific career as a playwright and master of short fiction, famously said that medicine was his wife and literature was his mistress. In a different use of the same analogy to a similar end Osler advised: "Live a simple and a temperate life, that you may give all your powers to your profession. Medicine is a jealous mistress." Just as when I'd left work to go to therapy, I never crossed the Charles River from Boston to Cambridge on my way to Extension without feeling that I was sneaking away.

Adding to this furtive feeling was an odd thought I had as I made my way from my car to Harvard Yard to my classroom: that, possibly, I might be mistaken for a student. Maybe not an undergraduate, but a graduate student. I was in my forties during those years, fifty-one when I finished, so this seems unlikely. Still, with my black-and-white checked Gap backpack and bright-blue Kleen Kanteen water bottle I felt somehow that I was passing.

◆ ◆ ◆

I was also, I understand now, healing. My relationship with reading had long been uneasy and fraught with shame.

I read on my own for the first time at about age six—not precocious. While playing at a neighbor's house I picked up a picture book in which the sentence "THE DOG SAYS WOOF!" appeared in large black letters on a white page. I read this aloud as "THE DOG SAYS WOLF!," knowing "wolf" wasn't quite right, but still pleased with myself for having performed the magic of transforming letters into words, silence into sound.

I became a competent enough reader, according to the color-coded tests administered in the 1960s by the New York City public school system and progressed from level turquoise to level silver along with the other kids in "IGC," the class for intelligently gifted children—that is, white and mostly Jewish. This designation was part of the school system's unofficial segregation, even after busing. In seventh grade, my parents sent me to an all-girls' private school, a fusty institution housed in a gothic hulk of a building where we sang Protestant hymns each morning and wore one-piece outfits for gym as if we were Gibson girls escaped from a rotogravure print. By ninth grade, protest anthems had replaced the hymns, and we'd traded the gym suits for tie-dyed T-shirts. My classmates and I started meeting after school for what we called "consciousness-raising" during which we mostly complained about our mothers. But when I arrived in the fall of 1969 I felt, for the first time in my life, like an outsider. Many of the girls at my new school were blond and slender. I learned there to my surprise, at the age of twelve, that Jews constituted a tiny minority of the world's population when I saw the blue specks marking Israel, New York, Miami, and Los Angeles on a map of the world's religions in *Junior Scholastic* magazine.

I responded to the insecurities brought on by a new school (and puberty) by retreating into reading, as many kids do. But the reading into which I retreated was somewhat of an act. I mostly *pretended* to read. In my bedroom I cleared off a shelf that I'd previously devoted to the dolls my parents had brought me from the airports of the many countries they'd visited during summer trips while my brothers and I went to camp and I began accumulating books, several borrowed from my father's collection. Each day I'd bring one to school and during study period hold it stiffly, with both hands, so that the bottom of its spine rested on my desk and everyone could see the cover. It was an odd assortment, those books I fake-read: Norman Mailer's *The Naked and the Dead* (I had high hopes, unfulfilled, for "naked"); *The Selling of the American President*, whose jacket featured Richard Nixon's scowling face emblazoned on a pack of cigarettes; *The Call of the Wild* by Jack London.

What I actually read, *all* I actually read, were a trio of predictable adolescent favorites, *To Kill a Mockingbird*, *Catcher in the Rye*, and *A Tree Grows in Brooklyn*, over and over again in rotation, plus whatever I purloined from my mother's stash: *Rosemary's Baby*, *Diary of a Mad Housewife*, and *Everything You Always Wanted to Know About Sex** (*But Were Afraid to Ask*).

In high school and then in college, I became not so much a reader as a student of literature. I saw poetry and fiction as puzzles to be solved, assignments to be completed. My paper-writing technique was to find a theme, flip through the text to gather quotes related to that theme, and then stick them together with the thin mortar of my own prose:

"Eyes in *The Great Gatsby*" by Suzanne Koven.

Once, when I was in high school, a family friend asked me at one of my parents' dinner parties what I planned to be when I grew up. To the laughter of all assembled I announced that I was still deciding whether to go into practice with my father the doctor or with my mother the lawyer. This was funnier back when fewer women were professionals. The punch line to a riddle popular then was that a surgeon couldn't operate on an injured child because the surgeon was the child's *mother.* I'd said what I said mostly to entertain. But there was some truth in it too. Though I knew my parents were happily married, as a child and teenager I ruminated about what they didn't have in common, and about whether, regarding a variety of traits, I resembled one more than the other. As a reader, for example.

Years after his death, when I picture my father, I picture him with a book. He sat in a worn red velour chair in my parents' bedroom, a large man in a starched dress shirt, boxer shorts, and black Ban-Lon socks, a powder-blue mohair blanket thrown across his white and nearly hairless legs, smoking a cigarette and reading. When ash fell on the blanket and singed its fibers he reached down and pinched out the flame without taking his eyes off the page.

My father loved words, the very sound of them. Though his accent was generally Brooklyn, he pronounced sexual in the British manner: *sex-sual.* He also liked "scotch broom," "Mercedes-Benz," "greenstick fracture," and any number of other names and phrases that he snuck gratuitously into his sentences for the mere enjoyment of saying them aloud. When my Aunt Paula was diagnosed with leukemia, my father informed me that it was of the rare hairy cell variety. I'm not sure that this was the precise diagnosis, but quite certain my father would have been unable to resist the pleasure of repeating that luscious term.

My father read what I thought of as men's books and periodicals: nineteenth-century travel journals; Henry Miller, Saul Bellow, and Donald Barthelme; *Art Forum* and the *Journal of Bone and Joint Surgery*; catalogs of rare volumes he bought at auction houses; and, his favorite, *Ulysses*. The only book by a female author I remember seeing on my father's shelves was one that I suspected he never read but whose provocative cover I think he must have liked to display, the title in large letters: *Sexual Politics* by Kate Millett. *Sex-sual.*

My mother was not a reader, or at least not in the same way that my father was. She loved to tell this story: when she and my father had been married a year, she asked him whether he had been in any way disappointed by his bride. "Darling," he answered, "marriage to you has been heaven, except for one thing: I wish you would read better books." This was my mother's embellished version; though my father adored her he never called her "darling" and he never called anything "heaven."

My mother's tastes, or perhaps her assessment of the limits of her reading ability, ran to bestsellers rented from the stationery store on Flatbush Avenue for a nickel a day, *McCall's* magazine, and the occasional how-to. When I was no more than ten, I teased my mother that I was reading her copy of psychologist Haim Ginott's book, *Between Parent and Child*, just to keep one step ahead of her. In her later years my mother's literary horizons, like many women's, were expanded by Oprah. She devoured Janet Fitch and Barbara Kingsolver, Ursula Hegi and Wally Lamb. She announced with a new clarity that she liked novels "about relationships." She joined a book club in which many of the women were several years younger than she was, and she counted her meetings with them—talking about relationships and about books about relationships—as some of her happiest hours, involving her most intimate and unguarded conversations with anyone other than my father and, I hoped, me. "As you get older you need to make younger friends" became one the many set pieces of advice my mother often repeated to me, which I found annoying, but which happened to have been true.

In addition to Oprah's picks my mother started going in for self-help. Stacked on her night table were *The Inner Game of Tennis* and several bridge strategy guides, plus cookbooks featuring low-calorie recipes. Other books that a casual observer might not have identified as self-help but which I recognized also fell into this category often appeared at my mother's bedside, including a collection of opera libretto synopses and several volumes on home landscape design. Tennis, weight, bridge, and gardening were among the many areas in which my mother deemed herself perennially in need of improvement.

Occasionally, a work of serious literature would find its way to the pile. Late one evening I found my mother, then in her seventies, in her nightgown and robe, with a cup of tea and a book, at the dining table in Boca Raton. My parents had bought a place in the '90s and had started spending longer and longer stretches of the winter there in retirement. She held a collection of essays by Elizabeth Hardwick upright, at an unnatural distance, as if she didn't quite know what to do with it. When I asked why she was reading this particular book my mother mentioned that a friend of hers whose intellect she admired had recommended it.

When I came home from college and flaunted my supposed love of Dickens or Woolf to my mother, she frowned and said she didn't like books with "lots of description," which I interpreted as her acknowledgment that I now inhabited a world that excluded her, a world of readers like my father and me. Even when I was a child my mother had seemed reluctant to engage me about books. Once, when I was eight or nine, I told her how much I'd enjoyed *Stuart Little*—one of the few books I read voluntarily in elementary school—and she made an unpleasant face and told me that she found the idea of a woman giving birth to a mouse repulsive.

My feigned childhood passion for books didn't impress my father or, more likely, he didn't notice it. For him, reading was solitary. My mother, on the other hand, seemed delighted to believe that I shared my father's love of reading. More than once she stood at the door of my bedroom and, finding me in bed with a book, exclaimed, "How lucky you are to be a reader!" Then she'd wave her hand to take in the light-blue walls and matching shag carpeting I'd picked out myself and say, "This room is a blue lagoon!" stretching the last syllable as far as it could go. She, too, took pleasure in words but it was a different pleasure than my father's. Hers was the storyteller's pleasure: not in the words themselves but in wrapping up life in them and presenting it, brightened and enhanced, to someone else. "You're floating in a blue la-*goooon!*"

Like my mother, I'm a storyteller. For a long time I resisted admitting this to myself because I'd rather have inherited my father's bookish self-containment. Perhaps it seemed conceited to me—even greedy—to imagine that I could possess what I saw as the most enviable qualities of each of my parents: my father's intellect and my mother's charm. As my future husband, a prodigious reader himself, and I sat down at the small butcher-block table that was one of the few pieces of furniture in our first apartment, I often began conversations by announcing: "The most interesting thing happened to me today!" He would respond, amused, that he often went *weeks* without anything interesting happening to him.

One afternoon a year or so after her heart attack, my mother was in the hospital again, this time with an infarcted spleen, a painful complication of her chronic leukemia. As I sat by my mother's bed and watched her sleep. I felt I couldn't bear her sickness, the hopelessness of her situation, her futile pinballing from one medical calamity to the next, a minute longer. I needed to bring something *not* sick into the dim, lifeless room. I reached into my bag for the current issue of the *New Yorker* and I asked my mother if she'd like me to read her an article. She half-nodded, her eyes closed.

I read in an animated, theatrical voice, an essay by Nora Ephron. Ephron reminded me a bit of my mother: something about her hair, her self-effacing humor, and her cashmere turtlenecks—or maybe she reminded me of how my mother might have been if she'd been born a few years later, a little more self-confident, a little less concerned with conventional appearances. In the essay, Ephron writes about moving from the Upper West Side apartment in which she lived for many years because the building was going condo. She riffs back and forth between her own story and the history of the city's housing market—a typical *New Yorker* piece: personal narrative/space break/reporting/space break/repeat.

The essay was long and I was certain my mother had fallen asleep. but I kept reading. When I reached the end I asked her, as I'd ask my Lit Med group about various works of literature starting a couple of years later, "Why do you think this essay works?" I expected no answer. My mother was taking strong pain medication and it seemed unlikely that she'd been able to follow what I'd read to her, even if she had been awake. But she surprised me. She opened her eyes, turned her pale face toward me and said: "I'll tell you why it works. Because it has stuff in it. It's not just all about *her*." To this day, years later, I blanch at what feels like criticism—I write more about myself than about *stuff*, after all—and yet, part of me knows, knew even then, that my mother was just passing along a truth, sharing a tip, one storyteller to another.

When I'd decided to go to medical school, my relationship with reading changed in an unexpected way. I believed, at that stage in my life, that one had to choose to be one type of person or another. I'd chosen to be the type of person who becomes a doctor, not the type of person who reads—an odd conclusion, in retrospect, given my father's profession and his literary proclivities. Perhaps I believed that only men had the luxury of being more than one thing. I now think I may have misconstrued the intended lesson of another story that my mother often repeated to me: When she entered high school, her father told her that she could either earn A's or have a social life, not both. She'd opted for the latter—lots of boyfriends and lots of B's. But, she told me, she'd always regretted it. When I was young, I thought my mother meant that she wished she'd chosen to stay home and study harder. Now I think she meant that she wished she'd ignored her father's advice altogether and just done everything she wanted to do. In any case, once I made up my mind to become a doctor and was thus freed of thinking of myself as a reader, I started to read. I plowed through several novels during the hours I sat between classes at a Roy Rogers franchise in the student center of the university where I completed my pre-med requirements.

◆ ◆ ◆

I see now, that even though I hoped to be mistaken for an under-graduate in Harvard Yard, at least part of the reason I enrolled in Extension was to prepare for my old age, just as my mother had found solace in her Connecticut book club as the losses of her later years accumulated. The most moving moment of my time at Extension occurred when Charles Segal, a recently retired Har-vard professor of classics who taught my Greek Tragedy course, spoke about how the Oedipus trilogy reminded him of Erik Erik-son's three stages of development. In youth, Professor Segal said, a person struggles to figure out who they are in relation to their parents (a real head scratcher in Oedipus's case). In middle age a person establishes their place in the community. And in the final stage—here the professor's voice cracked a bit—a person struggles against despair to remain creative.

In Sacvan Bercovitch's Jewish Modernism course I wrote a paper about how the story of the binding of Isaac, the *Akedah*, contained all the basic elements of Jewish humor: the deflation of authority, the self-aggrandizement, the *shlepping*. In that course I also wrote a paper comparing Kafka's *Metamorphosis* and *Portnoy's*

Complaint. I pointed out the echoes in Portnoy's chronic masturba-
tion of Gregor-as-insect's sticky effluvia. "Saki" and I kept in touch
after the course. We met occasionally for lunch in Harvard Square.
We traded Jewish jokes, he read sections of the memoir I wrote
about my father for my master's thesis, and he confided in me about
his medical conditions. I visited him at his home a week before he
died. He lay in a hospital bed in his living room, surrounded by
books. We drank tea and laughed as December darkness fell early
and hard and though saddened by the imminent loss of my friend, I
felt thoroughly comfortable, thoroughly myself.

Here is something very painful to recall: I neglected to tell my
husband the date and time of my graduation from Extension. When
I finally told him the details at the very last minute, he couldn't miss
work to attend. I said that there was really no need for him to be
there, that it was only Extension, that the degree meant nothing
to me. I wore my cap and gown and was called up to the stage to
receive the award for best student—I'd received A's in every course
I took during those eight years—and attended the buffet lunch—in
wonderfully arcane Harvard fashion, called "the spread"—without
him. I would have spent my graduation day alone entirely if my
daughter, then in college nearby, hadn't insisted at the last minute
that she skip class and be my "plus one." If I couldn't acknowledge
to myself how strange it was that I was going to my graduation
alone, then she would acknowledge it for me

Why did I engineer that day to make it impossible for my husband to come to the graduation? I think I simply felt too exposed.
I feared that I had finally, *finally* come closer to being fully myself
and that the person who knew me best would tell me that, no, I was

mistaken: that this was merely another fad, another phase, another fake. Of course, he wouldn't have. I was very unfair to him. My graduation, and other incidents like it, when I shut my husband out because I couldn't bear to be seen and possibly found deficient are the greatest regrets of my life.

◆ ◆ ◆

Lit Med, the first year I ran it, was a bit of a flop, I thought. Maybe, so soon after my mother's death, I was too exhausted and distracted to take on a new role, but that wasn't the only reason. As a facilitator I felt I was uncharacteristically stilted and the conversations I led were halting and awkward. The two hours did not fly; they limped. I think I was hamstrung by two things: first, I felt I needed to restrain my enthusiasm for the texts we read, which didn't do much for my effectiveness. I felt that the doctors and nurses who signed up for Lit Med wouldn't want to hear my thoughts about imagery and metaphor in a poem any more than I'd want to hear about their boats or their collections of rare coins. The other problem was that at first I believed that I needed to limit the selection of readings to texts strictly related to medicine. The list of really good poems, short stories, essays, and novels about illness is fairly short—as Virginia Woolf notes in this single remarkable sentence with which she begins her essay "On Being Ill":

> Considering how common illness is, how tremendous the spiritual
> change that it brings, how astonishing, when the lights of health
> go down, the undiscovered countries that are then disclosed, what

wastes and deserts of the soul a slight attack of influenza brings to view, what precipices and lawns sprinkled with bright flowers a little rise of temperature reveals, what ancient and obdurate oaks are uprooted in us by the act of sickness, how we go down in the pit of death and feel the waters of annihilation close above our heads and wake thinking to find ourselves in the presence of the angels and the harpers when we have a tooth out and come to the surface in the dentist's arm-chair and confuse his "Rinse the mouth-rinse the mouth" with the greeting of the Deity stooping from the floor of Heaven to welcome us—when we think of this, as we are so frequently forced to think of it, it becomes strange indeed that illness has not taken its place with love and battle and jealousy among the prime themes of literature.

Between those two self-imposed limitations I worried that the tone I struck was too apologetic, sheepish, even, as if I were trying to sell my colleagues a product I knew they didn't want or need.

Over the next few years, though, I found my bearings. I unabashedly assigned nonmedical readings, Shakespeare and Kafka and Yeats. Toni Morrison and James Baldwin and Kazuo Ishiguro and David Sedaris and Alice Munro. I waxed about narrative structure and diction and recurring themes with all my English major's heart. And the doctors and the nurses and the administrators *talked*. On survey after survey they reported that reading and discussing works of literature had made them feel less stressed, more connected to their patients and to one another.

Narrative medicine, the term coined in 2000 by Rita Charon at Columbia, is based on the idea that by studying literature closely, improving our skills in identifying tone, subtle shifts of mood, themes, and recurring metaphors, we become better at diagnosing and treating our patients. In her classic 2004 essay, "Narrative and Medicine," Charon, a primary care doctor, describes meeting a thirty-six-year-old Dominican man with back pain for the first time. Rather than homing in right away on his "chief complaint," she asks him to tell his life story:

> I listen not only for the content of his narrative, but for its form— its temporal course, its images, its associated subplots, its silences, where he chooses to begin in telling of himself, how he sequences symptoms with other life events. I pay attention to the narrative's performance—the patient's gestures, expressions, body positions, tones of voice. After a few minutes, he stops talking and begins to weep. I ask him why he cries. He says, "No one has ever let me do this before."

Elsewhere Charon recommends asking patients to tell the story behind each scar on their bodies.

Charon has a PhD in English. She'd been a biology major in college, happened to pick up a copy of Henry James's *The Wings of the Dove* after she'd been practicing medicine a few years, read it in three days, and marched into the English Department at Columbia to ask if she could take a course. She intuited that something about James, about the way James was able "to expand every nanosecond to reveal, to expose what is inside . . ." as she put it in an interview, had everything to do with caring for patients.

Many of the "discoveries" I've made while leading Lit Med

have been things I now know Charon had previously figured out: that it's unnecessary and undesirable to limit our readings to medically related texts (she notes that when reading *Ivan Ilyich* doctors get bogged down arguing about whether the title character of Tolstoy's novella had gastric cancer or pancreatic cancer, missing the point entirely); that literature helps dismantle the "hidden curriculum," the teaching that our patients are somehow fundamentally different from us and we from them; that immersing ourselves in imaginary worlds populated by imaginary people and investing emotionally in their problems is excellent training for empathy.

Most important, Charon emphasizes how therapeutic it is for patients to be given permission to tell their stories in the manner and, most especially, at the pace they want to. I have experienced this myself. Once, after I'd been shuttled to various busy specialists, a doctor sat down, leaned back in his chair, turned away from his computer screen, and said, "So tell me the whole story from the beginning." Like the Dominican man with back pain I nearly wept with relief. I've since adopted this line and use it with my own patients: *Tell me the whole story from the beginning.* I've come to believe that there is no act more therapeutic than asking someone to share their story. Joan Didion observed, "We tell ourselves stories in order to live." I think she meant that literally. I see now that Albert Blake, the first patient I ever interviewed in medical school, the man with leukemia who agreed to tell his story over and over to so many students, did so not just to pass the time, but to survive.

Something I read in an interview President Barack Obama had with Michiko Kakutani, then chief book critic at the *New York Times*, a few days before leaving office in January 2017, comes closest to expressing what literature means to me in medicine. Obama said, regarding the novels he read while in the White House:

> It was important to pick up the occasional novel during the presidency, because most of my reading every day was briefing books and memos and proposals. And so working that very analytical side of the brain all the time sometimes meant you lost track of not just the poetry of fiction, but also the depth of fiction.
>
> Fiction was useful as a reminder of the truths under the surface of what we argue about every day and was a way of seeing and hearing the voices, the multitudes of this country.

For "briefing books and memos and proposals" substitute "x-ray reports and lab values and physical exam findings" and there you have it. I can think of so many times when reading helped me understand the story obscured beneath a series of facts in a way that not only made me see a patient, but also myself, in a more compassionate and incisive way.

Many years ago I had a patient who was a handsome and successful businessman in his forties. He wore expensive suits, professionally laundered shirts, gleaming Italian leather shoes, and cashmere socks. Yet, oddly, when he came in every year for his annual physical he didn't hang his clothes on the hook provided but, instead, piled them haphazardly on a chair, crumpling his pressed suit, starched shirt, and silk tie. On top of the pile always sat the last article of clothing he removed, his underwear. You might think such a man would wear good underwear: pima cotton boxers, perhaps. But this man wore Jockey shorts, and not new or clean ones either. Year after year I was treated to a full-on view of my patient's yellowed, holey, shit-stained drawers.

What was this about? I asked myself. And by that I meant—though I only came to understand this much later, long after he stopped coming to see me for reasons I never knew—not only, why would an affluent and well-dressed man wear old, dirty underwear, but why did the fact that he wore them fascinate me so much?

During the years I saw this man I developed a theory about him. Despite his success he always looked kind of depressed, and when I asked him what was troubling him he said that he and his wife weren't very compatible, had almost no sexual relationship, and disagreed about almost every aspect of childrearing. Plus, he hated his job. When I suggested individual or couples' counseling he shrugged and said there really was no point since he couldn't leave his job or his marriage and neither would ever change. His prominently displayed underwear, I concluded, were a plea for help. He repeatedly rebuffed my offer to refer him for counseling and even my questions about how he felt about his marriage and his work—but the soiled underwear seemed to say: *Don't stop asking.*

A few years after the patient stopped seeing me a novel we read in Lit Med added to my understanding of this man and of myself. The novel was *Disgrace*, by J. M. Coetzee. It concerns a middle-aged college professor who has an affair with one of his students. When the affair is found out he is publicly humiliated and his life unravels. He loses not only his job but his home. His adult daughter is raped, a violent mirroring of the professor's predation of his student.

As we discussed *Disgrace* we considered how large and unspoken the role of shame is in medicine. How even the most blameless patient, the victim of an accident or a random illness in no way related to anything that person did and in no way preventable by them, feels shame. How the ill and injured body is a disfigured body, the object of disgust and self-disgust, of shame. We'd discussed this concept, too, when we read Kafka's *Metamorphosis*.

The day after this session I received an email from a nurse practitioner in the group:

So just to follow up on our discussion last night on the theme of shame . . . I saw a single young professional woman this morning with a new anal lesion. She had researched online what can cause anal lesions and freaked out. She was embarrassed talking about it. Turned out to be a hemorrhoid. I felt more inclined to be patient and more empathetic with her as a result of our discussion on shame. It made me more aware of how shame can accompany patients to their visits with us. Had we not had that discussion last night I might not have been as sensitive to her feelings.

Retrospectively, I had a similar insight about the businessman with the underwear—that what he was displaying on the top of that pile of expensive clothing was his shame, his feelings of failure about his work and his marriage. I honestly think that if I'd had that discussion about *Disgrace* while I was caring for this patient I would have been a better doctor to him. I now realize that every time I suggested therapy—totally reasonably and appropriately, of course—I was compounding his shame. If I'd been more conscious of his shame, more "sensitive to [his] feelings," as the nurse practitioner put it, I'd have worked harder to understand why he felt that his unhappiness was his own fault, why he deserved to wear such awful underwear.

But there's more, another layer. And it has to do with my own shame. The truth is, I didn't enjoy seeing this patient. I found his glum affect depressing, his refusal of therapy frustrating, his dirty Jockey shorts gross. I was glad when he stopped coming to me. And now I wonder if I'd been primed, by reading *Disgrace*, to think more about the role of shame in our interaction—his, for his own reasons; mine for my inability to help him and for the fact that I wished I didn't have to see him—I would have resisted him less and enjoyed caring for him more.

◆ ◆ ◆

Reading has enhanced my medical practice in yet another way, one that doesn't specifically have to do with medicine, one that I experienced long before I ever saw my first patient, in fact. When I sat in the Roy Rogers between pre-med classes one of the novels I read was *Anna Karenina*. I found myself less drawn to the ill-fated Anna than to the plodding landowner, Levin. I particularly liked the passage where he joins laborers in scything a field. Levin is enjoying the work, he's in "the flow," as we now call it, until he starts thinking about what he's doing, and then his back begins to ache.

The longer Levin mowed, the oftener he felt the moments of unconsciousness in which it seemed not his hands that swung the scythe, but the scythe mowing of itself, a body full of life and consciousness of its own, and as though by magic, without thinking of it, the work turned out regular and well-finished of itself. These were the most blissful moments. It was only hard work when he had to break off the motion, which had become unconscious, and to think.

I didn't fully understand it at the time, but Tolstoy had articulated my own experience. When I thought too much, I lost the joy in whatever I was doing, whether working through chemistry problems, listening to records late at night with my husband, or, in fact, reading *Anna Karenina*. Tolstoy had more than articulated my experience; he had anticipated it, even shaped it. A novel had moved me.

I'm often asked how, *exactly*, reading poetry, fiction, and memoir benefits healthcare workers. In addition to the growing body of work by scholars of narrative medicine, there are countless articles in the lay media about how reading increases empathy, decreases burnout, or even makes you a nicer person. These may be true, but for me, reading—now that I am truly a reader—has a more profound effect: it effaces the boundaries between me and my colleagues, between me and my patients, and also between me and my many selves. When I'm doing it right, reading makes me feel whole, more fully human, able, even if only for a few moments, to scythe my field with joy.

23

Mixed Emotions

Not long ago I sent a form letter to four hundred of my patients, many of whom I've known for decades, to tell them I'm not going to be their doctor anymore.

I began the letter: "It is with mixed emotions . . ." I went on to explain that I was reducing the size of my practice to spend more time writing and teaching (not *retiring*—somehow this was important to me to emphasize). I'd seen the phrase "mixed emotions" in various colleagues' letters announcing their intention to downsize or retire or move to another hospital or another city, and it had struck me as a cliché but also honest.

For months a draft of the letter and a spreadsheet listing the names of all of my patients in alphabetical order sat on my computer desktop unopened. Finally I printed out the spreadsheet, found three highlighters—green for "keep," pink for "reassign," and yellow for "not sure"—and quit in frustration when I'd filled up a few pages with green and yellow. I'd settle on criteria for reassigning my patients to a younger doctor: anyone under forty, anyone I hadn't known more than a few years, anyone who didn't have many medical problems . . . But then I'd get stumped by all the exceptions.

Yes, this man was only thirty-five, but I'd taken care of his parents and grandparents. Yes, this woman had only been my patient for two years but she'd just been diagnosed with breast cancer. Yes, this woman was healthy but she had a deep distrust of doctors and it had taken years for her to feel comfortable with me. I needed to reassign four hundred patients to fit my new, reduced schedule, and I was barely able to identify ten I could part with.

My practice was already fairly small. I'd started working part-time over twenty years ago when my kids were little and I hadn't expanded my practice as they grew up. I always knew, somehow, that I wanted to limit the amount of time I spent caring for patients and spend the rest of my time doing something else. That something else turned out to be writing, mentoring other clinician-writers, leading Lit Med, and organizing literary events at my hospital. I'd acquired this additional career fairly late. Now it's not at all unusual for doctors to begin their careers knowing they want to do something in addition to practicing medicine. In fact, a dean at Harvard Medical School tells incoming students to begin thinking from the outset of their careers about what their "hyphen" will be: Physician-scientist? Physician-educator? Physician-advocate?

I, too, had been trained to aspire to hyphenhood and, in fact, had initially rejected this training when I decided that after my chief residency I would become a full-time primary care doctor. When I told a senior attending my plan he seemed disappointed and asked me—not entirely in jest, I think—whether I might consider completing an immunology research fellowship first.

My role models in those early days of my career were the infinitely available internists, mostly men but a couple of women, who would come over to the hospital early in the morning and late in the evening, before and after office hours in their private practices and on weekends to check on their patients. This was the kind of doctor my father had been. When I started working at Mass General my older colleague Marty, who'd been in practice for over twenty years, told me that the three most important qualities in a physician are: accessibility, accessibility, and accessibility. Now I was violating this ideal in the most extreme way. How much less accessible could I make myself than by telling my patients I would no longer be their doctor?

At first, I attributed my reluctance to reassign my patients to guilt—a familiar guilt. I'd experienced it years earlier when I decided, not two years into practice, that I couldn't manage full-time work plus a toddler and an infant. I couldn't follow the example of my father and of my other role models. I made this decision one winter day as I walked out of the office of the director of my medical group. He'd just told me that he'd been reviewing the numbers and that if I continued to be as productive—that is, see as many patients—as I'd been the previous month I would be a great asset to the practice. I *had* been productive the previous month. I'd also been miserable. I was exhausted, I had a constant cough from the viruses my kids acquired at daycare, and the knot in my stomach tightened as the day wore on and the time to pick them up approached. I was the only woman in my department then who had young children and worked full-time, so my decision was hardly trailblazing. My husband didn't have the option of working part-time, plus, as I then told people, I was better suited to being home with the kids than he was since I enjoyed finger painting and glitter glue more than he did—not *much* more, but more.

Almost immediately after I started working less, I felt better. I literally breathed easier. Still, I had a nagging fear that I wasn't doing right by my patients. This fear was validated one day when I'd been working part-time for about a year and went to visit a hospitalized patient of mine who was recuperating from surgery. She was an older woman who'd started seeing me a few months earlier after her previous physician, Dr. Wright, retired. My associate, another woman with young children who worked part-time, had seen the patient the previous day, on my day at home, and now I arrived to discuss her follow-up with me after discharge. "That won't be necessary," the woman informed me. She went on to say that she'd decided to find a new doctor, preferably an older man. "Someone more like Dr. Wright," she said.

I returned to my office distressed. Marty asked what was wrong and I told him the story. "Well," he said, "she's right." This was not the consolation I sought. "You don't offer what Dr. Wright did," he continued. "But then again, I'm sure you offer things Dr. Wright didn't."

I brushed off Marty's reassuring words, but then I remembered that there had been another patient I'd inherited from Dr. Wright, an elderly woman who, I learned after many visits, had suffered abuse as a child. I'd referred her to a therapist and, in her eighties, she was finally coming to terms with decades of pent-up pain. She told me that she'd complained for years to Dr. Wright about her depression and anxiety and he'd merely told her to "keep busy."

Still, I couldn't quite let go of my guilt. Every experience I had as a patient or as the parent or child of a patient reminded me of how attached patients and their families become to doctors. I thought about the times I'd waited for a doctor's phone call or sat by the hospital bedside of a family member whose doctor was supposed to come by "later today." I recalled occasions where I'd scrutinized a doctor's facial expression or casual comment for clues to my or my loved one's fate. And though as a doctor I congratulated myself for having achieved work-life balance, I knew this balance was fragile and hinged heavily on my shortchanging my patients. I was a very good doctor when I was with my patients but I was not accessible, accessible, accessible.

Gradually, the guilt subsided. I built a practice made up of patients who knew my schedule and accepted it. I trusted the doctors with whom I shared coverage. The development of encrypted electronic records allowed me to look up patients' medical information and call them from home when necessary. It wasn't perfect— at home or at the office—but I considered myself lucky to be able to forgo some income to have more time for Little League, Play-Doh, and even occasional solitude, as many working parents would if they could.

Having made peace with my decision to work part-time when my kids were small, I was surprised at the depth of my alarm a few years ago when I read an op-ed in the *New York Times* in which Karen S. Sibert, a full-time anesthesiologist and mother of four, asserted that women physicians who work part-time are betraying their patients, their full-time colleagues, and the taxpayers who partially subsidized their medical education.

Sibert pointed to the projected growing shortage of physicians in an aging America—a deficit of up to 150,000 in the next fifteen years, by one estimate—as a reason why women who receive medical degrees should commit to full-time work. She noted that since women are more likely than men to enter fields such as internal medicine, family medicine, pediatrics, and obstetrics-gynecology, in which the shortage of physicians is greatest, and are more likely to work in underserved communities, the loss of work hours when female physicians cut back is most sorely felt. An illustration accompanying Sibert's op-ed depicted a female physician wearing high heels and a stethoscope and pushing a vacuum cleaner, a veritable "Physician Barbie."

It is true that just over 50 percent of American medical students now are women and in some fields, such as pediatrics, women now make up at least three-quarters of all trainees. Clearly, under the current system, if in a few years most of these doctors are practicing part-time, that would worsen the shortage. In surgical specialties, an additional concern arises: surgeons who work part-time perform fewer operations and may not acquire and maintain their technical skills as reliably as if they worked full-time. There's a grain of truth in an old surgical joke: the problem with being on call every other night is that you only get to perform half as many operations.

But it's unfair to expect women to work full-time simply because they happen to be the ones who disproportionately choose to work in fields where there's a shortage of doctors. It's also unfair that women often feel they need to work part-time because they, on average, assume more responsibility for childcare and housekeeping than their male partners. Plus, it's a misconception that female doctors are most likely to want to work part-time. One of the fastest growing subsets of doctors reducing their work hours are older men. The endlessly available solo practitioner no longer exists and when he did, even he signed out to take in a round of golf now and then. The reality is, while patients may become ill at any time, *all* doctors work part-time. As one physician responded by letter to Dr. Sibert's editorial: "The degree is a doctorate in medicine, not an application for martyrdom."

Around the time the op-ed was published I happened to see my patient Irene, a particular favorite of mine, a warm and intelligent woman in her seventies. Years earlier she'd been diagnosed with lung cancer while I was on maternity leave. In my absence, one of my colleagues had given her the bad news about her biopsy and had visited her after surgery. Now I asked Irene whether it had bothered her that I wasn't available when she'd needed me most. Her answer surprised me. She said that she felt well cared for because I had provided her with "an excellent proxy," as she put it. In other words, my absence hadn't gone unnoticed, but neither had I failed her.

I still find it hard to reconcile my deep belief in the healing power of the relationship between a doctor and a patient with the reality that we doctors are easily replaced. As fond as Irene was of me, as much as she trusted me and relied on me, it was not so terrible for her that I wasn't there when she had lung cancer.

Nor, it turns out, is it so terrible for my patients who I finally, after months of fiddling around with those spreadsheets and highlighters, reassigned. Some wrote me kind notes, a few begged me to take them back, many wished me well and asked if their new doctor would have access to their records. All of them will be just fine.

But will I? Who will I be when I have fewer patients? When I have no patients at all? It's often noted that "practice" as it relates to medicine has two meanings: the act of caring for patients and the doctor's never-ending process of perfecting his or her craft. But there's a third meaning, too, one I'm only now appreciating as I contemplate the end of my career. Medicine is a practice in the way that yoga or meditation is for many people, an activity repeated so often that it becomes a kind of incantation. I have, for so long, stood to my patients' right sides as physicians have done for centuries; palpated the lymph nodes in their necks, armpits, and groins; auscultated their hearts and lungs; asked the same questions I first learned to ask nearly forty years ago—*What makes the pain better? What makes it worse?* These rituals are for me an anchor without which I fear I might simply drift away. Of course I suspected all along that what I feared wasn't abandoning my patients, but myself.

When I think about retiring here's what I think about: not being able to write my own prescriptions; not being able to wander around the hospital, email or call any doctor I want to ask for anything I want, defenseless as an average patient; not being *me*. When my father was old and ill, my mother insisted that the aides who came to my parents' home to take care of him called him "Dr. Koven." Among the last words my father ever uttered before he died were addressed to the anesthesiologist about to intubate him. He asked the anesthesiologist: "So where'd you train?" Even near death my father couldn't bear to not be a doctor.

The younger colleagues to whom I've reassigned my patients tell me how much the patients miss me. My colleagues may just be saying that to be nice. Or, possibly, patients *do* tell them they miss me and *they're* just being nice. I'm not sure I miss them, not in the way I miss people close to me whom I've lost. Why? My patients share extraordinarily intimate information with me, which draws us close, in a certain way. We have intense and deeply moving interactions, but always within narrow boundaries. Some doctors socialize with their patients but I've never done this. My relationship with my patients has been confined to the exam room, the hospital ward, the telephone and the computer screen, occasionally the sickbed at home: the places where they remain in my mind and I imagine I remain in theirs.

Perhaps this is simply what I need to tell myself now.

Since downsizing my practice my feeling of loss has most often taken the form of curiosity. Physician and writer Abigail Zuger, who specialized for many years in treating people infected with HIV, expresses this feeling powerfully. Zuger knew it was time to quit when, with what she calls her "feeble old neurons," she found it easier to remember the names of HIV medications no longer in use than those of the current ones. Still, she anticipated a sharp and specific kind of grieving:

> When I close the door to my airless little clinic room for the last time, I will be closing hundreds of charts in the middle and walking away before the stories end. In all of medicine, is there anything more difficult to do than that?

My mother used to say something similar. She didn't fear death—in my experience few old people do. But she wished she could stay around long enough to know "how the story ends," as she put it: how her grandchildren and great grandchildren turned out; when America would finally elect a woman president, if her garden would ever be as lush as she'd always hoped it would be.

But the story never ends. When you leave, you always leave in the middle.

24

They Call Us and We Go

April 3, 2020

Do you remember a time before PPE and ventilator shortages; virtual grand rounds and telemedicine "exams"; elbow bumps and then the avoidance, even, of elbows?

A scene that keeps coming back to me during these sleepless nights occurred the first week in March, when I met with the staff of one of the inpatient units at Mass General. That day, as we sat crowded together around a small conference table—how quaint this seems now—I passed out copies of William Carlos Williams's poem "Complaint." Published in 1921, the poem features a doctor who is summoned late one snowy night to the home of a woman who may be in labor. Williams, a physician himself, begins, "They call me and I go . . ."

I invited the group to explore the various emotions we clinicians feel when we're summoned urgently by pager, bedside call bell, electronic message, or telephone to care for a patient. We generated an impressively varied list: pride, annoyance, curiosity, apprehension, gratitude, exasperation, and joy. Some reflected that at times we experience all of these. On this we agreed: like the doctor in "Complaint" who heads out into the cold and dark, no matter what we feel, when we're called we go.

Except barely two weeks later the call came for me and my first reaction was to ignore it. Because of the coronavirus pandemic, like many of my colleagues I was working from home. I'd settled into an easy chair in my living room with my laptop to refill prescriptions when I received an email requesting volunteers to work in a clinic that had just been created to evaluate patients with coughs, fevers, and other possible symptoms of Covid-19. Nearing the end of my career, I regarded this email the same way I view announcements about proposed IT updates: with the sense that it didn't really apply to me. Plus, I knew that because of my age if I contracted coronavirus I'd be at higher risk of complications. I wouldn't be much help to anyone if I ended up in the ICU. I'd be more useful, I reasoned, managing my patients remotely, continuing to facilitate discussion groups via video conferencing, and cheering on my younger colleagues.

I deleted the email.

Over the next forty-eight hours, though, I paced around my house uneasily as if I had a pebble in my shoe. When the pebble became a rock I decided that I needed to volunteer for the new clinic, that I couldn't live with myself if I didn't.

If this sounds brave I don't mean it to. I am not a brave person. As a child I hated recess. The school playground frightened me: the monkey bars were too high, the slide too slippery, the swing too . . . swingy. As an adult I'm no more physically courageous. If I were to respond to the challenge currently circulating on social media—

"name five things you don't like that other people like"—I'd put air travel, roller coasters, and skiing, all of which terrify me, as the top three, with bleu cheese and science fiction coming in at four and five. Still, in the hours after the email about the Covid-19 screening clinic arrived, I felt that however much I feared for my physical safety, the psychological distress I'd feel if I didn't volunteer would be far greater. I feared that if I worked in the clinic I would contract the virus and possibly die. But if I didn't work in the clinic I feared another kind of erasure: the denial of the doctor I had been for most of my adult life.

Where did this feeling come from? Medical school. Part of the curriculum, no less essential than anatomy and physiology, is the teaching that physicians do not turn away from human suffering. Others may avoid the sickly smell of bloody stool, the sight of a festering wound, the sounds of a grieving parent's wails—but not us. This is the doctor's and nurse's equivalent of the firefighter running into a burning building.

Unlike firefighters, healthcare workers usually do not put our own lives in jeopardy, though many of course have during wars, outbreaks of contagious diseases, and in other perilous circumstances. Often the cost of responding to the demands of patient care is relatively small compared with its rewards. I learned this thirty years ago, when I started in practice. My first weekend on call I was paired with a mentor, a beloved veteran internist. I was certain I'd need his assistance, as I was new to the hospital and not yet confident in my outpatient skills since my training had been heavily inpatient-oriented. But the weekend went smoothly and by Sunday night I was in my pajamas, ready to turn in, and rather pleased with myself. That's when my pager went off. Ms. B was in the emergency room.

She was a woman in her fifties who'd been assigned to be my patient and whom I'd not yet met. Ms. B was in the ER having survived a suicide attempt. She'd be transferred to a psychiatric hospital once she was medically stable. I hung up the phone and turned out the light, but I couldn't sleep. I dialed my mentor's number and, after apologizing for calling him so late, asked if I should go to the ER. "Well," he said, "you don't have to, but every time I've felt I *should* see a patient, it ended up being the right thing to do."

A couple of years later I would make up my own private name for this sound advice: The Rizzo Rule. Here's why: One Friday evening, before going on a week's vacation to the beach with my family, I'd meant to visit Mrs. Rizzo, a patient of mine who was in the hospital. I'd planned to tell her that I would be away and that I'd arranged for one of my colleagues to look in on her during the week. Except I got distracted—I was in a hurry to go home and pack for the trip—and I didn't go to see her. The next day I was walking on the beach but I couldn't get Mrs. Rizzo out of my mind. My colleague would explain who he was, of course, and everything would be fine. But what if it wasn't fine? What if Mrs. Rizzo felt I'd abandoned her? What if she died? I really should call her, I thought. But there were no cell phones then. I'd have to find a pay phone. It would be silly to leave the beach for that. And just then, a skinny teenage boy walked toward me. The sun was in my eyes so I didn't notice it at first, but as the boy passed me I saw that he was wearing a T-shirt with a single word printed across the chest: RIZZO. And I went to find a pay phone.

I got dressed and drove downtown to the hospital, where I found Ms. B. lying on a gurney in the emergency room. I introduced myself and she nodded sleepily. The doctor who'd paged me appeared puzzled as to why I'd responded in person to what was essentially an FYI. I felt foolish, realizing that Ms. B. wouldn't even remember that I'd been there.

But she did remember. Over the next twenty years, she frequently mentioned how much my presence had meant to her that night. Ms. B. moved away a while ago and recently died of breast cancer. Her husband called to tell me the news, saying she would have wanted me to know. I may no longer have been her "provider," he said, but I'd always been her doctor. I have no doubt that I earned this honor in large part because I'd shown up that night. That reflex to show up, instilled in me so long ago, must explain why I retrieved the email about the Covid-19 clinic two days after I deleted it.

The clinic isn't so scary after all. Unlike many less fortunate facilities, ours is well organized, well staffed, and well equipped. My colleagues' banter and the determination evident even behind their goggles and masks calm my jangling nerves. Camaraderie and singularity of purpose, it turns out, are highly effective anxiolytics.

I understand I'm not taking anything like the risks many of my colleagues are taking, especially those treating patients in intensive care units and emergency rooms; health workers who lack adequate protective gear; doctors and nurses older than me who've come out of retirement to serve; pregnant clinicians and residents working long hours with repeated exposures to patients infected with the virus. I recognize, too, that because of their own medical conditions or family situations, some health workers are unable to care for patients with Covid-19. But I also know something I didn't even a few weeks ago: that as averse to risk as I am by nature, I would take on more if called to do so during this crisis. The sentiments expressed by the narrator of *The Plague*, a novel by Albert Camus that I'd been assigned to read in high school, are no longer abstract to me: "I have no idea what's awaiting me, or what will happen when this all ends," says Dr. Rieux. "For the moment I know this; there are sick people and they need curing."

———

Women in STEM

"Letter to a Young Female Physician" appeared in the *New England Journal of Medicine* a month after I turned sixty. You might think that at this age I'd have outgrown imposter syndrome, that I would no longer feel I wasn't good enough or lacked a distinct identity; that I'd have long ago cast off feelings that, at various points in my life, in my own private lexicon of insecurity, I'd called "willowy," "the hanging plant," "asterisk," "the Answer," and "the unbearable aboutness of being." And, in fact, I mostly *had* cast them off. Still, when the essay was about to be published, when it was too late to change or retract it, I worried that I'd revealed too much, that I'd sounded too self-centered, that I'd mistakenly assumed my own demons, small and idiosyncratic, bedeviled others. I also fretted that I hadn't made my point clearly, that I had, in fact, made the opposite of the point I'd wished to make: I'd reassured young women of their worth by validating their soft, "womanly" skills rather than their toughness and intelligence—their equality to men.

The digital edition of *NEJM* is published online at precisely five p.m. every Wednesday. The week my essay was to appear I braced myself for a barrage of harsh comments leavened by a handful of polite congratulatory notes from my colleagues. Instead, almost immediately, messages began coming in via email and social media from around the world, not only from young female physicians but also from men, older doctors, and readers who didn't work in healthcare. Nearly all who wrote said, in one way or another, that they, too, felt like imposters. Many women of color told me that they viewed imposter syndrome as internalized racism and sexism. One of the saddest notes I received was from a Black female cardiac surgeon in Los Angeles who told me that she knew from the very outset of her career that nothing she accomplished would ever feel like enough.

Another reader pointed out something I hadn't considered: that imposter syndrome is a particularly American phenomenon. He may have been right. From Horatio Alger to Superman to Tony Soprano and Walter White, the hero (or antihero) who knows he isn't really what he appears to be has been a staple of American culture. Perhaps imposter syndrome is the inevitable downside of American upward mobility: the fear that just beneath one's riches will always lie rags.

Other than the usual handful of profanity-laced messages that I've come to expect no matter what I publish—my favorite, after I posted a blog about firearms as a public health issue: *Fuck you Feminazi Libtard, you don't know shit about guns!*—the only less-than-positive feedback my essay drew was from a women's studies scholar I admire who'd just turned eighty. "Imposter syndrome?" she asked, with dismay over coffee. "I thought we were all over that *decades* ago!"

Messages still arrive now and then. Just recently I received an email from a man who had been a few years ahead of me in medical training and whom I'd always thought of as the ultimate "Osler Marine," unflappable in his starched white coat and *Aequanimitas* tie. He told me he'd come across my essay in a stack of unread journals as he was cleaning out his office in preparation for closing his practice. He wrote: "After reading your piece I realized that part of the relief of retirement is that I will successfully escape before anyone finds out about my own impostership."

◆ ◆ ◆

A few months after the publication of "Letter to a Young Female Physician" I received an invitation to participate in a panel discussion about imposter syndrome to be held during an all-day conference for female undergraduates majoring in STEM (science, technology, engineering, and math). I chuckled as I recalled my struggles with these subjects. As my friend Marty likes to say, "life is nothing if not ironic."

I arrived on a cold, rainy Saturday morning, signed in, and received my swag which included an oversized package of blue and white M&M's, each imprinted with "STEM," and which I tucked into my black suede briefcase, which I'd brought not to carry papers but to show how put-together I am. I resolved not to eat the candy, but I ended up gobbling the whole bag on the way home when it turned out that Burger King, which I never go to *ever*, wasn't serving lunch at 10:45 a.m.

The auditorium was filled with women college students. On the panel, besides me, were a geologist, a physicist, and an aerospace engineer. The moderator was a woman who was an executive for an international biotech giant. She introduced the panelists, and we each said a bit about ourselves, which amounted to us competing about who was the biggest imposter. I'd thought I had that one pretty much sewn up, in this company. When it was my turn I said: "I don't even *like* STEM!" which drew a big laugh from the audience. I went on to confess that, as a doctor, I use more of what I learned from reading novels than from studying organic chemistry, which I got an A in, even though I don't know what it is. I'd used that line before, including at Harvard Medical School, and it had always gotten a good laugh. I delivered my greatest hits. I aimed to be the *best* imposter.

But the other women on the panel had good stories too. The geologist's parents were proud of her but had no real understanding of what she did, who she was. Once, she said, her mother visited her office in the university department where she was a professor and began crying. She'd never realized what her daughter had accomplished. The aerospace engineer was seated next to me. She told the audience that she sometimes thought she'd rather be a sculptor. The physicist's high school physics teacher had told her that a girl couldn't be a physicist.

During the Q&A a young woman with lots of piercings and jagged hair asked me how she could possibly feel confident when her parents didn't support, as she put it, her "life choices." I answered not as a doctor, or a writer, but as a mother: "Trust me," I said, "it may not seem like it, but all your parents want is for you to be happy."

The last question came from a young woman who wanted to know how to get over imposter syndrome. "It helps to get old," I said. This drew a laugh from the audience, which surprised me.

Were they amused by my bluntness? Or were they laughing because I'd implied that for young people it was pretty much hopeless, that they needed to wait decades to be relieved of this burden? Kind of like when someone compliments something you're wearing and asks you where you got it and you say Hong Kong or Paris and they snort: Hmph, fat lot of good *that* does me.

The moderator did not laugh. She sprang from the podium and interjected, with a tight smile: "We don't say 'old.' We say 'experienced.'" But I was on a roll. "Yeah," I said, "every month I go to the beauty parlor and tell the hairdresser: 'make me look less experienced.'" Laughter. Lots of laughter. Big Tush triumphs. Curly Curvy comes out on top.

Afterward, outside the auditorium, I accepted compliments from the organizers of the conference. We promised to keep in touch, follow one another on social media, collaborate on another event. I told them about my terrible sense of direction and they pointed me toward the parking lot. I'd almost reached my car when a student ran to catch up with me. "Can I hug you?" she asked.

◆　◆　◆

A few days after my mother's first stroke, the one in April 2008 when she lost her memory, I took her to the Morikami Museum and Japanese Gardens in Delray Beach. We sat outdoors at the museum's restaurant and I ordered salmon crusted with almonds, which more or less fitted in with my Kripalu diet. I forget what my mother had but remember that she didn't even bother looking at the menu, asked me to pick something for her, and cheerily pronounced it a winner.

It was a hot, sunny day. I borrowed a wheelchair despite the museum attendant's warning that it would be difficult to push along the gravel paths of the Japanese gardens. But my mother loved gardens, and the effort it took for me to slog the wheels through the gravel salved my need to feel that I could help her. Bending from the waist and pushing with my arms fully extended we made it through the bonsais and on to the Zen, a large rectangle of artfully raked sand, dotted with smooth boulders.

We sat under the sun for a long time, my mother and I. She didn't seem impatient to move. I was surprised, because other than the austere patio she'd had installed in 1970 when she ripped out the rosebushes and the picket fence in our backyard in Brooklyn shortly before she applied to law school, she'd favored blowsy, overgrown English gardens. This spare, flowerless expanse was not her taste at all. Finally, my mother turned to me and said the most fluent sequence of sentences she'd uttered since my arrival, the words I now longed to say to this student, this young woman in STEM who asked if she could hug me, who now looked at me so eagerly in the parking lot, as if I had the Answer. I longed to tell her what my mother told me that day in the Zen garden:

Don't waste your time on nonsense. Don't waste your life.

ACKNOWLEDGMENTS

"Writing is like driving at night in the fog," E. L. Doctorow once observed. "You can only see as far as your headlights, but you can make the whole trip that way." The same might be said of becoming a doctor—and a person. In my life and medical career, as in the long journey leading to the publication of this book, I have been aided by many people without whose encouragement and illumination I surely would have gotten stalled in the darkness.

This book began as a series of letters to my dear friend and writing partner, the brilliant scholar and biographer Natalie Dykstra. Natalie understood, long before I did, where those sprawling missives were heading. Without her insightful questions and suggestions and the confidence she lent me when my own ran dry, they never would have arrived there.

Joy Harris, my literary agent, has been a wise, kind, and infinitely patient guide as I navigated the unfamiliar terrain of publishing. Joy's colleague, Adam Reed, provided assistance that eased the path forward.

Jill Bialosky, my editor, foresaw the book that might emerge from a single essay. Without her sharp eye and gentle direction I could not have written that book. The Norton team, Lauren Abbate, Jessica Friedman, Ingsu Liu, Erin Lovett, Rachelle Mandik, Meredith McGinnis, and Drew Weitman, made a complex process easy and even fun.

Physician and writer Randi Hutter Epstein introduced me to both Joy and Jill, setting me on my way.

Dani Shapiro has been my fairy godmother: a role model and mensch upon whose steady counsel I have relied again and again.

Emily Rapp Black read the earliest and roughest versions of this book and emboldened me to press ahead anyway.

I benefitted greatly from the comments of Renée E. D'Aoust, David Groff, Mary Jane Nealon, Suzanne Spector, and Janet Sternburg, who reviewed drafts at various stages. I'm especially grateful to my younger medical colleagues who offered their perspectives: Giancarlo Buonomo, LaShyra Nolen, Colleen M. Farrell, and Emily Silverman.

I owe much to the editors with whom I first worked on many of these essays, particularly Thomasine Berg, Anica Butler, and Gideon Gil at the *Boston Globe*, Julien Crockett at the *Los Angeles Review of Books*, Debra Malina at the *New England Journal of Medicine*, and Joanna Palmer at the *Lancet*.

For help in verifying historical or medical information or sharing personal recollections I thank: Stephen C. Achuff, W. Scott Butsch, Erica Camargo Faye, David S. Jones, Nancy C. Haff, Alan W. Heldman, Gene R. Howard, Ralph H. Hruban, James Januzzi, Muryum Khan, Lee Kaplan, Martha Katz, Joan Kronick, Margaret A. Marino, Ellen S. More, Athol W. Morgan, Janice P. Nimura,

David B. Pearse, Adam Rodman, Carol J. Scott, John Sotos, Monique Tello, Katharine Treadway, Jack Turban, Judith Vick, Debbie L. Weaver, and Malissa J. Wood.

I thank physician and writer Gavin Francis for generously allowing me to borrow "science and kindness."

I have been challenged and lifted at every step by my writing and medical mentors: At Yale, the late John Hersey; at Johns Hopkins, David B. Hellmann and the late Henry M. Seidel; at Harvard Extension School, the late Sacvan Bercovitch and Grace Dane Mazur; at the Bennington Writing Seminars, Sven Birkerts, Susan Cheever, Dinah Lenney, Phillip Lopate, and Wyatt Mason; at Massachusetts General Hospital, James J. Dineen, Leonard M. Rubin, Mary McNaughton Collins, and Joshua P. Metlay.

Mary and Josh, along with our colleagues in the Division of General Internal Medicine, Shelli Mahan, Felisha Marques, Vivian Lee, and Libby Williams, supported me in the improbable and exhilarating endeavor of creating the Writer in Residence Program. Katrina Armstrong, physician-in-chief and chair of the department of medicine, and Peter L. Slavin, president of Mass General, along with Shea Asfaw, Patrick Rooney, and Peggy Slasman, made it possible for me to expand that program hospital-wide. Because of them my dream of bringing poetry and prose to health care workers has become a daily reality.

For thirty years my clinical home has been the Bulfinch Medical Group at Mass General. My medical and writing careers would not be the same without my BMG family, especially Robert A. Hughes, the founder and longtime medical director of the group;

our current medical directors, Caroline Birks and Li Tso; and my work sister and cross-covering partner, Barbara J. Kane.

My patients, many of whose stories appear in these pages in altered form, have trusted me with their deepest and most private pain, fear, and joy. I hope I have been worthy of that privilege.

Jane Saulnier provided expert and loving childcare during many of the busiest years of my medical career and I treasure her friendship still.

My siblings, David and Diane and Richard and Melinda and their families, have cheered me on in my second career as they did in my first. It's said it isn't easy to have a writer in the family, but they've never made me feel this was true for them. Of the many things we share, the legacy of my parents is the most precious. I've tried to convey in this book what a gift that legacy was and to honor their memories.

Sophie, Patrick, Giampiero, Giulia, Tony, and Giancarlo encircle me with love and laughter and bear my endless distraction with good humor. T/Mom/Grandma loves you, angels.

My husband, Carlo, to whom this book and much else I dedicate, has been, for over four decades, my life, my light, my heart.

NOTES ON SOURCES

INTRODUCTION: LETTER TO A YOUNG FEMALE PHYSICIAN

1 **In 1855, James Jackson:** James Jackson, *Letters to a Young Physician Just Entering Upon Practice* (Boston: Phillips, Samson and Company, 1855).

1 **More recent additions:** Richard Selzer, *Letters to a Young Doctor* (New York: Simon & Schuster, 1982); Perri Klass, *Treatment Kind and Fair: Letters to a Young Doctor* (New York: Basic Books, 2007).

2 **female physicians earn:** AB Jena, AR Olenski, and DM Blumenthal, "Sex Differences in Physician Salaries in U.S. Public Medical Schools," *JAMA Internal Medicine* 176 (2016): 1294–1304; AB Jena, D Khullar, O Ho, AR Olenski, and DM Blumenthal, "Sex Differences in Academic Rank in US Medical Schools in 2014," *JAMA* 314 (2015): 1149–1158; KP Richter et al., "Women Physicians and Academic Promotion," *New England Journal of Medicine* 383 (2020): 2148–2157; Robert Lowes, "Most Female Physicians Report Sexual Harassment at Job," *Medscape*, August 24, 2016, http://www.medscape.com/viewarticle/866853.

3 **A 2016 study suggested:** Y Tsugawa, AB Jena, JF Figueroa, EJ Orav, DM Blumenthal, and AK Jha, "Comparison of Hospital Mortality and Readmission Rates for Medicare Patients Treated by Male vs. Female Physicians," *JAMA Internal Medicine* 177 (2017): 206–213.

CHAPTER 1: RISK FACTORS

9   **in my first published essay:** S Koven, "The Ungifted Physician," *JAMA* 27 (1998): 1607.

16 **"It is the fellowship":** Richard Selzer, *Down from Troy: A Doctor Comes of Age* (New York: William Morrow & Co., Inc., 1992), 136.

CHAPTER 2: PREREQUISITES

18 **I'd just read Susan Sontag's *Illness as Metaphor*:** Susan Sontag, *Illness as Metaphor* (New York: Farrar, Straus and Giroux, 1978).

18 **She quotes an Auden poem:** "Miss Gee," in *WH Auden: Collected Works*, ed. Edward Mendelson (New York: Modern Library, 2007), 159.

CHAPTER 3: ADMISSIONS

26 **about a third of all mental healthcare:** M Olfson, "The Rise of Primary Care Physicians in the Provision of US Mental Health Care," *Journal of Health Politics, Policy, and Law* 41, no. 4 (2016): 559–583.

CHAPTER 6: WE HAVE A BODY

44 **Archival photographs document instances:** John Harley Warner and James M. Edmonson, *Dissection: Photographs of a Rite of Passage in American Medicine 1880–1930* (New York: Blast Books, 2009).

CHAPTER 7: THINGS SHAMEFUL TO BE SPOKEN ABOUT

60 **We recited the final lines:** W. S. Jones, *The Doctor's Oath* (Cambridge: Cambridge University Press, 1924, 2013 edition).

60 **More recent translations are sunnier:** Louis Lasagna, quoted in Rachel Hajar, "The Physician's Oath: Historical Perspectives," *Heart Views* 18, no. 4 (October–December 2017): 154–159.

CHAPTER 8: LINEAGE

69 **eight years before I started my internship:** Samuel Shem, *The House of God* (New York: G. P. Putnam's Sons, 1978).

69 **When I interviewed Bergman:** Suzanne Koven, "35 Years Later, Author Revisits 'The House of God,'" *Boston Globe*, September 2, 2013.

70 **I'm certain I would have seen myself:** Shem, *House of God*, 105.

76 **"There are three classes of human beings":** William Osler, quoted in Carol Lopate and Josiah Macy Jr., *Women in Medicine* (Baltimore: Johns Hopkins Press, 1968), 178.

78 **a series of black-and-white photos:** W. Eugene Smith, "Country Doctor," *LIFE*, September 20, 1948.

81 **the first female graduate:** Richard B. Gunderman, "Elizabeth Blackwell: First Woman of American Medicine," *Pediatric Radiology* 50 (2020): 628–630.

81 **until I came upon a copy:** Florence Haseltine, MD, and Yvonne Yaw, *Woman Doctor* (Boston: Houghton Mifflin, 1976).

81 **Haseltine's account of a brilliant college classmate:** Haseltine and Yaw, *Woman Doctor*, 10.

82 **"flooded [. . .] with fatigue":** Haseltine and Yaw, *Woman Doctor*, 8.

82 **The first pages of the book show:** Haseltine and Yaw, *Woman Doctor*, 3.

CHAPTER 9: THE LAST THREE POUNDS

84   **"One apple satisfies"**: Samuel Hazo, *And the Time Is: Poems, 1958–2013* (Syracuse: Syracuse University Press, 2014), 185.

85   **Though the American Medical Association**: Andrew Pollack, "A.M.A. Recognizes Obesity as a Disease," *New York Times*, June 18, 2013.

85   **Just four years earlier the National Institutes of Health**: "Methods for Voluntary Weight Loss and Control," Technology Assessment Conference Statement, March 30–April 1, 1992, National Institutes of Health, Office of Medical Applications of Research.

85   **By 1998 that rate would go up**: "Clinical Guidelines on the Identification, Evaluation, and Treatment of Overweight and Obesity in Adults: The Evidence Report," National Institutes of Health, https://www.nhlbi.nih.gov/files/docs/guidelines/ob_gdlns.pdf.

86   **the number of prescriptions dispensed**: Matthew Kauffman and Andrew Julien, "Scientists Helped Industry to Push Diet Drug," *Hartford Courant*, April 10, 2000.

86   **"Eventually"**: Gina Kolata, "How Fen-Phen, a Diet 'Miracle,' Rose and Fell," *New York Times*, September 23, 1997.

87   **Hippocrates cautioned**: D Haslam, "Obesity, a Medical History," *Obesity Reviews* 8, Suppl. 1 (2007): 31–36.

87   **Osler, whose only child**: William Osler quoted in Hugh Chaun, "Osler in Gastroenterology," *Canadian Journal of Gastroenterology* 24, no. 10 (October): 615–618.

89   **80 percent of American girls**: "Children, Teens, Media, and Body Image," https://www.commonsensemedia.org/research/children-teens-media-and-body-image.

92   **binge eating disorder**: *Diagnostic and Statistical Manual of Mental Disorders, 5th Edition: DSM-5* (Washington, DC: American Psychiatric Publishing, 2013), https://doi.org/10.1176/appi.books.9780890425596.dsm10.91

94   **I still have my mother's 1966 edition**: Jean Nidetch, *Weight Watch-*

ers Cook Book (New York: Hearthside Press Incorporated Publishers, 1966), 273.

99 **Denise suggested a book:** Jane R. Hirschman and Carol H. Munter, *Overcoming Overeating: How to Break the Diet-Binge Cycle and Live a Healthier, More Satisfying Life* (Boston: Addison Wesley Publishing), 1988.

102 **In 1997 the FDA:** Kolata, "Fen-Phen."

102 **Leptin was a bust too:** Bradley K. Fikes, "UCSD Study Reports Why Appetite-Suppressing Leptin Doesn't Work in Overweight People," *Chicago Tribune*, August 22, 2018.

104 **For a while, I followed the advice:** Rachel Naomi Remen interview by Charlie Rose, *The Charlie Rose Show*, PBS, June 29, 2001.

108 **After registering for the retreat:** Abraham Joshua Heschel, *The Sabbath* (New York: Farrar, Straus and Giroux, 1951).

108 **They'd tweaked the program again:** Taffy Brodesser-Akner, "Losing It in the Anti-Diet Age," *New York Times Magazine*, August 2, 2017.

CHAPTER 11: CURBSIDING

128 **"imposter phenomenon":** Pauline Clance and Suzanne Imes, "The Imposter Phenomenon in High Achieving Women: Dynamics and Therapeutic Intervention," *Psychotherapy: Theory, Research & Practice* 15, no. 3 (1978): 241–247.

130 **a book called *The Secret*:** Rhonda Byrne, *The Secret* (New York: Atria Books, 2006).

131 **I never actually met this doctor:** Christiane Northrup, *The Wisdom of Menopause: Creating Physical and Emotional Health During the Change* (New York: Bantam Books, 2001).

132 **Poet Leslie McGrath evokes:** Leslie McGrath, "The Dodo," *The Common* 19 (2020).

132 **On the occasion of the tenth anniversary:** Sandra Tsing Loh, "The Bitch Is Back," *Atlantic*, October 2011.

134   **In a 2008 review article:** AS Filho et al., "Does the Association Between Mitral Valve Prolapse and Panic Disorder Really Exist?" *The Primary Care Companion to the Journal of Clinical Psychiatry* 10, no. 1 (2008): 38–47.

134   **"although several studies have reported":** Sheldon H. Gottlieb, "Mitral Valve Prolapse: From Syndrome to Disease," *American Journal of Cardiology* 60, no. 18 (1987): PJ53–J58.

CHAPTER 12: AN INHERITED CONDITION

140   **"Alas," as Elizabeth Hardwick writes:** Elizabeth Hardwick, *Sleepless Nights* (New York: NYRB Classics, 2001), 91.

144   **In a landmark 1990 essay:** Bernadine Healy, "The Yentl Syndrome," *New England Journal of Medicine* 325, no. 4 (July 25, 1991): 274–276.

145   **coronary atherosclerosis is the number-one killer:** Lori Mosca et al., "Fifteen-Year Trends in Awareness of Heart Disease in Women," *Circulation* 127, no. 11 (2013): 1254–1263.

146   **A 1966 syndicated newspaper article:** Cara Kiernan Fallon, "Husbands' Hearts and Women's Health: Gender, Age, and Heart Disease in Twentieth-Century America," *Bulletin of the History of Medicine* 93, no. 4 (Winter 2019): 577–609.

146   **and my favorite:** Alton Blakeslee, "Heart Attacks Claim 1,400 Each Day—Want to Kill Husband? Try Atherosclerosis!" *Youngstown Vindicator*, March 6, 1966.

147   **"Physicians generally should not":** "Treating Self and Family," https://www.ama-assn.org/delivering-care/ethics/treating-self-or-family.

148   **I was reminded of this exchange:** "Save the Reaper" in Alice Munro, *The Love of a Good Woman* (New York: Random House, 1998), 146–180.

149   **cultures of illness:** Jerome Groopman and Pamela Hartzband, *Your Medical Mind: How to Decide What Is Right for You* (New York: Penguin Books, 2011).

152   **Geriatrician and writer Louise Aronson:** Louise Aronson, "'Good' Patients and 'Difficult' Patients—Rethinking Our Definitions," *New England Journal of Medicine* 369 (2013): 796–797.

160   **I recalled articles I'd read:** Elizabeth Mostofsky et al., "Risk of Acute Myocardial Infarction after Death of a Significant Person in One's Life: The Determinants of MI Onset Study," *Circulation*, 125, no. 3 (2012): 491–496.

CHAPTER 13: THE DISEASE OF THE LITTLE PAPER

165   **a novel extraction method:** *Time*, "Medicine: Stretching Penicillin," September 11, 1944.

165   **An article in the *New York Times* in 1984:** Ronald Sullivan, "Employees Strike at 27 Hospitals in New York City," *New York Times*, July 14, 1984.

166   **"an exhaustive list of purported ailments":** Quoted in Sanjiv Grover, "Don't Dismiss the Little Notes that Patients Bring," *British Medical Journal* 350 (2015), doi: https://doi.org/10.1136/bmj.h20.

166   **A disciple of Charcot:** H Meige, *Le Juif-Errant à la Salpêtrière: Étude sur Certains Neuropathes Voyageurs* (Paris: L. Battaille, 1893).

166   **"A patient with a written list":** William Osler, *Aphorisms*, coll. Robert Bennett Bean; ed. William Bennett Bean (New York: H. Schuman, 1950).

166   **one doctor updated:** JA Muir Gray, S de Lusignan, "National Electronic Library for Health (NeLH)," *British Medical Journal* 319 (1999): 1476–1479.

166   **John F. Burnum challenged the notion:** JF Burnum, "La Maladie du Petit Papier: Is Writing a List of Symptoms a Sign of an Emotional Disorder?" *New England Journal of Medicine* 313 (1985): 690–691.

170   **a self-described compulsive list maker:** Susan Sontag, *As Consciousness Is Harnessed to Flesh: Journals & Notebooks, 1964–1980* (New York: Farrar, Straus and Giroux, 2012), 219.

CHAPTER 14: THE NONCOMPLIANT PATIENT, RECONSIDERED

172 **fewer than half of all American adults:** "Flu Vaccine Coverage, United States, 2018–19 Influenza Season," https://www.cdc.gov/flu/fluvaxview/coverage-1819estimates.htm.

172 **the number of Americans who have had screening:** "Healthy People," https://www.healthypeople.gov/2020.

172 **a high percentage of patients didn't even recall:** "Care That Delivers – Future Health Index Report 2017," https://www.philips.com/a-w/about/news/future-health-index/reports/2017/how-can-global-health-systems-use-digital-technology.html.

173 **In a 2017 blog in *NEJM Journal Watch*:** Alexandra Godfrey, "'As I Lay Dying': Patient Readmission and Non-Compliance," https://blogs.jwatch.org/frontlines-clinical-medicine/2017/08/03/lay-dying-patient-readmission-non-compliance/.

173 **She quotes an intriguing 1984 article:** CW Flexner, et al., "Repeated Hospitalization for Ketoacidosis. The Game of Sartoris," *American Journal of Medicine* 76, no. 4 (1984): 691–695.

175 **"A plant which it has taken two centuries":** Henry David Thoreau, *A Year in Thoreau's Journal: 1851*, ed. H. Daniel Peck (New York: Penguin Books, 1993), 326.

CHAPTER 15: THE HATEFUL PATIENT, REVISITED

177 **a now-classic article:** James E. Groves, "Taking Care of the Hateful Patient," *New England Journal of Medicine* 298 (1978): 883–887.

CHAPTER 16: THE DOCTOR'S NEW DILEMMA

180 **Ridgeon's dilemma:** George Bernard Shaw, *The Complete Plays of George Bernard Shaw (1893–1921)* (Oxford: Oxford City Press, 2012).

182 **trust that, studies have suggested:** JM Kelley, G Kraft-Todd, L Schapira, J Kossowsky, and H Riess, "The Influence of the Patient-Clinician Relationship on Healthcare Outcomes: A Systematic Review and Meta-Analysis of Randomized Controlled Trials," *PLoS One* 9, no. 4 (2014): e94207-e94207.

183 **For several groups, I've selected "Communion":** Richard B. Weinberg, "Communion," in *Annals of Internal Medicine* 123 (1995): 804–805.

CHAPTER 17: OFF THE CHARTS

186 **the orderly progression of grief-related emotions:** Elisabeth Kübler-Ross, *On Death and Dying* (Abingdon, Oxfordshire: Routledge Press, 1969).

188 **I told her about an essay:** Donald Hall, "Between Solitude and Loneliness," *New Yorker*, October 15, 2016.

189 **Dr. James Jackson summed up their philosophy:** James Jackson, *Letters to a Young Physician Just Entering Upon Practice* (Boston: Phillips, Samson and Company, 1855), 25.

190 **"unprofessional behavior":** Scott Hardouin et al., "Prevalence of Unprofessional Social Media Content Among Young Vascular Surgeons" (RETRACTED), *Journal of Vascular Surgery*, December 24, 2019, DOI:https://doi.org/10.1016/j.jvs.2019.10.069.

190 **an impromptu Twitter campaign:** Emma Goldberg, "Women Doctors Ask: Who Gets to Decide What's 'Professional'?" *New York Times*, August 2, 2020.

192 **the term "client":** Raisa B. Deber et al., "Patient, Consumer, Client, or Customer: What Do People Want to Be Called?," *Health Expectations* 8, no. 4 (December 2005): 345–351.

192 **Baruch summarized our ambivalence:** Jay Baruch, "Hug or Ugh?," *Hastings Center Report* 40, no. 2 (March–April 2010): 7–8, 10.1353/hcr.0.0243.

192 **"The patient is the central object":** Jackson, *Letters*, 26.

CHAPTER 20: SCIENCE AND KINDNESS

212 **"Medicine is an alliance"**: Gavin Francis, *Shapeshifters: A Journey Through the Changing Human Body* (New York, Hachette Books, 2018), 4.

213 **Until a hundred years ago**: Regina Morantz-Sanchez, "The Gendering of Empathic Expertise: How Women Physicians Became More Empathic than Men" in *The Empathic Practitioner: Empathy, Gender, and Medicine*, eds. Ellen Singer More and Maureen A. Milligan (New Brunswick, New Jersey: Rutgers University Press, 1994), 41.

214 **"Foucault described the moment"**: Abraham M. Nussbaum, *The Finest Traditions of My Calling* (New Haven: Yale University Press, 2016), 36.

217 **"What *do* I want in a doctor?"**: Anatole Broyard, *Intoxicated by My Illness: And Other Writings on Life and Death* (New York: Ballantine Books, 1992), 40–44.

217 **It's a relatively new word**: Susan Lanzoni, "A Short History of Empathy," *Atlantic*, October 15, 2015.

218 **papers with distressing titles**: BW Newton, L Barber, J Clardy, E. Cleveland, and P O'Sullivan, "Is There a Hardening of the Heart During Medical School?" *Academic Medicine* 83, no. 3 (March 2008): 244–249.

220 **"Empathy"**: Danielle Ofri, *What Doctors Feel: How Emotions Affect the Practice of Medicine* (Boston: Beacon Press, 2013), 10.

221 **"seem to understand that empathy is"**: Leslie Jamison, *The Empathy Exams* (Minneapolis: Graywolf Press, 2014), 5.

CHAPTER 21: BURY ME IN SOMETHING WARM

228 **"I should have been buried"**: Philip Roth, *Patrimony: A True Story* (New York: Vintage International, 1996), 237.

236 **"This postmortem readjustment"**: Sally Mann, *Hold Still: A Memoir with Photographs* (New York: Little, Brown & Company, 2015), 173.

CHAPTER 22: EXTENSION

249 **I read in an animated, theatrical voice:** Nora Ephron, "Moving On, A Love Story," *New Yorker*, May 29, 2006.

253 **"Considering how common illness is"**: Virginia Woolf, "On Being Ill," *The New Criterion* (1926) Vol IV, Number 1, 32.

255 **"I listen not only for the content"**: Rita Charon, "Narrative and Medicine," *New England Journal of Medicine* 350 (2004): 862–864.

255 **"to expand every nanosecond"**: Rita Charon interview by Jon Parrish Peede, *Humanities* 38, no. 4 (Fall 2018).

256 **"We tell ourselves stories"**: Joan Didion, *The White Album* (New York: Farrar, Straus and Giroux, 2009), 11.

257 **"It was important to pick up"**: Barack Obama, interview by Michiko Kakutani, *New York Times*, January 16, 2017.

258 **The novel was *Disgrace***: J. M. Coetzee, *Disgrace* (New York: Penguin Books, 2000).

261 **"The longer Levin mowed"**: Leo Tolstoy, *Anna Karenina*, trans. Constance Garnett (New York: Sterling, 2003), 93.

CHAPTER 23: MIXED EMOTIONS

266 **women physicians who work part-time:** Karen S. Sibert, "Don't Quit This Day Job," *New York Times*, June 11, 2011.

268 **One of the fastest growing subsets of doctors:** "More Doctors Work Part Time, Flexible Schedules," https://amednews.com/article/20120326/business/303269974/1/.

270 **"When I close the door"**: Abigail Zuger, "Moving On," *New England Journal of Medicine* 378 (2018): 1763–1765.

CHAPTER 24: THEY CALL US AND WE GO

272   **William Carlos Williams's poem:** William Carlos Williams, *The Collected Poems of William Carlos Williams, Vol. I: 1909–1939* (New York: New Directions, 1986), 153.

277   **"I have no idea what's awaiting":** Albert Camus, *The Plague*, trans. Stuart Gilbert (New York: Vintage, 1991), 127.

LETTER TO A
YOUNG FEMALE
PHYSICIAN

Suzanne Koven

LETTER TO A YOUNG
FEMALE PHYSICIAN
Suzanne Koven

DISCUSSION QUESTIONS

1. *Letter to a Young Female Physician* grew from an essay by the same name, first published in 2017. Why does Suzanne Koven begin the book with this particular essay? As you were reading, did you think of the book as a letter?

2. Koven opens *Letter to a Young Female Physician* with two quotes, the first from Sir William Osler and the second from her mother. Why do you think Koven chose quotes that seem to contradict one another? What do these quotes suggest about her approach to both writing and medicine?

3. As a child, Koven recounts feeling that, though she did not want to be a man, she did not necessarily want to be a woman either. Does this feeling connect to Koven's experience of "imposter syndrome" as a female medical student and physician? How does Koven come to see traditionally feminine qualities as an asset in her work?

4. In chapter 6, "We Have a Body," Koven describes an autopsy subject encountered on a high school field trip as her "first patient." How does the fact that her first patient is a cadaver shape Koven's conception of the relationship between patient and physician, and how does that conception evolve throughout her career? Does Koven view patients differently after the illnesses of her parents and her son?

5. Why is Koven drawn to Susan Sontag's *Illness as Metaphor* during her pre-med coursework? How does she understand the roles of language and narrative in the practice of medicine?

6. Physicians request "family history" to build clearer and more complete pictures of patients. What would Koven's own family history look like? Beyond her relatives, who does she consider part of her lineage?

7. What does Koven mean when she writes that "the experience of the body is never only about the body"? (p. 135) How does she go beyond the body when treating patients, and what are the benefits and potential pitfalls of doing so?

8. When she first begins leading Lit Med, Koven discovers that "the list of really good poems, short stories, essays, and novels about illness is fairly short" (p. 253). What might explain this scarcity? How does exposure to "nonmedical readings" inform Koven's work as a doctor?

9. Koven returns to her mother again and again throughout *Letter to a Young Female Physician*, concluding with her death in chapter 21, "Bury Me in Something Warm." How does Koven's experience caring for her mother during her final illnesses affect their perennially tense relationship? Why do you think Koven might instinctively imagine writing about her mother's passing even as she is present at her deathbed?

10. *Letter to a Young Female Physician* is replete with apparent binaries: male and female, doctor and patient, the art and the science of medicine. How does Koven call the distinctions between these categories into question? Why might it be important for her to do so?

11. Koven feels that she has "many selves," while also fearing at times that she lacks a discernable identity. How do Koven's multiple identities as doctor and writer, mother and daughter intersect and influence one another? What part does writing play in Koven's sense of herself?

12. Koven agrees with physician and essayist Gavin Francis that "medicine is an alliance of science and kindness," (p. 212) but questions whether one component in the alliance takes precedence over the other. What do you think? Does Koven suggest that it might be possible to value scientific acumen and compassion equally?

13. In chapter 22, "Extension," Koven references Erik Erikson's three stages of human development: determining one's identity in relation to one's parents; establishing one's place in the community; and, finally, struggling against despair to remain creative. Do these stages correspond to the life history that Koven unfolds in *Letter to a Young Female Physician*? How does Koven approach the final stage, old age?

14. Koven writes of her mother's death, "The story never ends. When you leave, you leave in the middle" (p. 271). How do the final essays of *Letter to a Young Female Physician* leave readers in the middle of the story? Would you have preferred a more conclusive ending?

15. In her decades as a doctor, what shifts does Koven observe in the medical field? Despite the new challenge presented by the Covid-19 pandemic, which elements of the practice of medicine remain, for her, a constant?

16. In chapter 9, "The Last Three Pounds," Koven writes that "no one would buy a book about weight by a doctor who offered no advice about how to lose it" (p. 104). Can *Letter to a Young Female Physician* be read as an advice book? Does Koven offer readers "the Answer" and, if not, why?